NORTHERN BOUNTY

NORTHERN BOUNTY

A Celebration of Canadian Cuisine

Edited by Jo Marie Powers and Anita Stewart

Random House of Canada

Published in 1995 by
Random House of Canada Limited, Toronto

Canadian Cataloguing in Publication Data

Northern bounty: a celebration of Canadian cuisine

Proceedings of symposium held at the Chefs School,
Stratford, Ont. in Sept., 1993.

ISBN 0-394-22431-0

1. Food – Congresses. 2. Diet – Canada – Congresses.
3. Food habits – Canada – Congresses.
4. Cookery, Canadian – Congresses.
I. Powers, Jo Marie, 1935– II. Stewart, Anita.

TX360.C3N6 1995 641'.0971 C95-930219-0

Book design: Gordon Robertson
Cover illustration: Sandra Dionisi

Printed and bound in the United States

10 9 8 7 6 5 4 3 2 1

The editors' proceeds from this book
have been donated to Cuisine Canada.

A WORD OF THANKS

On behalf of Cuisine Canada and all the participants of the Northern Bounty conference, we extend a heartfelt thank-you to James Morris and Eleanor Kane of the Stratford Chefs School in Stratford, Ontario, for their unflagging support. The Stratford Chefs School is known across Canada for its dedication to excellence in culinary education. That dedication was showcased throughout the conference with the help of their excellent staff, and in particular, Ann Marie Moss, Neil Baxter, Deborah Reid, Bryan Steele and Elisabeth Lorimer.

The editors do not believe that this book would have come about without the initial support for the idea of the Northern Bounty conference. For this we would like to thank Elizabeth Driver, for her insights, perseverance, and knowledge; Dr. Robert McLaughlin, for his continued support; Julia Aitken, for her encouragement; and Donna Messer, for her enthusiasm and for the office space she provided.

From the beginning, Doug Pepper of Random House of Canada realized the importance of documenting the many facets of Canadian cuisine. But, the person who was responsible for carrying the project from beginning to end was Sarah Davies, our Random House editor, whom we cannot thank enough.

The editors would also like to say thank you to the John Morris Law Office in Elora, Ontario; Karen Leachman and Lisa Fodor, of the secretarial staff in the School of Hotel and Food Administration at the University of Guelph; Barbara Brooks, for her translation from French to English; and to all the student volunteers from both the University of Guelph Hotel School and the Stratford Chefs School.

CUISINE CANADA

Mission Statement

To actively promote the growth and study of our distinctly Canadian food culture.

Objectives

To foster knowledge and understanding of our unique Canadian food history and the multicultural and regional diversity of Canadian cuisine.

To provide a forum for communication and interaction for Cuisine Canada members through national conferences, regional functions, newsletters, and publications.

To advocate the use of quality Canadian products within Canada and internationally, and to encourage their research and development.

To nurture young members of Canada's culinary community by providing inspiration, information, and educational support.

CONTENTS

The Regional Cuisine of the Prairies

The Regional Cuisine of Ontario

INTRODUCTION

TO BECOME truly sovereign, a nation must nurture its culinary arts, discuss them and exchange opinions on them. Here in Canada, the intellectualizing is spiced with the practical. We have survived . . . and in doing so have forged a respected identity for ourselves among nations. We have fine dining experiences with many great chefs. We have multitudes of honest country kitchens with cooks who not only understand the land, but also shop it. Our First Nations have traditions that hark back millennia. Our ingredients are among the finest in the world simply because our farmers and fisherfolk are. In our farm markets we can savour each particular region and revel in the first tastes of each season.

The conference Northern Bounty gave us a crystalline glimpse of Canada's culinary reality in 1993. Northern Bounty was about awareness, national pride, and possibilities. From all parts of Canada, visionaries and risk takers, purists and dreamers, converged upon Stratford, Ontario, at the height of the harvest.

This book is the aftermath, organized as the conference was, by region. We asked ourselves, "Who can tell us what we want to learn? What meals will best reflect the reality of each region?" The answers follow! Our book *Northern Bounty* is a flag-waving exploration of Canadian cuisine, and a turning point in our collective awareness of it. Never before have our culinary professionals shared their intimate understanding of our culinary past, present, and future. We present this book with great pride for all Canadians to treasure.

The future is very bright. But it will not come easily. In order to continue our quest for understanding, we have created Cuisine

Canada, a professional alliance for those Canadians involved in all aspects of our culinary world, with chapters in every region and a written mandate to celebrate the culinary riches of each. The founding meeting was held—appropriately, we think—at Le Château Champlain, in Montreal on October 26, 27 and 28, 1994. For three days, the joint boards met and hammered out our charter and savoured Quebec.

It has become clear over the years leading up to the Northern Bounty conference and now, with the simultaneous launch of this book and Cuisine Canada, that Canadians' limits are self-made and the dream can be ours!

Anita Stewart and Jo Marie Powers
December 1994

INTRODUCTION TO THE REGIONAL CUISINES OF CANADA

CAROL FERGUSON

Our Northern Bounty

Northern Bounty will take you on a gastronomic odyssey across our vast and bountiful land. In a coast-to-coast celebration of our splendid Canadian foods and unique regional heritage, this book will surely put to rest once and for all that old question "Is there really such a thing as Canadian cuisine?"

The longstanding dilemma of defining our cooking is understandable. What do you call the cuisine of a country that spans some 8,000 kilometres and encompasses a dozen dramatically different regions and three centuries of culinary traditions? A cuisine as modest as shortcakes baked up by a rural church group for a strawberry social and as spicy as the jerk chicken at a Toronto Jamaican jump-up? As traditional as fish-and-brewis in Newfoundland and as innovative as steamed gooseneck barnacles at Sooke Harbour House? You call it Canadian, that's what.

Canadian cooking is defined by its diversity. We're country-style cosy and city-street sassy. We're butter tarts, Nanaimo bars, chili sauce, and figgy duff. We're *poutine* and perogies and pasta. We're curries and tacos and *tiramisu*. And the evolution continues today.

But we've never been a real melting pot. There's no denying our far-flung geography, and each of our distinct regions has its own culinary personality, reflecting the climate and local ingredients and the varied backgrounds of the people who settled there. Canada has always been a land of immigrants, and each wave has added new flavours to the old, as people first figured out how to cook what they found locally, then gradually adapted their traditional dishes, creating brand-new ones, and finally swapped recipes with one another.

Thus we have our unique regional food styles. There are even regions within regions. In the Atlantic provinces, for instance, many traditional specialties remain distinctly local, from oatcakes in Cape Breton to rappie pie in northern New Brunswick to cod au gratin in Newfoundland. On the Prairies, community suppers have always been an international smorgasbord of Ukrainian, German, English, French, Scandinavian, and many other traditions (with saskatoon pie for dessert). British Columbia cuisine is an eclectic blend of lotus-land flair on the coast and rib-sticking ruggedness in the interior. Northern and Southern Ontario food styles are as diverse as their long multicultural history. Quebec has three centuries of traditions, now classified into a dozen different culinary regions.

Of course many foods are familiar coast to coast: apple pies, cinnamon buns, and lasagna; lobster, beef, cheddar cheese, and McIntosh apples. But the sources of many of our finest and often world-famous products are undeniably regional: Arctic char, Okanagan peaches, Lac St-Jean blueberries, Peace River honey, P.E.I. mussels, Manitoba golden caviar. Even the "official" Canadian menu that used to appear at diplomatic functions—maybe it still does—salmon, fiddleheads, wild rice, and maple mousse—represents a mix of regions, not a national cuisine.

Regional cooking is not unique to Canada. Think of Italy, France, China, all with diverse regional cuisines based on local ingredients. Even the so-called melting pot south of the border has spawned fashionable new waves of regional cuisines in the Southwest, Southeast, and Pacific Northwest.

Canadian chefs, too, are exploring their regional roots, updating local traditions and creating dazzling new dishes with the finest of fresh, local, seasonal ingredients. Country inns and bed-and-breakfasts coast to coast are serving up a great variety of local specialties. But many of the best-kept secrets of regional Canadian cooking are still tucked away in the home kitchens of our heartlands.

Each of the five Canadian regions explored in this book begins with an overview from culinary authorities who really know their regional stuff. They set the stage for the specialists who follow. These are many of Canada's top-notch food professionals: producers, marketers, chefs, restaurateurs, vintners, food writers, teachers, historians. All have unique perspectives on where we've been and where we're going.

The lineup of topics for each region follows the cycle of food products all the way from the original sources, through gathering, processing, and marketing, to cooking, serving, and eating. Food is many things—sustenance, sensuality, sociability, politics, economics, science, art. *Northern Bounty* will give you a taste of all of them.

You'll read about our homegrown ingredients—from Saanich Peninsula herbs to Bay of Fundy herring. You'll be inspired by flourishing new food-marketing methods at farm gates and farmers' markets as important tie-ins to tourism. You'll find treasured traditions alive and well in many regions, including Waterloo County Mennonite favourites, Winnipeg European classics, and Acadian and Loyalist specialties in the Maritimes. Gentler times in the dining cars of the great transcontinental railways that tied us all together in the first place will be relived. New perspectives will be gained on our First Nations food cultures as we explore their traditional links with nature.

As we approach not only a new century but a new millennium, it's an appropriate time to be looking ahead but also to be looking back. We can't know where we're going until we know where we've been. Our foodways are a direct reflection of our social and cultural history, of family and regional ties, and our collective identity as Canadians.

But digging up our culinary roots is not an easy task. Food gets very short shrift in our history books and archives. This is partly because food was long associated with domestic life and thus not considered important, but also because Canadians are traditionally self-effacing about such things. We seem to prefer the understated, the modest approach. This can be very endearing, but there comes a time for stronger stuff.

And the nineties is it. It's a perfect time to do some flag waving. I hope *Northern Bounty* will inspire greater pride in our culinary past, present, and future. Canadians could certainly use some cheering up, some reminders of how much we have in this country, and appreciation of who we really are as a people. We need comforting, but we also need excitement. Our best Canadian cuisine can provide both—with soul-warming traditional dishes and the creative new styles of fresh-market cooking. We need consuming passion, not fashion. We don't need gastronomic pretension or regional affectation when we can have the real thing.

But along with all the pleasures, we recognize the problems. Our food resource industries are facing massive challenges. The Atlantic fishery is in serious crisis. Canadian family farms are becoming an endangered species. There are difficult choices to be made, both nationally and globally. With increasing debate about trade and tariff barriers, global environment, food safety, and distribution, it's clear that politics, science, and technology somehow have to be balanced by a profound concern for the human spirit and for the Earth itself.

Canadians are in a unique position to carry that philosophy into the twenty-first century. When Margaret Fraser and I were researching our book, *A Century of Canadian Home Cooking*, it was clear that Canadians have special ties that bind them to the land and sea. As one farmer simply stated: "Our roots are terrible deep here."

So, to quote from *A Century of Canadian Home Cooking*,[1] I would like to conclude with these thoughts about the future: "We are still close enough to our rural roots, to natural wilderness and the rhythm of the seasons to pass along to our children a respect for the sources of their daily food. We are also a society of richly diverse culinary traditions, with a long history of sharing that began with our first pioneers and has continued down through all the decades. Today as in the past, our Canadian cooking doesn't need defining; it needs sharing. When we pull our chairs up to each other's tables, we understand a little better who we are. Sounds like a good start for a brand-new century."

Carol Ferguson is a Toronto-based food writer, editor, and consultant. She is a professional home economist and was food editor of *Canadian Living* magazine for more than ten years, editor of *Canadian Living's Food* magazine, and author/editor of *The Canadian Living Cookbook*. She is co-author, with Margaret Fraser, of *A Century of Canadian Home Cooking*, an illustrated cookbook/culinary history of Canada through the decades of the twentieth century, and author of *Really Cookin'*, a cookbook for students and other novice cooks. Her current projects include development of food programming for specialty television.

THE REGIONAL CUISINE OF BRITISH COLUMBIA

EVE JOHNSON

Historical Influences on West Coast Cooking

SUPPOSING we all agree that such a thing as West Coast cooking exists—if only in the minimal sense that there are people who live on the West Coast who cook. What is it, then, that distinguishes this cooking? It has something to do, of course, with being in a specific place on the Pacific Rim.

Before contact with European culture, B.C.'s coast supported the most materially wealthy hunting and gathering societies the world has ever seen. Everywhere else people needed agriculture to accumulate wealth. We had salmon—along with an entire world of other sea creatures—and we still do.

Asian flavours are another part of the mix: strong and getting stronger. Close to 25 percent of the people who live in the Lower Mainland understand the word *homeland* to mean somewhere across the Pacific, not the Atlantic.

We have a busy fermenting food world that includes our own monthly magazine for food enthusiasts, Rhonda May's *City Food.* We have restaurants—the best known being The Raintree—that consciously work at forging connections with growers and serving local food in season. And we have delis where you can get soups, sandwiches, sushi, and *samosas.*

If we're all agreed that this eclectic, rich, Asian-influenced stew is what we mean by "West Coast cooking," then I can quickly explain its historical antecedents. And they have about as much to do with food in early Vancouver as the science and democracy movement in early-twentieth-century China had to do with Confucianism. In that case, Chinese university students came back from study abroad fired with a belief in Western scientific culture. In this case, we haven't had to travel—although the fact that many more people have eaten good food elsewhere doesn't hurt. Instead, the revolution has come to us. Aside from the removal of racial restrictions on immigration during the 1960s, the one biggest influence on today's West Coast cooking is California, as presented through the food media.

Call it the "Alice Waters-Chez Panisse" effect. But here's the paradox for you: our interest in fresh, local food comes from the new orthodoxy of the international food world. It comes from *Bon Appetit* and *Gourmet*, from the sudden shift in North American understanding that made it okay to think and talk about food as something more than fuel. If you'd like a convenient date for the revolution in Vancouver, try 1980, when Granville Island Market opened. Suddenly we had a successful city market where there was always something new to taste.

Now, here's the really puzzling part. Why did it take so long for us to show this level of interest in our own food? We've had the same natural resources since the 1880s, when settlement began. There were 100 Chinese living in Granville in 1886, when it became incorporated as Vancouver. Japanese and East Indian immigrants were not far behind. Yet the wok came to us as an exciting new piece of kitchen equipment in the 1970s, and it was well into the 1980s before you could reliably find fresh ginger in large produce departments. Why is it that before 1970, our best known culinary achievement was the Nanaimo bar?

Where I propose to lead you is into the black hole of West Coast cooking before the revolution, a lightning tour of the years between 1880 and 1980. This is, more specifically, urban mainstream cooking, as reflected in newspaper food pages. My approach is, necessarily, anecdotal, but it has its advantages. Last spring, while doing research for a historical essay for my book *Five-Star Food*, a collection of recipes from the pages of the Vancouver *Sun*, I had a revelation. Suddenly I understood why a newspaper might want to call itself the *Daily Mirror*. A newspaper is a mirror, with one fragment broken off and delivered to your door every morning. A newspaper survives by appealing to the tastes of its readership.

Just to let you know how far we're travelling, I'd like to show you a particularly jagged piece of the daily mirror. This one was authored by Edith Adams, who, from 1912 until 1979, was the newspaper's voice of homemaking authority. (We still have a recipe-finder column called "Edith Adams Answers," though we no longer use her byline or answer the telephone as Edith Adams.)

In 1947, Edith had her greatest moment. The *Sun* opened a self-contained suite of rooms on the main floor of the old Sun Tower on Beatty Street, with a separate entrance, a test kitchen, a demonstration kitchen, a model living room, and five full-time home economists. In December of that year, the newspaper ran a recipe contest, offering $500 in prizes for the best B.C. recipes.

From 3,486 submissions, judges picked as a grand-prize winner Fraser River Salmon Royal—a salmon stuffed with oysters, larded with bacon, and baked at 400 degrees Fahrenheit for twenty-five minutes a pound. If you had any left over, presumably you could always use it as wood filler.

But the recipe I'd like to draw to your attention is Vancouver Island Salad—which won a special award. The ingredients are grated cabbage, apple, carrot, and celery, sprinkled with icing sugar, mixed with three-quarters of a cup of whipping cream, moulded, turned out onto lettuce cups, decorated around the base with banana slices, topped with cream-cheese-and-nut-stuffed celery cut into slices one-third of an inch thick, and, finally, finished off with a dollop of whipped cream and a maraschino cherry.

Here are Edith's comments: "No meal is complete without a vitamin-and-mineral-rich salad." Cabbage, it turns out, was the most often used salad ingredient among the contest entries. As far as Edith was concerned, by trimming and decorating cabbage, the Vancouver Island Salad "really raises the humble vegetable to the plane of the more exotic."

So how did we get to Vancouver Island Salad? How did we come to eat such bland, sugary food? And why did we eat it for so long?

The Europeans who came to the West Coast were traders, not farmers. They wanted sea-otter pelts first, then lumber. From the beginning, Vancouver was a transportation and trade centre. The city grew because it was situated where the trans-Canada railroad met the Pacific steamers. That gave it a very different growth pattern from the city that comes into being to serve a prosperous agricultural region.

When I began my research for my essay, I wanted to find out when we first started eating California fruit. I got my answer reading the Vancouver *News* for August 11, 1886. Both Blake Bros. on Carroll Street and Harme's Bakery advertised "fresh California fruit," a dividend, we assume, of the thriving steamship traffic between San Francisco, Seattle, Vancouver, Victoria, and Nanaimo.

Vancouver never depended on local agriculture. In 1912, Maxwell Smith, writing in the Vancouver *World*, described the province's agricultural assets and asked: "With these splendid natural conditions . . . why do we have to import upwards of $20 million worth of foodstuffs annually?" Vancouver, by the way, had just reached 100,000 in population. His answer—"Too many of our so-called farmers and fruit growers are in reality simply land speculators."

This may or may not be true. (Certainly land speculation continues to be a more reliable route to wealth than farming.) But I can testify that it was easy, growing up in Vancouver in the 1950s and 1960s, to lose sight of the fact that we lived on the coast. We ate canned salmon, breaded fish sticks, and the occasional piece of fresh cod. Fresh salmon arrived on the table when my brother started working as a commercial fisherman. The single biggest West Coast element in our diet was the summer's succession of berries, beginning with strawberries, ending with blackberries.

From the beginning, the urban West Coast was able to by-pass the dependence on local food that might have led us to develop a distinct culinary tradition. We could eat what we wanted, and unfortunately, that meant British colonial food—the food you get when you take the natural conservatism of British cooking and put it in an environment in which fears for cultural survival run high.

Let's not forget, in this age of global eating, that for most of human history, people have defined their cultures, in some ways, by what they don't eat and others do. Food comes encased in culture. Here's Henry Beard and Roy McKie in *A Cook's Dictionary*—a very British book—defining "very light" use of garlic: "one or two sides of Enrico Caruso singing Cavalleria Rusticana, played at moderate volume on a small kitchen hi-fi placed not too close to the cooking pot."

In Paul Yee's book, *Saltwater City: An Illustrated History of the Chinese in Vancouver*, there's a garlic story from closer to home. Sister Theresa Fung, Vancouver's first Chinese nun, tells of cooking during the 1930s for destitute men at Mount St. Joseph's Oriental Hospital. "Before I came," she says, "the sisters did all the cooking with water. They boiled up chicken and rice and vermicelli and that was considered a Chinese meal. But the men wanted salt fish steamed with pork. They liked the taste of dou-see and meen-see [bean sauces]. They liked roast pork and salt shrimp sauce and tofu, so one day, I heated the big pot and fried up the garlic and the salt shrimp. And then the sisters came running, crying, "What are you doing? It stinks."

British Columbia's period of officially sanctioned racism lasted from 1875 to 1949, the year Chinese citizens finally won the right to vote in municipal elections. If our food culture was hermetically sealed, despite the early presence of Chinese, Japanese, and East Indian immigrants, look here for a reason.

Those who belong in the mainstream lose status if they eat the same food as people of lower status. People who, for example, are barred from voting; running for political office; becoming lawyers, pharmacists, or chartered accountants; joining the police force; practising forestry; or even working in the post office.

It was 1962 before the federal government started to remove racial references from Canada's Immigration Act; 1967 before Chinese and South Asian immigrants were considered on the same basis as Europeans and Britains. This holds even truer for food of the coastal First Nations. By 1880, when settlement began in earnest, disease had swept through native populations, reducing the Haida, for example, from an estimated 9,000 to under 1,000 by the turn of the century.

Our second founding cuisine, perhaps even more unfortunate than the first, began to make its presence felt in the early years of the century: American home economics. By the end of the Second World War, it had become a more powerful presence on our tables than even our British heritage. And with television, and the Kraft kitchen, it triumphed.

This is a cuisine that put nutrition, as it was then understood, highest in its values. Next came sanitation, best expressed in the phrase "untouched by human hands." Nothing, of course, could beat the sanitation of packaged food produced in modern factories. Economy was next on the list of virtues, a nod in the direction of what was often the most powerful determinant of a narrow diet. Taste ran a poor fourth, if it was considered at all.

From this perspective, the delight with which Edith Adams greeted the Vancouver Island Salad seemed only natural. It was a "vitamin-and-mineral-rich salad," after all. And what could be cleaner and more refined than icing sugar? The basic ingredient, cabbage, is as economical as vegetables get.

What carries over across the gap between the fifties and the eighties? I think there are two main influences: one of them negative, one positive.

In the past fifty years, transportation systems have only become faster and more efficient. Agricultural land is threatened because farmers can't compete against California, with its low production costs and long growing season. In the summer of 1992, farmers dumped loads of iceberg lettuce on the steps of the legislative assembly in Victoria to protest iceberg lettuce dumping of another kind that was going on at the border. But every year we witness the annual berry desecration, when you can get California berries in every supermarket and B.C. berries only in specialty stores, as though eating what grows around you were some sort of difficult and expensive affectation.

The positive is that even if we managed to stay largely unconscious of the Asian food cultures around us, when we finally did wake up to the joys of *mirin* and *hoisin*, everything was there for us. If West Coast cooks, on the whole, are open to experiments in fusion cooking, it's at least partly because we never have to send away for anything. If you want it, you can get it.

This isn't, I admit, a flattering picture of West Coast culinary development. But in its outlines, it's a true picture of the way most urban people ate on the West Coast in the years before there was any discussion of something called West Coast cooking. We aren't drawing from a strong tradition of making the best use of native and local foods. Instead, we're consciously creating a West Coast way to eat.

Historical Influences on West Coast Cooking

Eve Johnson has a master's degree in history from the University of British Columbia. Since 1987, she has worked in the food section of the Vancouver *Sun*, first as food writer, then as food editor. She now writes about agriculture, as well, for the newspaper. She is the author of *Five Star Food*, a cookbook, and a co-author of *Vancouver: A City Album*, a visual history of the city.

STEPHEN WONG

Asian Flavours

FROM frozen broccoli to fresh organic greens, from HP sauce to aisles full of exotic condiments and flavourings from around the world, Canadians no longer have to look much farther than their neighbourhood supermarkets to see the signs of change in the way they eat. Not only are we more aware of nutrition and the sources of our foods, but we are blessed with an unprecedented variety in ethnic cooking styles and tastes. An evening meal at home or out can easily be roast beef and gravy, fettucine alfredo, or a Thai fish curry, depending on our mood. In the Lower Mainland around Vancouver, ordering out for Chinese on Boxing Day, can be as traditional as having a Christmas turkey. Ethnic celebrations such as the Greek Festival on Broadway or the Chinese New Year parade in Chinatown are as permanent on the family calendar as Thanksgiving or Mother's Day. The broadening of tastes is leading the way to more colourful lifestyles and new, evolving food ways. This expanding collage is part of the Canadian Experience, unique and inherent in our legacy and in our commitment to be a multicultural society.

The question of whether we have a national cuisine is ultimately a trivial one. The daunting task is in describing its complexity. The reason for telling the self-indulgent story that follows is that I believe it to be germane to the topic at hand. It depicts how ethnic influences evolve and contribute to the development of Canadian cuisine. For me, the experience of change was up close and personal.

I arrived in Calgary, Alberta, on September 4, 1973. The trip from Hong Kong was a gruelling thirty-hour ordeal that included a tour of a handful of major airports on both sides of the Pacific. I was exhausted. I could hardly stomach the bowl of noodles my sister offered. I barely noticed that strange vegetable that looked like a large cluster of choice *gailan* flowers bunched together. It turned out to be broccoli, which I've since grown to adore.

The next evening it snowed—those large, fluffy, first-of-the-season prairie snowflakes. Life for the adventurous youngster that I was was off to a great start. The world that had previously existed only in Christmas cards and movies was now at my doorstep. I pulled on my new, soon-to-be-obsolete, made in Hong Kong parka, slipped and slid past the few blocks of slumbering suburbia, and plunged into the bright lights of the nearest strip mall, eager for my first night out in a strange country. To my disappointment, the stores were closed. But I found myself bathed in the irresistible golden glow of a pair of giant yellow neon arches and was inexorably drawn toward the slick, well-lit eatery below. I was ravenous, and it was time for evening snacks anyway. And so it happened that I had my first Filet o' Fish and French fries, washed down with a Coke, of course. My apprenticeship in Canadian living had begun.

I might have been only one of millions served by the fast food giant that was soon to captivate billions around the world, but for me, it was the one giant step that marked the beginning of my Canadian food odyssey. Once I embarked on it, I never looked back. In the next few months, guided by my new friends from college, I ate hamburgers; fried, barbecued, and cacciatoreed chickens; thin- and thick-crusted pizzas; spaghetti with meatballs; fish and chips; even tuna salad sandwiches.

But before too long, I began to notice a yearning in the pit of my stomach (which, as we all know, is where the soul resides). I missed the smell of freshly cooked rice, its special chewy texture, the way it soaks up and spreads the flavour and juices of other foods across the tongue. That's when I remembered the electric rice cooker my mother, against my most emphatic protestations, had painstakingly packed into my luggage when I left home. It had been sitting in the corner of my tiny basement-suite kitchen, quietly gathering dust—patiently waiting for the inevitable. And so I found myself, in my new ski jacket, trekking across what by then had become a full-blown winter-wonderland landscape, looking for the familiar. This time I headed for the nearby Safeway.

I had my heart set on a simple stir-fry with *gailan* and chicken, and a couple of eggs fried with green onions and Chinese sausages, which I would steam over my rice for flavour. The Chinese sausages were another "don't leave home without it" gift, this one from my aunt. They came packed together with the dried mushrooms from a family friend. The doting instructions said that I was to share the bounty with my sister when I got to "Ga Na Dai" (Canada). Both items had been sitting at the back of my refrigerator, awaiting their moment of glory.

The rice was easy. I picked it after only brief deliberation, opting for the "unconverted," bagged in plain plastic, over the "converted," despite my admiration for the colourful packaging. The meat, eggs, and vegetables were next. I went to the meat counter, marvelled at the neatly wrapped chicken, poked at the rather pathetic-looking shrimp, picked up some eggs, and came to a halt, puzzled, at the gleaming and meticulously stacked vegetable counter. Things were beginning to get complicated. The vegetables were strange to me and the selection, in the middle of a prairie winter, was slim. I pinched, then rejected, the glossy but underripe tomatoes; searched in vain for fresh ginger. Finally, after getting some strange looks from fellow customers and a store clerk, I decided on celery, carrots, and mushrooms. The resulting meal was different from what I had started out to make, but satisfying nonetheless.

It was sometime later, when I took a job with the Canadian Pacific Railway as a relief train operator and began travelling among the small towns of Southern Alberta, that I discovered that I had, like so many others before me, reinvented the North American version of chop suey, which contrary to popular belief is not an American invention but an adaptation of a classical Cantonese dish—a fact that reflects the inventiveness of Chinese cooking as a *method.*

No different from many other cultures, the Chinese have had a long history of food ways that are inextricably woven into their way of life. Food is much more than something that merely satiates hunger—it profoundly affects one's well-being.

For the Chinese—and the Chinese enculturated into Canada—food is medicine. The Chinese take the expression "you are what you eat" almost literally. Many of the most expensive Chinese foods and the strange inventory you will find in the drawers and jars of Chinese apothecary shops, such as sharks' fins, birds' nests, and dried sea cucumbers, may have great reputations with only dubious curative powers to match, but they feed the soul. Eating gelatinous foods will keep you supple; eating a soup made from dried geoduck siphons can improve your virility—true or false, there's a lot to be said for the psychological edge.

Food is what appeases the gods (of course, after offering it to them, what's left over, you get to eat). Food is for festivals, celebrations, and funerals. Foods are omens: eating the right things during the New Year celebration can affect your fortune in the coming year. Foods as gifts are effective social lubricants—they may improve the mood of a cantankerous boss, provide incentive to faithful employees, or act as a simple calling card. Food-related rituals, such as your place at the banquet table or being offered a choice piece of chicken, can be an indication of your current social status. These are only some of the Chinese food-related beliefs.

It was reported that during the most restrictive times of the Cultural Revolution, great expenses were not spared for banqueting. Even for the poorest peasants, banqueting represented a diversion from their back-breaking toil and, perhaps more important, a supplement to their otherwise meagre diet.

In Canada, especially in the West, Chinese food ways have become one of the roots of a blossoming tree that is modern Canadian cooking. In fact, the tree has turned out to be a magical one that will bear fruits of all colours and flavours—a fairy tale to thrill all for generations to come.

It is no coincidence that this remarkable achievement is rooted in the rich soil of our nation's history. It all began with our commitment to the social philosophy of multiculturalism, which allows our nation to be enriched by continual waves of immigrants. Cultural food ways, cooking methods, and flavourings imported by immigrants from their parent cultures are the seeds from which the roots germinate. Almost without exception, the new immigrant modifies the methods and concepts of his or her cooking to adjust to the availability of ingredients—and in this way, the seedling is planted in the soil. After a certain time has passed, as they acclimatize to Canadian life and gain a surer footing in the socioeconomic firma of their adopted nation, the "homesick syndrome" happens: the immigrants begin to yearn for the staple or "comfort foods" they had in the Old Country. For immigrants who came from countries that have an established history of well-integrated food ways, rituals, and traditions, this yearning can be very strong indeed. Soon, in order to satisfy this longing, foods are imported; those that can be cultivated and produced here are transplanted and developed into budding businesses. Foods discovered here are carried to their native land on visits. A wonderful exchange begins to happen to the benefit of all—the young sprout fleshes out into a vibrant young tree. Before too long, as social circles expand and mature, these new food ways are gradually introduced into the mainstream population and the young tree begins to bear fruit. This is what seems to be happening now, and has happened in the past few decades, in the Asian Canadian communities on the West Coast. New flavours and new dishes have been developed and integrated into the mainstream diet—the fruits are ripening into what can now be justifiably called Canadian cuisine.

Examples of new food marriages abound. A First Nations recipe of dried clams calls for soya sauce and sugar instead of molasses from an earlier version. A Filipino *sinigang* remains rich and flavourful, but becomes a brilliant showcase when West Coast salmon is substituted for the traditional pork ribs. Black cod and roasted pork braised with garlic has become a new hot-pot classic in Chinese restaurants. Geoduck sashimi is now coveted both in Japan and Hong Kong, almost at the peril of local stocks. The list goes on.

Chronologically, Asian influences on the Western Canadian food scene began as early as the days before Confederation, with the Chinese leading the pack. In the late 1800s, many Chinese immigrants were employed in restaurants and hotels in the Lower Mainland and on Vancouver Island. Soya sauce began to flavour First Nations recipes, and the festive foods of the Chinese New Year were always a popular diversion. A hundred years later, in the postwar years of the late forties and fifties, a great number of Chinese-Canadian restaurants dotted the nation, even in the most remote and unexpected places. When I worked for CP Rail in the early seventies, I was surprised to find chop suey, egg foo yung, chow mein, and fried rice on menus in virtually every hamlet and town in Southern Alberta. These hybrid Chinese restaurants had been there for many years and were very much part of the community. The widespread acceptance of Canadian-Chinese restaurants established some basic, but important, flavour references in the Canadian psyche. The taste of soya sauce and the salty, sweet, and sour balance present in many Asian dishes were no longer totally alien.

The liberating sixties brought gradual increases in Asian immigration quotas, especially from Hong Kong, Japan, Thailand, and Vietnam. In the seventies, increased demand for authentic ingredients by immigrants led to a boom in imports, market gardening, and food-processing activities in the Lower Mainland near Vancouver. A healthy economy and busy lifestyles brought increased spending in restaurants. Dining became entertainment as different types and styles of ethnic restaurants began to flourish alongside traditional steak houses. Dim sum and sushi, with their unique presentations and "point-and-order" accessibility, became popular. In the eighties, the entertainment aspect of dining flourished through increased coverage by the media. Food trends began to take on a dimension not unlike that of the fashion carousel—with ethnic cooking styles like Thai and Vietnamese joining the parade. Demands within the new Asian immigrant communities brought further increases in the varieties of imported foods from Southeast Asia, many of which were snack foods and prepared sauces. With interest piqued and taste buds primed, when Western Canadians, whether by necessity or by choice, retreat into our cocoons in the nineties, we may be packing oyster sauce and sesame oil for our stir-frys, *hoisin* for our barbecues, and *wasabi* for our homemade California rolls.

When we do go out to restaurants, we are more likely to encounter yet another patch of our expanding food quilt. Young Canadian chefs who grew up steeped in the flavours of this rich ethnic mosaic are now eager to add to the complex picture with their own signatures. Truly creative dishes that pundits have called eclectic and confusing are now commonplace and presented with justifiable pride. Traditional recipes and methods from Western and Eastern traditions are deconstructed and fused into new and original creations that defy easy classifications. Some may not work, but many do—with ground-breaking brilliance and ingenuity—enticing us with exciting combinations of flavours, textures, and presentations. To complicate matters, as part of this development, regional characteristics are beginning to emerge. Differences in produce and cultural demographics are blossoming into discernible regional styles, each a celebration of this fresh meeting of the minds and each a tribute to the divergent roots of our land. While Pacific Rim flavours are dominant in the West, European and Caribbean influences remain strong in the East. In the meantime, all across the country, in their pursuit for the ingredients that fuel their creative impulses, chefs are acquiring a better awareness of our food resources and a heightened concern for local agricultural issues. And their enthusiasm has begun to affect the public and change the way we eat. Whatever Canadian cuisine is and will become, one thing is clear: these are interesting times in the history of Canadian food.

Stephen Wong is a food journalist, restaurateur, and food and beverage consultant. Born in Hong Kong, he immigrated to Canada in 1973, and soon became immersed in the Vancouver restaurant industry, opening and managing restaurants including the Raintree and Cheyna Restaurant and Bistro. He has contributed to books, magazines, and newspapers in the Northwest, including *Pacific Northwest Magazine*, *The Northwest Palate*, *Northwest Best Places*, *Vancouver Magazine*, *Cityfood*, and many others. His work ranges from essays and newsletters on food and wine to recipe development for cookbooks, such as *Pacific Northwest: The Beautiful* Cookbook. Currently he is the freelance Pacific Rim food correspondant for the Vancouver *Sun*. He was invited to Japan recently to demonstrate Canadian food products.

NANCY J. TURNER
SINCLAIR PHILIP
ROBERT D. TURNER

Traditional Native Plant Foods in Contemporary Cuisine in British Columbia

ABORIGINAL PEOPLES in British Columbia used a wide variety of plant foods to supplement their staple diet of seafood, fish, and game. Most of these plant foods, over 100 in all, are not only flavourful, but also nutritious. Unlike some eastern plant foods, such as wild rice and maple syrup, hardly any of the western wild plant foods have become incorporated into the mainstream commercial food market. However, the potential of some of them for use in contemporary cooking, both for aboriginal and nonaboriginal people, is very good.

British Columbia aboriginal peoples were traditionally hunters, fishers, and gatherers. They tended their wild plants carefully, and some prime gathering and harvesting areas owned by individuals and families, were passed down from one generation to the next. Because aboriginal peoples were good managers of their food resources, they were able to maintain a fairly constant and predictable supply of food.

At Sooke Harbour House Restaurant on Vancouver Island, and in other regional cuisine restaurants, a major effort is being made to feature some of these plant foods in a modern context, often in traditional food combinations, but also incorporating new dishes and flavour variations.

Here are some traditional plant foods, their use historically, and some ideas for preparing and serving them in regional dishes.

Green Vegetables

Stinging nettle (*Urtica dioica*) This plant is obviously not eaten raw, but when the shoots are still young and tender, they are picked and cooked as a potherb, purêed for sauces, or used to make a rich, deep-green broth. They are an excellent and tasty accompaniment to fish, especially halibut. Before the coming of Europeans, nettles were valued mainly for their medicinal qualities, and for their fine, tough stem fibre, which was twined and used for cordage and fish nets.

Miner's lettuce (*Montia perfoliata*) This small, succulent-leaved annual can be grown from seed, and often readily self-seeds. Its leaves, with flower buds and stems, make a very pleasant salad green, and can be served alone or in salad mixes. The early miners and prospectors used it primarily, but aboriginal people in California also used it.

Thimbleberry and salmonberry sprouts (*Rubus parviflorus* and *R. spectabilis*) The tender young shoots of thimbleberry and its relative, salmonberry, were, and still are, highly appreciated as springtime green vegetables. Only the sucker shoots are used. When they can no longer be snapped off readily with the fingers, they are considered too tough and woody to eat. Once picked, they are peeled and eaten raw (or, in the case of salmonberry shoots, cooked), traditionally with a dressing of sugar and ooligan (eulachon) grease or some other type of animal oil. At Sooke Harbour House they are a delicately flavoured vegetable accompaniment to seafood, but can also be used in salad mixtures. Thimbleberry leaves, which are large, soft, and maplelike, make excellent serving surfaces. Traditionally they were used for drying berries on and for makeshift berry containers. The bright-pink flower petals of salmonberry are also edible.

Wild Berries and Fruits for Desserts, Preserves, and Sauces

Thimbleberries (*Rubus parviflorus*) Thimbleberries themselves are edible, and are still used by aboriginal people. They are soft and fine textured, with a sweet, pleasant flavour. In contemporary cuisine, their bright-red colour and sweet flavour can be employed to advantage in sauces for cheesecake and other desserts.

Salmonberries (*Rubus spectabilis*) One of the most common, and the earliest fruiting, of all the West Coast wild berries, salmonberry comes in a variety of attractive colours, from golden to ruby red. The berries can be served raw in salads or as a garnish, or cooked to make sauces.

Salalberries (*Gaultheria shallon*) Salal is one of the most common understory shrubs of the Pacific Coast temperate rain forests. It is in the heather family, and has tough, leathery evergreen leaves, and soft, sweet, dark-blue berries hanging from an elongated stalk. These are among the most important of all the wild fruits for Northwest Coast aboriginal peoples. They are picked in large quantities in the late summer and early fall, and were formerly cooked to a jamlike consistency using red-hot rocks, then spread out on skunk-cabbage leaves to dry in cakes for winter. Because they are sweet, they were sometimes used with other, more tart, fruits to enhance their flavour. Today many people make jam and jelly from salalberries. They yield a rich, bright-purple sauce that makes an attractive and delicious dressing for fish and other dishes. They also can be used in drinks, sorbets, cheesecake, and other dessert dishes.

Red Huckleberries, oval-leaved blueberries, evergreen huckleberries, and black huckleberries (*Vaccinium parvifolium, V. ovalifolium, V. ovatum*, and *V. membranaceum*) These and other species in the genus Vaccinium are among the most popular of all wild fruits. All of these were, and still are, used by aboriginal people, both fresh and dried for winter. As restaurant foods, they all lend themselves to a variety of main-course dishes as garnishes and sauces and to desserts. Every year the

Warm Springs Sahaptin people of Oregon celebrate the ripening of the black huckleberry with a "First Fruits Ceremony." These berries are so esteemed among some groups, such as the Nuxalk of Bella Coola and the Lillooet, that the name for black huckleberries in their languages simply means "berry."

Saskatoonberries, or serviceberries (*Amelanchier alnifolia*) These are a truly Canadian fruit. The city of Saskatoon is actually named after the Cree Indian word for these berries. They and related species occur right across the country. They reach their peak flavour and production on the Prairies and in central British Columbia. Several commercial varieties have been developed, and can be purchased in nurseries. Saskatoon jam and saskatoon syrup are made by Summerland Sweets and other processing companies, and can be purchased in some places. There are many varieties of these berries recognized by aboriginal peoples of south central British Columbia. Some are best suited to making juice, some to drying like raisins, some to drying in cakes. Dried saskatoons are a major ingredient in pemmican, and are known as an energy-rich food that can be cooked with meat or salmon, as well as used in a variety of dessert dishes.

Wild crab apples (*Pyrus fusca*) These are the only apples native to British Columbia. Hanging in clusters, they are small and quite tart, but they are very pleasant when ripe. They were harvested in large quantities in late summer and early fall by the aboriginal peoples, and eaten fresh or preserved. They are served with oil and a little sugar or "grease," a treasured oil from the eulachon fish. In the modern kitchen, they can be used fresh or pickled, as a garnish or to make sauces for main courses or dessert.

Soapberries (*Shepherdia canadensis*) Soapberries, or soopolallie, are small, very bitter berries that contain traces of saponin, a natural detergent that gives them the special property of whipping into a firm froth when mixed with water. This froth, sometimes called "Indian ice-cream," is a traditional British Columbia native food that is still made and eaten today, especially for feasts and parties. A lemonadelike soapberry summer drink is also made. Both of these are currently sweetened with sugar; formerly they would have been sweetened with sweeter types of berries. The soapberries can never be allowed to come in contact with oil or fat, or they will not whip up properly. Whipped soapberries have a slightly bitter taste, but it is well appreciated by many people. Soapberries are also widely traded and used as gifts. Soapberry whip, with its unique texture and flavour, can be used as a topping, or as a side dish for desserts in regional restaurants. The Quilicum West Coast Native Restaurant in Vancouver serves a soapberry-raspberry whip that is delectable.

Red elderberries (*Sambucus racemosa*) Many people consider these rather tart berries to be inedible, but in fact as cooked berries and sauce they formed an important component of the traditional diet of aboriginal peoples of the Northwest Coast. They have a unique flavour, and can be used as a specialty sauce or beverage flavouring.

Wild "Root" Vegetables

Edible blue camas bulbs (*Camassia quamash, C. leichtlinii*) These plants, in the lily family, have grasslike leaves, long stalks of bright-blue flowers, and edible bulbs that were a staple food of many aboriginal peoples of western North America. In British Columbia they occur mainly on the southeast coast of Vancouver Island, where they were formerly harvested in large quantities by the Coast Salish. They were traditionally cooked in underground pits, using red-hot rocks. The pits are lined and interspersed with various types of vegetation, such as fern fronds and salal branches, which both flavour the food being cooked and protect it from getting burned or dirty. The cooking time for foods like camas is normally about twenty-four hours. This extended period of cooking apparently maximizes the conversion of the major carbohydrate in these bulbs, *inulin*, into the sweet-tasting, easily digested fructose.

Camas bulbs have been served at Sooke Harbour House and have been greatly appreciated as a side dish to fish or meat, especially when the bulbs are smoked. They can be cultivated, but most of the bulbs available commercially come from Holland, where they were introduced and are now grown for worldwide distribution.

Caution: Care must be taken not to confuse the edible blue camas species with the very poisonous death camas (*Zigadenus venenosus*), plants with tight clusters of cream-coloured flowers and bulbs very similar to those of edible camas.

Wild nodding onions (*Allium cernuum*) Wild nodding onions were used by the interior peoples of British Columbia. Like camas bulbs, they contain inulin and are pit-cooked to soften and sweeten them. They were harvested in spring, and often braided together like garlics. They grow well in garden settings, and can be used as flavourings in salads and sauces. The bright-pink flowers are also edible, and can be used to replace chives in salads.

Indian rice, or mission bells (*Fritillaria camschatcensis*) The ricelike bulblets of this plant have been an important vegetable for Northwest Coast peoples. Slightly bitter in flavour, when served with a dressing of oil they were—and in some places still are—highly appreciated. Efforts are being made to propagate them and incorporate them into restaurant use at Sooke Harbour House. The rhizomes of the native springbank clover (*Trifolium wormskioldii*) and the roots of Pacific silverweed (*Potentilla anserina* ssp. *pacifica*), which often grow together with Indian rice in saline marshes and estuaries along the coast, also have potential as modern root vegetables. Efforts are also being made to propagate them and grow them in garden settings.

Flavourings, Seasonings, and Beverage Plants

Grand fir (*Abies grandis*) Traditionally used to make a tea, the needles of this plant have a citric, slightly resinous flavour. They are used at Sooke Harbour House as a flavouring for sorbet. The needled branches are also roasted until crisp and brown and used as a seasoning and garnish for other dishes.

Yerba buena (*Satureja douglasii*) Related to savory, this small, creeping mint has a strong aromatic flavour. The Straits Salish and Halkomelem of Vancouver Island made tea with it, which they drank as a beverage or used for medicinal purposes to treat influenza and colds. It can be used in herbal tea mixtures, as well as to flavour salads, soups, and sauces.

Indian celery, or Indian consumption plant (*Lomatium nudicaule*) This plant is aptly named, because its leaves and seeds have a strong celery flavour. The very young leaves, before the plants flowered, were harvested and eaten raw, or cooked as a potherb, by many of the aboriginal peoples of the southern interior of British Columbia. They also used the dried leaves and seeds as a flavouring for tea and tobacco. The peoples of the southern coast used the seeds more as a medicine and protective agent against disease and evil influences. The name "Indian consumption plant" derives from the use of the seeds in preventing and treating tuberculosis. They were chewed and the juice swallowed for colds and coughs, used to purify and disinfect homes where there was illness or death, or burned as incense in ceremonies relating to the coming of the first salmon. This plant has potential as a unique flavouring in salads and sauces. The seeds can replace fennel, caraway, or cumin seeds in Northwest cuisine.

Licorice fern (*Polypodium glycyrrhiza*) This small fern has sweet, licorice-flavoured rhizomes. The compound yielding the sweetness has been determined to be 600 times sweeter than sugar by weight. The rhizomes were traditionally used, in small amounts, as a mouth sweetener and appetizer, and to alleviate hunger. They were also chewed, made into a syrup for colds, coughs, and sore throats, or used to sweeten bitter-tasting medicines. They have potential as a sweetener for beverages, liqueurs, and dessert sauces.

Labrador tea (*Ledum palustre* ssp. *groenlandicum*) The leaves, and sometimes flowers, of this plant from peat bogs and muskegs have been used widely in Canada for making tea, which is also said to be excellent for colds and sore throats. Even when very dilute, the tea has a sweet fragrance and pleasant, soothing flavour.

Caution: Care must be taken to identify this shrub correctly. Other, related plants, such as bog laurel (*Kalmia* spp.) are toxic and can be confused with Labrador tea. Also, Labrador tea should not be made too strong, because it contains alkaloids that could be harmful in high concentrations.

Concerns about conservation and proper identification of these foods need to be addressed. Many of these plants can be propagated and grown in garden settings, rather than harvested from wild populations, which may be vulnerable to overexploitation. Partnerships between restaurant owners and aboriginal peoples could be developed, as is happening with buyers and harvesters of wild mushrooms, to provide employment opportunities for First Nations people.

Further research and development of these new "old" food sources is needed. Canadians need look no farther than their own countryside to find a wealth of nutritious, flavourful, and well-tested foods to incorporate into their cuisine.

Nancy Turner is an ethnobotanist and professor in the environmental studies program at the University of Victoria, British Columbia. For the past twenty-five years, she has been working with First Nations elders in British Columbia, documenting traditional botanical knowledge. She has authored more than fifteen books and monographs, including two handbooks for the Royal British Columbia Museum on *Food Plants of British Columbia Indians* and a series of four books on *Edible Wild Plants of Canada*, with Dr. Adam Szczawinski. Her latest is *Traditional Plant Foods of Canadian Indigenous Peoples: Nutrition, Botany and Use*, with Dr. Harriet Kuhnlein.

Sinclair Philip, an innkeeper on Vancouver Island for fifteen years, holds a Ph.D. in microeconomics from the University of Grenoble, in France. His inn, Sooke Harbour House, has been rated among the top ten in Ann Hardy's *Where to Eat in Canada* for eight consecutive years, and has been featured in numerous magazines throughout the world. Dr. Philip is an expert on West Coast shellfish and edible flowers. His organic gardens supply his inn daily with fresh produce.

A biographical sketch for **Robert Turner** can be found on p. 75.

HARRY McWATTERS

British Columbia Wines Take On The World

MOST PEOPLE would say that the British Columbia wine industry is new. But grapes have been grown in British Columbia since the 1860s. With a few grape cuttings, Father Charles Pandosy, an Oblate missionary, planted North American varieties near Okanagan at the mission south of Kelowna. Although Father Pandosy made wine from these grapes, he probably should have made jelly.

In 1922, the first contract was written between a winery and a grower. The winery was called Calona Wines and By-products. I've always been puzzled by what the by-products were, but they may have been more palatable than the wine Calona produced.

How our product line has evolved! In the 1960s, a forty-ounce bottle of wine called "Zip" sold for ninety cents. The name "Zip" seemed inappropriate and the wine was renamed "Zing." With the name change the price was increased by a nickel a bottle. Since women appeared to be buying wine, the wine makers coloured it pink, called it "Contessa," and increased the price to $1.05. Thus the slogan "Come alive for $1.05" was born.

The sad saga continued! Because the wine was not the most sophisticated, the makers thought that if it was mixed with other beverages, it might be more marketable. "Ginju" was the result: a clear version mixed with gin, with a 20 percent alcohol content!

In the meantime, genuine wine makers were quietly pulling out native North American grapes and planting hybrids in their place. In the 1960s, some of the French hybrids that came in were of exceptional quality. They grew well in British Columbia, were winter hardy and disease resistant, and they made a much better wine.

In 1966, Casabello Winery was established by a group led by Evans Lougheed, a businessman and my mentor, and Tony Biollo, a grape grower. They not only planted hybrids, but also began to experiment with European vinifera grapes, solely to produce quality wine. They were the first in British Columbia to produce vinifera grapes of any consequence. In 1968, I joined them, and in that year we sold 17,000 gallons. It was very progressive at the time to sell quality wine!

The signing of the Free Trade Agreement radically changed the British Columbia wine industry. It was recognized that if we wanted quality wines in our future, we would have to remove less desirable hybrids and plant European vinifera. So a collective decision was made by the federal and provincial governments, grape growers, and wineries to remove two-thirds of the grape acreage. This reduced our grape-growing lands from 3,400 to 1,000 acres—hardly an industry at all! But a number of us were committed to producing excellent wines and we refused to proclaim the death of the British Columbia wine industry. From a consumer's perspective, pulling out the hybrid grape vines was the best thing that has ever happened.

Today many people are dedicated to producing high-quality wines. Since the "pulling out" program, we have doubled the size of our vineyards to 2,000 acres, and plan to plant 250 to 300 acres of vinifera grapes this spring. The principal vinifera varieties produced in British Columbia are Chardonnay, Riesling, Pinot Blanc, and Pinot Noir.

British Columbia now has four wine regions. The largest and oldest wine is the Okanagan Valley, where wine history dates back to Father Pandosy's grapes. To the west through the mountains, is the high desert valley of the Similkameen region. Near the city of Vancouver, the expansive Fraser Valley farm community enjoys a temperate climate. Our newest wine region is on Vancouver Island, an hour's drive from Victoria. In each of these four regions, back-road explorers can discover wine makers who come from around the world, who produce exceptional wines.

British Columbia wineries are grouped into three categories: farm gate, estate, and major commercial. Farm-gate wineries are those that produce up to 45,000 litres a year; 75 percent of the juice used to make the wine must be from their farm. Estate wineries produce up to 180,000 litres of wine, and 50 percent of the juice for the wine must be estate produced. Major commercial wineries bottle unlimited quantities; at this time there are six large ones.

Wineries and growers from the four British Columbia regions now work together with the British Columbia Wine Institute to assure quality through an appellation standards program called the VQA (Vintners Quality Alliance). In the 1980s, when we began to develop standards for our industry, we could not decide whether to call our organization British Columbia Appellation or Appellation British Columbia—somehow we had trouble envisioning the letters "ABC" on the bottle's logo. At about the same time, a group of Ontario wine growers who were developing their own set of standards approached us and suggested that there could be unique marketing opportunities if we entered into a joint venture. We signed a contract with them to use the Vintners Quality Alliance (VQA) designation and we've agreed that in export markets there will be harmony in standards.

Since the British Columbia Wine Institute was established, some differences have existed between British Columbia and Ontario VQA standards, but the basic criteria are the same. For both provinces, from the beginning grapes have had to be 100 percent British Columbian or Ontario grown to qualify for VQA status. As well, if a bottle of British Columbia or Ontario wine claims to be, for example, Chenin Blanc, it must contain a minimum 85 percent of that varietal grape. If a bottle has a vintage year on the label, it must contain a minimum 95 percent of that identified vintage.

However, the Ontario and British Columbia VQAs go about evaluating wines differently. In Ontario, the VQA consists of volunteers from an organization of wineries that have contracted to produce wines to the standards of the VQA. These wines are scrutinized by a tasting panel.

In British Columbia, our standards are legislated by the British Columbia Wine Act of 1990. Our VQA wines are subjected to a tasting panel, but unlike in Ontario, where the tasting is done under the scrutiny of the Liquor Control Board of Ontario (LCBO), in British Columbia tasting takes place at the Agricultural Research Station. Our tasting panel consists of four wine makers (not necessarily the same wine makers at all times) and two people from the British Columbia Liquor Distribution Branch. To qualify for the panel, individuals must go through a screening process at the Agricultural Research Station to ensure that they can identify flaws in wine and varietal characteristics.

The highest quality VQA wine from British Columbia is awarded the VQA Gold label, as determined by the Liquor Distribution Branch. Wine writers and restaurateurs who have proven themselves knowledgeable about wines comprise the panel that judges the Gold. Their mandate is twofold: first, to identify the VQA Gold and market the VQA Gold as British Columbia's best. Second, if they find a wine that they consider flawed or that does not make the quality statement the industry is claiming, they must send it back to the first tasting panel.

To give you an example of how the VQA system works, in a 1993 tasting of 156 wines, twenty-two were awarded VQA Gold. The 1992 vintage was exceptional. However, the industry thought that the number awarded gold was light, considering the excellent vintage year. At the same tasting, they identified two wines, less than 1.5 percent of the wines, that were "tired"—they'd been in the market for some time. Since the VQA has created a friendly cooperation between the wineries, the producers, and the institute, the wineries did not hesitate to recall those two wines, thus maintaining the standards.

We have found that the severest penalty that can be imposed on wineries that violate the standards is loss of the VQA certification on the label. This penalty can be imposed for up to three years, and products bearing VQA can be ordered removed from the system at the winery's expense. In our experience, this has been a total deterrent. We've had two minor infractions in our first three years that could be deemed accidental. However, penalties were imposed. In one case, a winery had VQA tank approval, which is preliminary approval giving them the right to put VQA on the bottle, but not the right to sell it until it had been properly certified. The winery shipped their bottles to the Liquor Distribution Branch on a Friday, because it was their experience that it normally took a week or ten days for the bottles to be shelved. The wine was due to be ratified by the tasting panel on Tuesday. That particular week, the Liquor Distribution Branch displayed an unheard-of efficiency and the bottles were on the shelves by Monday! Although approved by the panel on Tuesday, this was a violation nonetheless. The product was taken off the shelf and no shipments were accepted from the winery for one month. The winery thought that was a severe penalty—the industry thought it was a pretty good slap on the wrist—and I can assure you that no one has shipped wine early since then.

The introduction of the Goods and Services Tax (GST) in January of 1991 was a blow to the wine industry as a whole. In British Columbia total wine sales fell 7 to 8 percent. But at the same time, VQA wine sales increased by 45 percent. In 1992 and 1993, VQA wine sales continued to improve by more than 30 percent a year, and that growth was in volume, not dollars. Obviously the program was overdue: Canadians have responded with confidence. Our sales of VQA wines came not because of aggressive marketing, but because consumers recognized that VQA takes the "wine roulette" out of purchasing British Columbian wines. VQA on the label makes it easy to identify wines that are both British Columbian and of high quality.

Our grape-growing regions, with their long, hot days and cool nights, have also become major tourist attractions. Today in the Okanagan, most tourist inquiries (65 percent) are about touring wineries and activities related to the wine industry. (Golf and skiing inquiries take second place, and we have found that skiers and golfers often buy our wines, too!) Special events celebrate wine culture throughout the year, such as our fall wine festival in the Okanagan Valley. Tourists enjoy our well-known wines, but more so, they prize discovering lesser known, distinctly flavourful wines.

Chefs and restaurateurs have found it profitable to carry British Columbian wines on their menus. They seek out local ingredients and wines grown in British Columbia that reflect the agricultural base of their community. The clean, crispness of British Columbian wines inspires chefs to create complementary dishes from regional ingredients. Pinot Blanc paired with salmon is a classic match.

In the international market, our wines are sold actively in New York and London, and are doing well in Asia: Japan, Hong Kong, Taiwan, and Malaysia. And although most people by definition wouldn't consider Ontario an export market for us, it's a lot farther away in mind-set. My mission is to unite this country through wine. The British Columbia Liquor Distribution Branch and the Ontario LCBO are now exchanging VQA wines.

What about all the interprovincial trade barriers? Each province has its own jurisdiction over wine sales, and if we want to sell wine in Alberta our wines get the same treatment as wine coming from anywhere else in the world. We simply are not given special treatment, as in British Columbia, where British Columbia producers receive a preferential markup (and were a target under the Free Trade Agreement). If there were trade barriers that could come down, the only thing I'd like to see as a producer is the right to ship by mail order to any Canadian. (Of course, that would also mean that any producer anywhere in the world would have the same opportunity.) However, many provinces would have to give up tax revenue to do this, so I don't see it happening.

Perhaps the best wine value is to buy direct at the farm gate. The returns to the small farm producer who sells to the customer from the winery are much greater, and, of course, there are no distribution costs. Restaurants search out their unique wines, not readily available anywhere else. As a result, there are some great buys on these very special unlisted wines.

We have shown that a demand for good British Columbia wine exists (beyond our expectations), even when sales of "pop" wine were plummeting. The gamble we took when we ripped out our old established vines paid off. Everyone has benefited—the consumer, the restaurants, the grape grower, and the wine maker.

Harry McWatters is president and co-owner of Sumac Ridge Estate Winery Ltd. His entry into the wine industry after a successful stint in business was in 1968 with Casabello Winery. Presently he is chairman of the British Columbia Wine Institute. In 1987, he chaired the conference of the International Society of Wine Educators in Vancouver. He was the founding chairman of the Okanagan Wine Fest, an annual ten-day festival now in its fifteenth year, with more than fifty sanctioned events, including visits to wineries and wine tastings.

NOËL RICHARDSON

An Herbal Journey

THE HERB GARDEN at Ravenhill Herb Farm is now fifteen years old. This is the story of how it came to be a great source of inspiration for my cooking; for writing cookbooks, newspaper columns and restaurant reviews; and for my local political activity, too.

Fifteen years ago my husband, Andrew Yeoman, and I purchased ten sloping acres on the Saanich Peninsula, overlooking a beautiful valley and the Saanich Inlet, and decided to become farmers. I was returning to the island of my birth, where members of my family had lived since 1886, when they first came from England. Several generations of them are laid to rest in a local graveyard, and this has always given me a sense of roots that I get nowhere else. My Yorkshire-born husband, after years in the oil business and the financial world, had experienced a great urge to create a garden. Being pragmatic sorts, we needed to grow a crop we could sell. Our mutual love of food and cooking, inspired by our travels to Europe and California, persuaded us to choose culinary herbs as our cash crop.

During our first summer we collected mother plants and Andrew sketched and designed the future garden. He made raised beds and terraced the vegetable and herb garden. We had paths and walls built near the house to enclose the flowers and create a private patio area for outdoor living.

The next summer, after a winter of dreaming and reading countless herb and garden books, we sent out a letter to prospective chefs about our fresh herbs. Only one replied, but at the end of the summer we had four customers, and during the next few years our clients increased to twenty-six. Friday became "herb day," a dawn-to-dusk enterprise. We did not advertise, but a chef told us that when chefs gather to drink wine and eat after work, they swap sources of good ingredients. That is how our name was passed around.

In our first few years we had our heads down, facing the earth, and were not too aware of the outside world. Then the single shop that sold our herbs asked for a pamphlet explaining the culinary uses of our herbs. I collected sixty favourite recipes and Andrew, with his trusty calligraphy pen, made a little book, which we collated around the dining-room table. We sold it for two dollars, and with its folksy charm it sold well—more than 2,000 copies. I took it to a cookbook seminar given at Simon Fraser University and met a publisher, who asked me to expand it into a full-sized book. I did this, and a local botanical artist, Joan Ward Harris, did line drawings and the cover. The creation, *Summer Delights*, went into the world, taking me with it, and it is now in its fourth printing. To promote the book, I offered a few free cooking classes at a local kitchen shop that became quite popular. After our kitchen was renovated, I began to give classes and herbal dinners at the farm. People loved seeing the garden and connecting it to the food on their plates. I started to give talks at garden clubs and to women's groups, and groups began to ask to visit the farm.

With Andrew's careful planning and hard labour, the garden was becoming a work of art. Today it is an enchanting mix of herbs, shrubs, vegetables, and flowers, framed by old Douglas firs and copper beeches, with a wonderful view of the valley, sea, and forest. It is strictly organic, and we raise sheep and chickens as a source of manure—and food, of course. We began to open on Sundays, and sold plants, cut herbs, and my cookbook. And people could walk through the garden. After this public exposure, several magazines asked us to write about the farm and our life. We had created a bucolic fantasy that seemed to touch a need or dream in many people. I enrolled in some writing courses and nervously started to send out articles. I received rejections, but I took the advice of a teacher who told me to write for free in the beginning—anything to get my foot in the door. So I wrote in a deli newsletter belonging to a friend—chatty little notes about cooking with herbs. Shortly thereafter, for the vast sum of thirty five dollars a month, a new newspaper hired me to write a food column. I leaped at the chance and for a year happily wrote articles, until one day when I went to deliver an article, the door was locked, the paper gone, and they owed me for three stories. Sadly I felt my writing career was over and I would be pulled back into the dreaded weeding. However, fate appeared in the form of a lifestyle magazine that asked me to be a restaurant reviewer. With some trepidation, I agreed, and have struggled with the limitations of restaurant reviewing since (the phrase "my companion ordered the lamb" fills me with yawning boredom). I try to write about life as well as about the restaurant I review, because sometimes the people are more interesting than the food. The editor of a new magazine in Vancouver who had done a story about the farm asked me to do a "country cooking from the garden" column—and to write the way I talk. This comment was both inspirational and validating for me as a writer and a person. She knew that urbanites, having an Edenic rural fantasy, relish reading about it, but prefer not to live it. For most, gardening and feeding chickens are too grubby.

About this time, certain events menaced our serene Eden. Dreaded developers were eyeing the forested land behind us and urban sprawl was becoming a genuine threat to our beautiful peninsula. Ordinarily the quiet, reserved gardener, Andrew began to organize politically. With much campaigning and the help of many people, the battle against the developers was won. I was appointed to a local heritage committee and began to work to save old barns, farmhouses, and buildings erected by the first settlers over a hundred years ago. Since we had both become more and more rooted in our farm and its life, our community involvement increased. Andrew helped organize a successful farmers' market with a completely volunteer committee, which has added much to the community. We started to have art shows in the barn, and donated the proceeds to charitable causes, usually for heritage goals such as a new roof on the pioneer museum. In November we hold a charitable craft fair. We fill the barn with boughs and lights, then put a fire in the wood stove to heat apple cider. The sheep, goat, and donkey come in and the chickens wander around. It is pure country theatre and hundreds of people come to see and enjoy this earthy, nonplastic Christmas event.

Following our first craft fair, I wrote my second cookbook, *Winter Pleasures: Preserving Herbs for Winter,* a companion volume to *Summer Delights.* About the same time, Andrew did a small calligraphy-penned volume about composting, and dedicated his earnings to the preservation of the farmland. With his fifteen years of experience on the farm, he is now working on a gardening book about how to grow herbs and vegetables organically for the cook and the kitchen. It will have a West Coast flavour, and be written with our cool marine climate in mind, since food can be grown year-round here.

What does the future hold for us? My younger daughter is a chef and will continue to join me in cooking classes in the farm kitchen. We plan to give more art shows in the barn to raise funds for local heritage causes. We will keep on gardening organically without chemicals—Andrew says he grows enough for us, the chefs and the bugs. As the soil is enriched by compost, every year the bugs seem fewer and the plants healthier. We both hope to write more and stay involved in environmental issues that affect our community: preserving farmland from urban sprawl, farming organically, fighting pollution in our streams and inlets, and preserving historic buildings and sites. Who would have thought that growing herbs for culinary, gustatory pleasure would lead to political activism? But the fact is, one act leads to another and there is a logic in the sequence of events. As our old age approaches, we should become more radical about caring about the land. The environment gives rich meaning to our lives, and happily we can share it with others through their visits to the garden and our writing.

Noël Richardson was born in Comox, British Columbia, graduated from the University of British Columbia in English literature and history, and became a school librarian. Fifteen years ago, she and her husband, Andrew Yeoman, started Ravenhill Herb Farm, near Victoria. She has written two herbal cookbooks—*Summer Delights* and *Winter Pleasures*—and is a restaurant reviewer for Vancouver's *Western Living* magazine. "Cooking from the Garden" is her monthly column for *City Food.* Ravenhill Herb Farm is a constant creative stimulus for her writing and her talks about the history and use of herbs. She is actively involved in local heritage preservation, and is committed to environmental issues concerning farmland and food production in British Columbia and Canada.

THE REGIONAL CUISINE OF THE PRAIRIES

BEULAH (BUNNY) BARSS

The Chuckwagon Tradition in Prairie Culture

STUDYING Canadian traditions has value for many reasons. It illustrates how people in a frontier society coped with and adapted to a changing environment. It helps us understand existing habits, and it instills in us an appreciation of our Canadian heritage. Food and cooking played important roles in the development of this country, and many traditions emanated from them. Such is the story of chuckwagons in the settlement of the West. Invented to provide meals to hungry cowboys working far away from the home ranch, they grew into an interesting, romantic Canadian tradition.

The use of chuckwagons on the range is a thing of the past. Today meals are sent out from ranch kitchens in the backs of half-ton trucks. Chuckwagons, however, are rolled out for special occasions, and the beef and beans served from them taste like culinary masterpieces. Chuckwagon breakfasts of bacon, flapjacks, syrup, and coffee are specialities at race meetings, fairs, and rodeos across the country. These breakfasts originated at the 1923 Calgary Stampede, and have become a symbol of "western hospitality."

Chuckwagon racing is now a major competitive sporting event featured at rodeos throughout the West. At these events, chuckwagons, each pulled by four well-trained, spirited horses, race at breakneck speeds around a track. The spectacular sight is a reminder of by-gone days at roundup time, when chuckwagon cooks raced their wagons and half-wild horses across the grasslands to win the best site for setting up camp.

The chuckwagon tradition lives on through these races and celebration meals.

Texan Charles Goodnight is credited with developing the first chuckwagon. He purchased a government wagon left over from the American Civil War and had it rebuilt to make a rolling kitchen. It provided meals for working cowboys, becoming their home-away-from-home for weeks and months at a time as they trailed cattle over the vast ranges of the early West.

Chuckwagons accompanied cattle drives to the prairies and foothills of Western Canada in the late 1800s. At that time, ranches were not fenced and the cattle roamed as they fed. During severe storms cattle drifted and became separated. It was necessary to organize roundups several times a year to gather them together for branding and to select beef for market.

A ranch had its own roundup, or five or six ranches got together for a general roundup, with every ranch bringing its own outfit and chuckwagon. Each outfit consisted of twelve or more cowboys and each cowboy had a string of six to twelve horses.

The chuckwagon served as kitchen, dining room, social centre, and hospital and home for the cowboys. It was a light mountain wagon, with high wheels and wide-gauged axles that had been strengthened to withstand wild rides over rough country. The bottom and sideboards were made of the roughest wood available. Wooden bows were arched over top so that a canvas sheet could be pulled over for protection on rainy days. The tailgate was removed, and in its place a "chuck-box" was installed. Approximately four feet high and three feet deep, this box was fitted out like a pantry, with shelves and divisions and drawers. Its hinged door was let down to rest on a wooden support leg, thus forming a work table for the cook. A curtain could be lowered over the end of the box to keep out the dust. Once the table was in place a cook tent was pitched so that the tent opening was right up against the table.

The wagon was packed with enough supplies to feed sixteen to twenty men for several weeks at a time. Shelves and drawers in the box were stocked with staples such as coffee, sugar, salt, baking soda, baking powder, and lard. Sacks of flour, beans, rice, cases of dried fruits, kegs of syrup and molasses, milk, canned tomatoes, and creamed corn were placed in the bed of the wagon. Cooking and eating utensils were stowed in the chuck-box compartments. Heavy cooking pots were stored in a compartment underneath the wagon or simply hung from the side. Empty, clean flour sacks were stuffed into a drawer, to be used for towels and aprons. There was also a drawer for medicines and simple remedies such as liniment and a needle and thread for sewing. A tin stove was attached to one side of the wagon, a water barrel to the other side. Strapped to the back of the wagon was a Winchester carbine. The wagon also carried bedrolls, ropes, axes, and extra gear. When the roundup was really large, a separate wagon was outfitted to transport bedding and gear other than food.

The chuckwagon cooks were versatile, talented men. They organized the supplies and packed the wagons; they prepared three meals a day in a small space with limited resources. It was the cooks' job to keep the harnesses mended and the wagons repaired. They were expert teamsters, capable of driving four half-wild broncs over rough country. Sometimes they acted as doctors to ailing cowboys, or sewed on buttons and refereed fights. Cooks got up earlier than anyone else to get the fire going and have the breakfast ready; they worked longer hours, as well. For this they received top wages, more than the average cowboy. They were not young men. Many of them had been cowboys, but because of an injury were no longer able to spend long days in the saddle. They loved ranch life and overseeing the chuckwagon was a way of remaining part of that life.

It has often been said that only a fool argues with a skunk, a mule, or a cook. In spite of the wagon cooks' reputation for being cantankerous, they achieved a special fame that has lived on in folklore. Ed Larkin was considered to have made the best raisin pies ever. Charlie Lehr was remembered for his steaks; Billie Grier for his sourdough. Billie "Forks" Houston was remembered because his wagon was pulled by mules instead of horses and he threw most of the wagons' forks at them trying to speed them up. Understandably, the wagon was short of forks by the time roundup was over! Dirty Dick, Death on the Trail, and Poison Bill Findlay need no explanations. Stone Roberts, renowned for his wit, retired to a piece of land outside of Calgary, where he liked to reminisce about his cooking days. He recalled how annoying it was to start his yeast bread, then receive orders from the foreman to pack up and move camp. He had to keep the pan of rising dough on the wagon seat beside him so he could punch the dough down when necessary. "I suppose," said his listener, "that you stopped at some stream of water to wash your hands before punching it down." "Hell no," replied Stone. "I'm not like some of those dirty chuckwagon cooks, always having to be washing my hands."

It was a big task to prepare meals on a small work table at the back of a wagon in all kinds of weather. The ingredients on hand were those items that kept well over a long period of time. Beef was the only fresh meat, and generally it was available only on a large roundup or when an animal injured itself. Keeping the meat fresh was a challenge. A quarter of beef was placed in a gunny sack and raised by a pulley and rope to the top of a thirty- to fifty-foot pole, where the breeze was cool and the meat safely above the range of blow flies. Beef steaks were sliced off the quarter and pounded in flour to tenderize them, then fried in hot melted beef fat until crispy brown on the outside. Beef stew might have canned tomatoes added to it, or onions and potatoes if available. Tough cuts of meat such as shank or neck were boiled. Beef that was corned or pickled so it would keep in the summer months would also be boiled, then sliced for serving or made into a corned beef hash.

Beans were eaten on more cattle drives and roundups than any other food. They were served so frequently that meals were often referred to as "bean time." Dry beans were easy to store and they kept indefinitely on a chuckwagon. They were cooked in a heavy Dutch oven in the evening to be ready for eating the next day, in sufficient amounts to last for several days. Generally salt pork and molasses—sometimes canned tomatoes—were added for flavour.

Chickens were scarce in ranch country, and eggs, if available, were considered too fragile to pack. Neil McKinnon, however, recalled that the LK chuckwagon cook packed eggs inside the oat barrel, where they were somewhat cushioned for the rough ride.

Canned milk was used on the chuckwagons and on many ranches, which surprises many people. But the cows were range cows and would have had to be roped and thrown in order to be milked. Cowboys would not be caught milking a cow if they could help it. That work was considered beneath them. Ranchers such as Willie Cockrane of the famous Cockrane Ranching Company, which ran 20,000 head of cattle, drove to town and loaded their wagons with cases of canned milk.

Most cooks prepared special desserts when possible. Pies were popular: raisin, dried apple, dried apricot. When the cook located some saskatoon bushes and had time to pick a bucketful of fresh berries he would make a pie. Rice pudding was a standby. When raisins were added, it was known as Spotted Dog.

When chuckwagon cook Mulligan Jack wanted to be especially nice to the "boys" on a roundup, he served a Son-of-a-Gun-in-a-Sack. This was a steamed or boiled pudding that required considerable ingenuity to prepare out on the prairie in blowing winds or cold rain. He'd drop a clean, smooth stone into the bottom of a sugar sack and make a hoop from a willow branch to hold the top open. The sack was dipped in water and dusted with flour. Then he'd spoon in the mixture, remove the hoop, and tie the top. The pudding and sack were immersed in a pail of water and boiled for several hours. When cooled, the sack was peeled off and the pudding sliced for eating.

Similar to the Son-of-a-Gun was the Duff and Dip, which was a type of steamed plum pudding. "Duff" was the pudding, "Dip" the sauce to pour over it. It was so tasty that it was talked about long after the roundup was over.

Sourdough was brought along on the wagon in an enamel pail or keg, and from it the cook made biscuits, bread, and pancakes. Sometimes camp biscuits were called "belly busters," and according to old range hands that was not a jest. Careless baking and the use of soda in most quickbreads led to more than a few digestive problems. In the early days bread and biscuits were baked in Dutch ovens over coals of the fire. When portable reflector-type ovens became available, baking was much easier.

Another delicacy, served only at roundup when bull calves were castrated, was Prairie Oysters. The calves' testicles were collected in a pail, washed, skinned, soaked in saltwater for about an hour, rinsed again, then rolled in seasoned flour and fried in hot fat until the outsides were crisp and the insides tender.

Cowboys had a great sense of humour, and it was often directed at their food. Fortunately J. D. Higinbotham, a Lethbridge pharmacist, always kept a little book in which he recorded words and expressions that he found peculiar to the times:

baked wind pills (baked beans)
flapjacks (pancakes)
CPR strawberries (prunes)
tin cow (condensed milk)
red lead or red paint (catsup)
dough-gods (dumplings)
rattlesnake (bacon)
a million on a platter (beans)
paperweights (hot biscuits)
tent pegs (frozen beef strips)
yesterday, today and forever (hash)
sowbelly (pork)

There were many other descriptive chuckwagon expressions, such as "lick" for molasses; "Charlie Taylor," a butter substitute consisting of syrup and bacon grease mixed together; "sinkers" or "hot rocks" for biscuits; "wrecker," the round pan for piling up the dirty dishes.

When the cook got up in the morning, as early as three o'clock, he'd put the wide-bottomed, smoke-blackened, five-gallon coffeepot on the fire so that the aroma of coffee would lure the cowboys out of their warm bedrolls. Although wagons operated by men from the British Isles served tea routinely, coffee was the acknowledged drink of most outfits and tea was regarded with disdain as something akin to poison. Jim Spratt was American-born, and a noteworthy character even for a cowboy. One evening when his outfit was camped near a big alkaline lake in Saskatchewan and all hands were sitting around yawning as usual, Jim stepped up to the stove and lifted the coffeepot to fill up his cup. The cook cautioned, "It's tea—we're out of coffee." Jim pulled out his six-shooter, peppered that pot full of lead, and warned, "You have coffee for breakfast or you'll get that, too." Coffee was in the pot for breakfast.

The chuckwagon cook was boss of the wagon and the space around it. There were unwritten rules regarding manners and deportment.

When riding into camp a cowboy always stayed downwind, and woe betide the unlucky one who stirred up a cloud of dust or tethered his horse too close to the wagon. A visitor to the outfit would not dream of helping himself to a snack or cup of coffee until invited to do so. When a meal was ready the cowboys held back until the cook yelled "Come 'n' get it," or gave some other signal for them to help themselves. Then they'd fill their plates, sit down on their bedrolls, and begin eating. They did not wait for others to serve themselves, nor did they make polite conversation. "Eat now and talk later" was the rule. Hungry men could go back for seconds, but they never took the last portion of food unless everyone else had been served first. Generally they ate with their hats on; only when eating at a proper table in the presence of a lady did they remove their hats, though if they left them on, this was not regarded as offensive. Only a greenhorn broke these rules, and then just once.

In the days of the open range a well-run chuckwagon was highly regarded. Not only did it attract good cowboys, but it reflected a well-managed ranch as well. It can be said truly that chuckwagon cooks made a significant contribution to our history and deserve a place of honour in our folklore.

Beulah (Bunny) Barss completed a B.A. in home economics at the University of Saskatchewan, qualified as a dietitian at the Royal Victoria Hospital in Montreal, and received an M.A. from the University of Calgary. She is the daughter of a Saskatchewan pioneer family and now resides in Calgary with her husband. Her interests include preserving the rich heritage of ranching and pioneer experiences, particularly those relating to food and cookery. She is the author of three historical books about Canadian food and two souvenir cookbooks.

MARGARET FRASER

Canada's Breadbasket:

Decades of Change

FRESHLY BAKED BREAD, whether the pioneer's staple, yesterday's comfort food, or today's source of complex carbohydrates, has long been Canada's staff of life. The Prairies, with their vast, waving wheat fields, have for many years made Canada one of the world's major wheat-exporting countries. Since the turn of the century, Prairie baking has varied from region to region, even from family to family. Our cooking has always been tied to our lifestyle: where we lived, in rural areas or in urban, whether we were affluent or not, a settler or a sodbuster; and, perhaps more than anything else, our ethnic heritage. Through the decades our cooking has reflected the yield of the land, for there have been years of plenty and years of naught.

Let me tell you about Prairie baking through the twentieth century.

The First Decade

As the railway crossed the western interior, a veritable sea of immigrants, as well as Eastern Canadians, moved onto homesteads. Towns sprang up along the rail lines. In just seventeen years (1896–1913) more than a million newcomers passed through Winnipeg, "the gateway to the West." They came in waves: German-speaking Mennonites, Icelanders, Scandinavians, Americans, trainloads of settlers from all over Europe and the British Isles.

But life for the hopeful farm owners was not as wonderful as the posters and the speeches had promised. In fact, it was harsh. Much of the land required breaking, and indeed would have been better left for grazing. Clearing the land was slow, back-breaking work, done without proper equipment, by men—and women—who often knew nothing about farming.

Those who arrived with "ten dollars and a dream" had little else but the thought of a bountiful harvest to keep them going. In the face of drought, prairie fires, grasshopper plagues, dust storms, blizzards, rust damage to grain, and poor quality seed, crops were more often than not a disappointment.

City dwellers and townsfolk fared better. Many settlers made cook stoves with ovens a priority in their homes. Some even had iceboxes, running water, and a "hired girl" who lived in. But the majority still relied on kerosene lamps, a backyard pump for water, and a wood stove, where Mother baked all the bread.

Farm folks came to town by horse and buggy to buy oatmeal, flour, sugar, molasses, beans, and prunes (called CPR strawberries in the West). Those far from town made it in only two or three times a year to load up with supplies. When these supplies ran out, they had to use coarse hand-ground flour, which made dark, uneven breads. Small privately owned flour mills gradually appeared across the Prairies, though they were few and far between. In 1909, a mill on the banks of Thunder Creek in Moose Jaw, Saskatchewan, began to turn out a flour named after an English hero—Robin Hood. This hard-wheat, all-purpose flour was packed into 100-pound cloth sacks stamped with a guarantee of "Absolute Satisfaction or Your Money Back Plus a 10% Premium." Not a bad deal . . . although the 10 percent premium has since been dropped from the company's money-back guarantee.

Using flours like this, with homemade yeasts or starters such as sourdough, potatoes fermented with sugar and flour, boiled hops, or barm (a fermented soft dough of flour, salt, and warm water), bread was on the table in most Prairie homes morning, noon, and night. Doughs were made by the "sponge method," a two-stage mixing with three risings. The process took all day or overnight. Loaves were baked in ovens where temperatures were gauged by how the oven felt as you stuck your hand in briefly. The results of this baking were willingly shared by Western Canadians. They broke bread with family, neighbours, the local schoolteacher, and the preacher. Often loaves were rough and heavy, but nothing was wasted.

Bannock, the simplest of breads, could be made with little more than flour, water, and a bit of lard, turned into a frypan and baked over a campfire. Red River settlers made a frugal bannock, now offered annually at Winnipeg's Folklorama, and a Saskatchewan firm markets a bannock mix. With much the same ingredients, a little baking soda, and sour milk, the Scots made scones. A biscuit dough, lightly handled, it was fried in a heavy griddle and turned once for a golden crust top and bottom. In many regions of Canada today these scones appear with raisins or cheese, made with whole-wheat flour or wheat germ in place of some of the flour, and often with the addition of cranberries or blueberries.

Lots of variety characterized the early sweet baking. The baked goods were mostly brown in colour from the brown sugar and molasses in them, and they were usually spicy. Lard from rendered pork fat was used to fry doughnuts. Fruitcake, cookies, and cakes laced with cinnamon, ginger, and cloves were favourites and good keepers. Pies, generally double crusted and full of apples or wild berries, were also popular. And yes, they made butter tarts. Pancakes or flapjacks, dumplings, cobblers, steamed puddings, rolled cookies, and, at Christmas, shortbread or special ethnic favourites, all attested to the availability of first-rate flour.

But special occasions or not, Westerners baked with a hard-wheat, all-purpose (bread) flour. (Soft wheat was grown more in the East, hence the more common use of a blended or cake and pastry flour in Eastern Canada.)

By the end of the first decade, Canada was the fastest growing country in the world and the world's largest exporter of wheat. A major breakthrough for western wheat farmers came in 1904 when Charles E. Saunders developed the rust-resistant *Marquis* wheat. Canadian wheat was considered the finest in the world winning gold medals at the 1904 St. Louis World's Fair. Wheat was indeed the gold of the West, and one of the foundations of Canada's economy.

The Second Decade

Immigration slowed during the second decade, but life on most of the Prairies still centred around the one-room schoolhouse or the community church. There were picnics, ball games, curling, Christmas concerts, sleigh rides, and dances. For all of these, home-cooked food and plenty of baking were the highlights.

Steam-powered tractors and threshing machines made their appearance in farm country. Bumper harvests meant wealth for mill and railroad companies, though little more than hard work for the homesteader. As for women, their work was never done. Relegated to the home, they were responsible for running the household: cooking, cleaning, laundry, child rearing, and caring for the sick. On the farm they also split wood for kindling, banked fires, took out ashes, fed the chickens, tended the garden, pumped water, milked cows, separated the cream, baked six or eight loaves of bread, maybe even bagged the dinner. After a day's work they often attended a suffrage or temperance movement meeting. Prairie women have always been outspoken campaigners for social justice and women's rights.

World War I overshadowed this decade. Although Canadian wheat flour had established its supremacy, the best was shipped overseas and home bakers were often left with a poor-quality wheat that made "war bread." Posters urged citizens to "Save Canada's Wheat." Commercial bakers were required to stop making fancy breads.

Milling companies promoted Five Roses, Purity, and Ogilvie's Royal Household flours with cookbooks that have been treasured and passed down through generations.

Gems were a favourite food of the decade. Similar to muffins, but baked in fluted pans called "gem pans," they were sometimes made with graham flour, a whole-wheat flour slightly coarser than regular grind. Pound cakes, originally baked with a pound each of sugar, butter, eggs, and flour, were made plain or studded with raisins, currants, candied cherries, or preserved ginger. An eggless, butterless, milkless cake simply called War Cake was a spicy, boiled raisin cake sturdy enough to tote to meetings.

The Twenties

Popular images of the twenties—flappers, the Charleston, and bathtub gin—were beyond the experience of most Canadians, particularly on the Prairies. A postwar slump and a series of poor crops dominated life until middecade. In the cities, men still carried lunch pails to work, women baked for church bazaars, and Sunday often meant a Flapper Pie (a vanilla cream filling in a graham-cracker crust with a meringue topping). Those fortunate enough to take a train trip enjoyed a taste of regional food served with impeccable style, in a flurry of white linen, with polished silver, in dining cars.

But at home, family supper fare included old favourites like stews, pot roasts, roast beef with Yorkshire pudding, and freshly baked biscuits or bread. Grain growers formed wheat pools and threshing time still meant tremendous quantities of baking for the many extra men who helped harvest the wheat. Twenty to forty loaves of bread, ten lemon and ten raisin pies, and good substantial cakes were the order of the day, along with rib-sticking entrees, of course, and gallons of tea and coffee. Threshermen often rated farms by the quality of the food served.

During this decade a new domestic efficiency began to grow. Homemakers' Clubs (similar to Women's Institutes) were organizing demonstrations and cooking courses. Electricity and natural gas were replacing coal stoves in towns. And flour companies published new editions of their popular cookbooks. *The Western Producer* and *The Grain Grower's Guide* featured articles about labour-saving kitchens, fireless cookers, hot school lunches, and feeding the threshers.

Local commercial bakeries began to deliver right to the door in horse-drawn wagons. Breads, buns, and cakes would be exchanged for pre-purchased tickets. But lots of homemakers continued to bake. Cheap, reliable, compressed fresh Royal Yeast Cakes were on the market, and the uncertainty of using homemade starters was over.

Baking-powder biscuits were popular, plain and dainty for ladies' luncheons, or split, buttered warm, filled with strawberries, and topped with softly whipped thick cream—the western version of strawberry shortcake. Tea breads like date nut loaf or banana bread were thinly sliced and served buttered. Sponge cake, the basis of a good trifle, was baked in a tube, square, or jellyroll pan. Basic white cake was served plain or frosted, or used to make upside-down cake with canned pineapple rings. Honey cake, Ukrainian in origin, was a nut- and raisin-filled cake usually made with buckwheat honey.

The twenties were also the era of royal cakes: the Prince of Wales, Prince Albert, King George, and King Edward cakes. And there were other "theme" cakes: Scripture cake, railway cakes, watermelon cake, ribbon cakes . . . the list goes on. The cookbooks from that time are full of them, but usually with very vague baking instructions—no pan size, no oven temperature, no doneness test; often only "bake as usual."

Just as the twenties were roaring at last, paper profits and too much wheat ended it all on Black Thursday at the Winnipeg Grain Exchange five days before the New York stock market crash on October 29, 1929.

The Thirties

The thirties were a decade of "use it up, wear it out, make it do, or do without." Ingenuity, plenty of belt tightening, and lots of bread-and-gravy or bread pudding were the order of business, along with soup kitchens, bread lines, and relief vouchers. Flour sacks were recycled as tea towels, curtains, even dresses. Flour companies offered patterns for sewing all manner of fashions from them. For the Prairies, the Hungry Thirties became the Dirty Thirties as drought turned "the breadbasket of the world" into a dust bowl. Along with the drought and wind came grasshoppers, Russian thistle, and hail to finish off what little crop remained. Yet through it all there was always enough to set an extra place at the table or offer a handout at the back door. Despite hard times, women baked their hearts out and still found a way to serve a tasty meal at the annual Thanksgiving Harvest Home Supper.

Domestic-science courses and Homemakers' Clubs on the Prairies continued to stress standardization in home cooking. Schoolteachers were mainly of British heritage and home economics classes taught familiar, not "foreign," foods. Unfortunately, we missed wonderful foods that should have been shared and not hidden in the kitchens of the ethnic districts. Although I grew up in Saskatoon, where there was quite an ethnic mix, I never tasted baklava, perogies, or Ukrainian

Easter bread until I went east. My parents, a Scottish mother and an Ontario-born father of British parents, cooked the kinds of foods their parents had. So the thirties to me meant chicken and dumplings (heavy on the dumplings), rolled oats or porridge bread (or one made with Red River cereal), banana bread, chocolate cake with brown-sugar fudge icing, sour cream raisin pie, matrimonial cake (date squares in the East), and at Christmastime shortbread and steamed carrot pudding. (My grandmother's recipe was called Six Cup Pudding, with a cup each of flour, carrots, brown sugar, bread crumbs, currants, and candied fruit.)

Had I grown up in a home with parents from Eastern Europe, I might have eaten buckwheat perogies, cheese dumplings, Russian potato cakes, and lots of cabbage rolls and sauerkraut. But regardless of our background we all ate saskatoon berry pies and smothered our bread with chokecherry or pincherry jelly.

Though we rarely shared recipes with neighbouring ethnic kitchens, there was a great sharing of agricultural advances aimed at ensuring sound future crops. Research in field husbandry helped farmers to control soils, and fertilizers and pesticides (which at the time seemed to be the better way) promised bumper crops.

Change was brewing on the home front, as well. Women asserted their independence and became busier outside the home. Along with Kraft Dinner came canned cream of mushroom soup, pudding mixes, and sliced bread. Talk about emancipation! In 1939, the best crop in eleven years made our spirits soar. The Prairie drought was over. Eastern manufacturers were eager to sell us modern new stoves and refrigerators as well as remarkable farm machinery.

But as crops were harvested that fall, Canada was once again at war.

The Forties

As World War II began, the first self-propelled combines enabled farmers in the West to harvest a record half a billion bushels of wheat, still Canada's leading export. The Wartime Prices and Trade Board announced a wage and price freeze and food rationing began in Canada. Nevertheless, life seemed grand compared with the Depression.

Bread baking continued in lots of rural homes, while cities and towns were now serviced by large commercial bakeries like McGavin's. Hundreds of white and brown sandwich loaves were filled and decorated for an endless stream of showers and weddings, both wartime and postwar. Besides the elegant party sandwich loaves, we made pinwheels, ribbons, and checkerboard fancy sandwiches for teas, and hundreds of big, hearty sandwiches to serve with coffee to "the boys." Small, light rolls were popular for luncheons: Parker House, cloverleaf, bowknots, crescents or butterhorns, fantans or simply pan buns (if you were in a hurry). And I wish I had a nickel for every cheese dream I made.

By the late forties, active dry granulated yeast was an alternative to yeast cakes. Developed during the war, this yeast did not require refrigeration and was simply activated with a little sugar and warm water. Also new was the "straight dough" method, which simplified bread making by cutting down the time required for rising.

Postwar recipes from flour companies also included recipes for a refrigerated yeast dough. This dough used water instead of milk, called for little or no kneading, and could be stored in the refrigerator for up to a week, making the use of only a portion at a time for fresh rolls very enticing. When prepared with twice the amount of sugar, butter, and eggs, this dough made a wonderful sweet dough for fruit-filled tea rings and cinnamon buns.

Boxes and bags of soft-wheat flour were in vogue out west at this time, specifically labelled "cake" or "cake-and-pastry" flour. Chiffon cakes (an innovation from California) hit the baking scene, and angel food cakes became popular, as well. Icebox cookies, the original slice-and-bake refrigerated cookie dough, was popular, especially when kitchens were streamlined and even farm kitchens had electricity.

The Fifties

The fifties were the Boom Years, the Fat Fifties. Happiness was a family, a house, a "baby bonus" cheque, and a television set. Convenience was the norm: electric frypan, waffle iron, kettle, blender, countertop mixer; built-in kitchen cupboards, Arborite countertops, garburetors, wall ovens.

Homemade bread took a back seat as the patio barbecue became the place to cook and the recreation room was the spot to entertain. Although local restaurants across the Prairies continued to serve traditional hot beef sandwiches (always on store-bought white bread, with gravy, mashed potatoes, and canned peas) or short-order specials like grilled cheese or club sandwiches, at least the flour was enriched, a condition of Newfoundland's joining Confederation in 1949.

A new wave of immigration was changing the multicultural food styles in big cities. Across the country, ethnic groups, proud of their food heritage, began to acknowledge their distinct contribution to our culinary history. One of the first cookbooks with a bit of Canadian history was *From Saskatchewan Homemakers' Kitchens.* In it was an account of "the rural home" from 1912 to the fifties. And Savella Stechishin, the first Ukrainian woman to graduate from the University of Saskatchewan, encouraged pride in her heritage with *Traditional Ukrainian Cookery,* a complete collection of Ukrainian-Canadian recipes. This cookbook is still a national treasure.

Canada's giant food and utility companies, as well as producers' associations, opened test kitchens and home service departments. Their home economists crisscrossed the country, giving cooking demonstrations and offering recipe brochures. With these books and pamphlets in hand, we filled angel cakes and whipped up one-bowl cakes (made possible using new emulsified shortenings to replace the traditional creaming method). We made Wacky Cake right in the baking pan and baked dozens of squares and bars.

The Sixties

The sixties were a whole new bag . . . everything from Flower Power to colour television to Pop-Tarts. Baby boomers protested and joined the back-to-the-land movement. Home cooks began to take "ethnic cooking" seriously, even though "international" often meant Hawaiian (anything with pineapple and coconut), Italian (tomatoes, garlic, and green peppers), or Oriental (soy sauce). Organically grown foods, "natural" ingredients, and health-food stores initiated a distrust of food additives.

On the other hand, Madame Benoît instilled in readers and television viewers her great love of our regional Canadian foods. *The Laura Secord Cookbook*, a Centennial project (now out of print) was one of the first books to create an interest in regional Canadian cooking. Some of the bread recipes included an almond-filled yeast bread called Dutch Kringle Bread; French bread, the crusty classic adapted to Canadian flour; and Greek Easter bread, a cloverleaf- (cross-) shaped loaf filled with candied fruit peel and raisins. Other treasured ethnic breads in this book included a Christmas sweet-dough bread of Ukrainian origin called *Makiwnyk* and the rich Ukrainian Easter bread called *Paska*; hot cross buns, originally an English tradition—which was served on Good Friday; a Polish bread with rolled oats, graham flour, and caraway seeds; a braided Finnish bread called *Pulla*, with cardamom and a shiny glaze of hot coffee and sugar; and Hungarian coffee cake, filled with cinnamon, nuts, cherries, and raisins.

Along with these ethnic breads were oatmeal bread, rye bread, sourdough bread, 100 percent whole wheat bread, and bannock. And those were just the yeast breads that greatly expanded the importance of wheat and flour.

Although not mentioned in the Laura Secord book, batter breads or casserole breads, made from a no-knead dough with a higher proportion of liquid, became popular during the sixties.

Following on the heels of Expo '67, there was a feeling in the land that we could be justly proud of things Canadian.

The Seventies

With the seventies came a need to try anything and everything, from Nouvelle Cuisine to the health-conscious "natural" foods to international gourmet fare. Whether because of travel, multiculturalism, or TV gurus like Julia Child, our gastronomic horizons expanded. It was the decade of the Cuisinart, and with it came food-processor doughs for breads and pizzas.

Interest in our own culinary heritage continued to expand. Food fairs and folk festivals like Winnipeg's Folklorama and Edmonton's Heritage Days offered taste teasers from many lands. Traditional breads from Eastern Europe and the Ukraine vied with pitas from the Middle East and pizzas from Italy.

Technology produced microwave ovens. Canada went metric, or at least started. (We're still stuck halfway there!) Test kitchens devised recipes using granola, bean sprouts, yogurt, and tofu. Sugar, salt, and white flour became the bad guys; healthy eating was the fashion for food in the seventies. Even carrot cake was made with whole wheat flour replacing half the white flour and with oil instead of butter.

The Eighties and Nineties

At first it was muffin mania, pasta machines (after all, Canadian durum wheat makes the best pasta), and oat bran in everything. The Prairies kept up with trends, and even created some, like adding pea flour to increase fibre in bread. Being closer to the West Coast (and California) Westerners often are aware of the "what's in and what's out" before Canadians in the East are. The emergence of ethnic restaurants, food shops, and Prairie farmers' markets offered even more opportunities to eat and cook well.

Bread machines and rapid-rise instant yeast, in-store bakeries, even bread baking in space are here. Familiar flours with a difference, like those with added bran or oats, are popular. Canada's new *Food Guide to Healthy Eating* is making our grains and breads fashionable once more. Recession and the desire for the comfort of familiar foods mean that our old standbys are reappearing, albeit with new twists. Seven-, nine-, and twelve-grain loaves of bread are the norm now. Soda bread may have rye flour and caraway seeds in it. Cakes are often less sweet, pies made free-form.

And through it all, in spite of the trends that come and go, Canadian home baking is still based on our old favourites, our traditions. As Prairie farm women seek recognition for their contribution, and Canadian farmers, women *and* men, work to keep family farms going, let us give thanks for our daily bread. Let us continue to share our diverse culinary heritage from our early western pioneers through the decades of change.

Margaret Fraser's most recent book, *A Century of Canadian Home Cooking* was a landmark endeavour co-authored with Carol Ferguson. It was the first book to document the history of twentieth-century Canadian home cooking. As a consulting home economist, Margaret Fraser writes for *Canadian Living*, and is now coordinating yet another book for them. *Canadian Living* cookbooks with her name on them include *Microwave, Barbecue and Summer Foods, Rush-Hour*, and *Light and Healthy*. In 1986, she was awarded the Toronto Culinary Guild's Silver Ladle Award (with Elizabeth Baird) and Toronto Home Economics Association's Honour Award (shared with Carol Ferguson). But her first love is baking cookies with any or all of her four grandchildren or barbecuing in Muskoka.

JUDY SCHULTZ

Development of the Prairie Palate:

The Red-Meat Eaters

WHILE we are all a part of this sprawling northern bounty called Canada, over time each of us identifies with a smaller region, our home turf, that special place that has helped to make us in some way unique. As we attempt to examine this country's culinary heritage, I'd like to share with you a small part of my own particular turf—the Prairies. The quirks of the Prairie palate are no accident; they are the result of a geography of formidable distances, a climate that ranges from moderate to extremely harsh, and our short history.

Any serious discussion of food on the Prairies must begin with the people of the First Nations. When the fur traders arrived on the Prairies, they would not have survived if the native people had not taught them how to deal with the extremes of distance, climate, and supply. Not surprisingly, these early traders had few culinary skills or gastronomic interests. For one thing, there were few women among them, and none carrying *Mrs. Beeton's* or *Fannie Farmer* cookbooks with flaky pastry recipes in their pockets.

The early settlers who moved west brought with them the customs, habits, and traditions from their recently vacated homelands, but they, too, lacked the skills and specialized knowledge necessary to deal with a food supply that was a cycle of feast and famine.

Settlers began to plant gardens as early as 1788 in what is now Manitoba and Alberta. Their seeds were not adapted to the short growing season and it must have been disheartening to watch young plants freeze and turn black before a single bean or pea could be harvested. Far away from major population centres, and faced with this harsh climate, the settlers had only one reliable food: red meat. But even that was not a given—they had to catch an animal or they would go hungry. Hunger proved to be a powerful teacher, and the pioneers were a quick study. The importance of meat is evident in records from 1823, when the standard daily food ration at Fort Chipewyan was ten pounds of meat for a man, and five pounds for a woman or a dog.

What a contrast between life on the plains and life in a Canadian city at the turn of the nineteenth century. In Montreal there were restaurants and grocers who cared about the ripeness of a cabbage or a cheese. There were bakers and butchers with an established clientele. People gave dinner parties. Toronto was small, but it had big ideas. A group of its ritzier women were getting ready to publish a cookbook from Upper Canada, with a section devoted to keeping domestic staff in line.

Although there were very few white people on the Prairies at that time, and not even many aboriginal people, there were, according to historians, some sixty million buffalo. These magnificent beasts roamed from the eastern shores of Lake Winnipeg, in Manitoba, to the slopes of the Rockies, and from the southern end of the Great Plains of the United States all the way into the Northwest Territories.

Members of the cattle family, and the largest land mammal in North America, bison stand six feet high at the shoulder, and weigh around 2000 pounds at maturity. There are two distinct species, the wood bison and the sweetgrass or plains bison, but the differences are subtle. At the beginning of the century, the bison was the Prairie's "one-stop-shop." It was the main source of food for the Plains Indians, the Métis, the incoming traders, and the settlers. It was not the only food source—the aboriginal people, traders, and settlers ate other meat, as well, when it was available. Or fish. However, bison was preferred for its excellent quality, either as a roasting meat or in a stew, or as the defining note in pemmican, one of the more exotic Prairie concoctions. Red meat, in particular, bison meat, sustained our fledgling Prairie population through a critical period of settlement.

Bison are sociable creatures, and they typically banded together in families or groups of fifteen to twenty. Eventually many bands linked up, forming herds numbering in the thousands. Skittish beasts, bison were easily stampeded. The Plains Indians understood this behaviour and capitalized on it with an organized hunting method, the "buffalo jump." The Indians deliberately stampeded the animals through a complicated series of coulees, driving them into a narrow, V-shaped lane, then over a cliff. A historic site in Alberta known as "Head-Smashed-In-Buffalo-Jump" was used as a communal kill site 5,700 years ago. If you fly over the Prairies today, you can still spot the ancient drive lanes of the bison.

Tribal customs for the hunt differed, but generally among the Plains Indians, the women followed the men to butcher, skin, and transport the bison back to camp. This was no small task. First they had to turn the enormous animals onto their backs to skin the hide. Using bone knives and their bare hands, they cut off or tore off the limbs, even chopped the ribs off the backbone. The meat and marrow bones were then folded in the hide for transport back to camp. Internal organs were wrapped separately. The most coveted bison parts were the tongue, shoulder, hump, the fat from the teats, the heart, and the fatty tissue along the crest of the hump known as "dépouille."

Some parts of the buffalo had religious or spiritual significance. The liver was removed and eaten raw. Occasionally, so were the muzzle and part of the kidneys. The blood was drunk warm by the men so that they would be brave in battle, and the tongues were given to medicine men to ensure a safe hunt.

When the women got back to camp, their first task was to preserve the meat. They accomplished this in three ways: drying the fresh meat, rendering the fat, and preparing pemmican from the dried meat and a portion of the grease.

To dry the fresh meat, they first cut it into thin spiral sheets less than a quarter inch thick, then hung them to dry over simple drying rods made of two tripods with a number of horizontal poles. If the sun shone, no fire was needed, but if it rained, the drying rods were moved into the tipi and set over a fire of buffalo chips. Anywhere from two to nine days later, the meat was dry. It was much like beef jerky in texture and flavour, but considerably leaner than beef. The brittle, dark, curled strips were then tied in bales or stored in rawhide sacks. This dried bison meat lasted for months and could be eaten as it was, broken into stews and soups, or toasted over the fire and eaten warm. The toasting process softened the dried meat and brought fat to the surface, making the meat much more palatable. During the period of early settlement from 1800 to 1870, dried buffalo meat was the basis of the Prairie diet.

The favourite fat for frying, cooking, and using as a substitute for butter was the rendered marrow fat from buffalo bones. As the bones boiled, the fat rose to the top. It was poured into a buffalo bladder, which was then sewn or tied shut. The fat from two buffalo cows filled one bladder and weighed about twelve pounds.

The most important dietary item provided by buffalo meat or any other red meat was pemmican. Although it originated with the native people, history books have an annoying habit of dismissing it as strictly an aboriginal favourite. It was a mainstay of the aboriginal diet, but its importance in the diet of the fur traders and settlers should not be underestimated. In fact, pemmican was consumed in such quantities by the Red River settlers that in January of 1814 the governor of Assiniboia, Miles Macdonell, banned its sale or trade from the colony for one full year. Called the "Pemmican Proclamation," the reason for this decree was to encourage settlers to plant gardens. With more settlers due to arrive near harvest time, starvation was almost a certainty if they relied only on pemmican. Since the fur traders and the local Métis provided the bison used to make pemmican, Macdonell's decree did not go over well.

Then, as now, not every cook was a great cook. The quality of the pemmican varied with the skill and imagination of the cook, the season in which the animal was killed, and the method of slaughter.

The first step in making pemmican was to pound some lean dried meat. Toasting the dried meat before beating it with stone hammers (malls) or hardwood sticks produced a finely chipped or powdered beef.

Meanwhile, the marrow fat from the bones would be rendered out, then mixed with the best of the tallow from around the kidneys. The concoction would be melted over a slow fire so that it would not burn.

Next, the powdered meat, known as "beat meat," would be mixed with berries—such as sweet, juicy saskatoons, tart little sand cherries, or even the seedy, pucker-power chokecherries—and whatever wild mint leaves or herbs that might be available. The melted fat would then be added and the resulting mixture poured into a buffalo-skin bag known as a parfleche. While the fat cooled, the bag was turned occasionally so that the ingredients would not settle out. Once the pemmican had solidified, it was ready for transport or storage. The proportion of fat, meat, and berries depended on many factors: the season, the success of the hunt, and the ingenuity of the cook.

Pemmican became the original western fast food. By adding just enough water to the pemmican to make a thick mass, along with herbs, additional berries, or even onion if available, "rubaboo," was the resulting trapper's variation. One pound of top-grade pemmican had a food value equivalent to five pounds of fresh meat.

Prairie cooking begins with outdoor cooking and communal feasting. Put these together and you have a barbecue. On the Prairies the word takes on a larger meaning: it embodies the tradition of hospitality for pioneers who settled the vast, empty grasslands and suffered as much from isolation and loneliness as they did from a sparse diet. For us on the Prairies the barbecue is a gathering of friends and strangers to share in the bounty of an outdoor feast during a time of plenty. It is a social ritual. The favourite adjective of many Prairie cooks is "barbecued," which is used to describe our favourite preparations of meat or vegetables cooked over open coals.

Barbecue includes three cooking methods: grilling, spit roasting, and pit roasting. Each has its roots in our early Prairie cooking.

From recorded anecdotes and oral histories, we know that meat was often placed on hot stones, or directly on coals, especially ribs. This seared the outside of the meat, leaving the inside juicy and rare—the original method of grilling on the Prairies!

When an animal was spit-roasted, its large intestine was cut into sections, dried, and broiled over coals. Sometimes the large intestine was filled with a mixture of blood and fat and the ends of the intestine tied off. This impromptu sausage was roasted in the ashes until it congealed. One recipe called Crow-Indian-Guts was considered a particular delicacy. A section of small intestine was drawn over a long strip of meat, the ends tied, and the whole supported over the fire by a forked stock so that the meat cooked in its own juices while the smoke permeated the membrane. Care was taken to keep the intestine from bursting and losing the juices.

Originally, pit roasts took place during the buffalo drive. A hole was dug in the ground, many hot stones were placed in the bottom, and a layer of sweet grasses and willow branches were laid over the hot stones. Several foetal or newly born buffalo calves were then placed on the hot stones and covered with grass and earth. About twenty-four hours later the meat was cooked.

As popular as buffalo meat was on the Prairies, within a short seventy-year period, the buffalo, the Prairie's original and best source of red meat, nearly became extinct. The great population of 60 million bison dwindled to a few thousand. There are theories about why this sustainer of life nearly disappeared. One is that the fur trade brought a new technology, the rifle, and the bison were overhunted. Another is that the series of cold, harsh winters in the 1830s contributed to their demise. Normally blizzards or cold, deep snow do not bother bison. They are born foragers who live exclusively on plants. With their shovel-shaped heads, they can simply dig out their dinner in a moderate winter. But the winters of the 1830s were abnormally severe. Finally, there is the theory that bungling by the Canadian government also played a part in the demise of the bison. In trying to protect the wood bison, the government unknowingly introduced disease and hybridized the wood bison stock in Wood Buffalo National Park. While the truth is likely a combination of these factors, one thing is certain—we nearly lost them.

But now they're back. Bison are again thriving, albeit in a cautiously controlled way, across the Prairies. The bison ranches are large and often contain densely wooded areas where the animals roam freely until a specific number are harvested. On the 7,000 acre North Country Bison Ranch at Smoky Lake, Alberta, the Bob Plum family care for between 400 and 500 head at a time. The bison take from twenty-four to thirty months to reach marketable weight. After culling, the herd continues to live and grow in its own natural way. Once again, Prairie cooks value buffalo meat for its flavour, its nutrient density, and for just plain good eating.

Prairie people have been meat eaters since they first arrived in the West. Although we think our lamb, pork, and chicken are exemplary, it was the cowboy with his omnipresent ten-gallon hat, his boots, and his faithful horse who became the symbol of the West. As any Westerner will quickly tell you, cowboys did not herd chickens, pigs, or sheep. Cowboys herded beef on the hoof. Cattle. More red meat. Thus the traditional western meal has always been built around red meat in some form. Today it might be the ubiquitous burger in the backyard or a steak fry. It might be a spit-roasted baron of beef, or a huge, savory stew; or if you are lucky enough to be in a crowd and with a pit-boss, a pit-roasted side of beef. If the meal is part of one of our other western traditions (a trail ride or a rodeo) other western foods—baked beans, sourdough biscuits, lashings of beer, maybe a discreet tipple of rye whisky—will be included.

But the defining ingredient of the feast will always be red meat.

Judy Schultz is the food and travel editor for the *Edmonton Journal*. A native of the Prairies, she loves food and festive occasions celebrated around the table. Her hobby is visiting kitchens, markets, and vineyards around the world. She is a frequent radio and magazine commentator and has taught courses on Prairie cuisine.

ROBERT D. TURNER

To Travel Hopefully:

Dining with the CPR in the West

BEFORE the Canadian Pacific Railway (CPR) across Canada was completed in 1885, then opened for service the following year, no means of convenient travel across the country existed. A journey between central Canada and the Pacific coast required a long detour through the United States or via Panama. The CPR changed everything about travel in Western Canada. A trip from Montreal to Vancouver could be completed in under a week and, for those with financial resources, in relatively comfortable surroundings. One could sleep on the train and be assured of reasonable meals en route. Nonetheless, travel across Canada was still a time-consuming, tiring adventure.

Passengers were vital to the financial survival of the new transcontinental railway, and the scattered settlements across the vast, almost unpopulated country offered few facilities for travellers. CPR management recognized that it would need to attract travellers and establish the facilities to make their journeys and visits enjoyable. This imperative was the basis of the CPR's hotel and dining car services. The famous Banff Springs Hotel and the Chateau Lake Louise were established in Banff National Park, Canada's first national park, primarily as a means of attracting tourist revenue to the CPR.

Steep grades in the Rocky and Selkirk mountains and the limited ability of early locomotives to handle the passenger trains prompted the CPR to build small hotels and restaurants at Field, east of Kicking Horse Pass, at Glacier in the Selkirks, and at North Bend in the Fraser Canyon to the west. The hotels were named Mount Stephen House, Glacier House, and Fraser Canyon House, and were opened soon after passenger service began. As crews changed or the train equipment was serviced, passengers could have a brief rest from the trip and a pleasant, if often hurried, meal. However, when two trains arrived at one of the meal stops at the same time, as apparently happened all too often, the facilities were seriously overtaxed, passengers were hurried, and service fell below standard. Later these early facilities were expanded and travellers were encouraged to stop over for a few days and explore the surrounding mountains.

Another factor for the CPR in having meal stops instead of dining cars in the western mountains was the high cost of purchasing, equipping, and using the cars. A fully equipped dining car could cost more than a new locomotive, and it was seldom profitable. Moreover, because seating space could not be sold on the dining cars, they were "dead weight" on the trains, which in the mountains meant higher fuel and locomotive costs. Short of funds following the heavy expenditures for construction and for improvements to the line during the 1880s and early 1890s, the CPR did, nonetheless, proceed to develop its dining-car services. The company took delivery of its first dining cars in 1885, and by the end of the century had a small fleet of sixteen. However, these were insufficient to replace the meal stops at the smaller hotels in the mountains.

The small dining-car fleet expanded rapidly in the early 1900s, a period when the railway experienced enormous growth in traffic and a major expansion of routes throughout the country. By the beginning of the First World War, eighty-eight more dining cars had been acquired. There were also various types of parlour and observation cars equipped with small buffets or cafés. With more cars and larger locomotives available, the meal stops at Fraser Canyon House, Glacier House, and Mount Stephen House were discontinued, and dining cars were run with the trains through the mountains. This produced some efficiencies, flexibility in scheduling, and far greater convenience for travellers. No longer were meals as rushed or passengers forced to wait for meals if trains were delayed. At the same time, there were major developments in the company's hotel system, with new hotels being built in Victoria, Vancouver, and Winnipeg and major additions made to the hotels in the Rockies. By the late 1920s, the CPR system was one of the most extensive in the world, and in Western Canada, the railway or its steamships reached nearly every major centre except for areas to the north along Canadian National's main line.

Food service on the CPR provided meals for everyone. Although meals were priced between seventy-five cents and a dollar, this was equivalent to half a day's wages for many people in 1900. In many communities at major division points, simple restaurants or lunch counters were set up in train stations or nearby. Another popular innovation were the cooking facilities in "tourist" and "colonist" cars for people to prepare their own food. These were sleeping cars with simpler interiors and fewer amenities for the travellers. In addition, sandwiches and similar snacks or light meals were sold by "newsies" on the trains. In later years, snack bars and lunch-counter services were instituted on many trains.

Dining cars required a large staff to service the substantial numbers of meals that needed to be prepared each day. The normal complement was eleven: steward; chef; second, third, fourth, and fifth cooks, and five waiters. Each had assigned duties and responsibilities. Dining-car staff could equal the number required to operate the rest of the train. A railway dining car provided very limited working and serving space. Normally the cars were about eighty feet long and ten feet wide, with at least half the car devoted to seating space for thirty to forty patrons. The pantry, kitchen, and stores were compressed into the other end of the car.

At peak meal times, the situation could appear chaotic. Staff had to be able to serve at least three seatings for each meal. However, with as many as eleven staff to serve thirty to forty patrons, there were sufficient people to provide attentive table service and individually prepared meals. This high staff-to-patron ratio was one means of ensuring quality control.

Table service—except during wartime, when some economies and shortages affected standards—was formal and carefully supervised. The CPR developed its own china patterns with special monograms for their dining cars, hotels, and steamship services. Similar decoration was engraved or stamped on the silver plates and cutlery. In many instances, company emblems or crests were woven into the linen tablecloths and napkins. Staff were instructed to lay out the china, silver, and cutlery carefully, so that the crests were at the top, not covered with food, and attractively displayed. Menus and other items also often displayed the company crests.

The supply and preparation of foods for the dining cars and dining rooms were major concerns, and critical to the system. Local, fresh foods were favoured whenever they were available. Economy was important, and it was stressed to staff that food was not to be wasted. CPR regulations stated that "Fruits that have become too soft to be served at table must be turned over to the chef to be cooked immediately. This material can be used to great advantage for making pies, short cakes, fruit sauces for puddings, etc., and is superior to all extracts, flavoring and colorings."

Menus and surviving recipes provide some further insights into the types of foods offered to travellers. Dining-car menus often included dishes with local or regional names or descriptions, such as Esquimalt Oysters on Half Shell, Baked Okanagan Apple with Cream, Winnipeg Goldeyes, British Columbia Potatoes, Canadian Maple Syrup, Individual Canadian Comb . . . Honey, and Lake Superior Trout or Whitefish.

Many other menu items were also clearly local in origin. Salmon, smoked salmon, and halibut were traditional foods on B.C. Coast Service menus and were featured, as well, on the B.C. Lake and River Service vessels. Vegetables were varied, and the selection sometimes noted as simply "Fresh Vegetables in Season." Entrees were meat or fish dishes, cooked and served with simple garnishes or gravies. On the interior steamships, live chickens were often carried on the freight deck, immediately available to the galley.

Of course, not all dishes were fresh, particularly in the late 1800s and early 1900s before modern refrigeration was available. Menus note jams, corned beef, sardines, and similar foods that presumably were preserved. Canned vegetables were used when fresh produce was unavailable, but cooks were instructed that the vegetables "must be removed from the can, the water discarded. Under no circumstances must they be heated in the tin or cooked in the tin water or allowed to stand in the can." Sources of supply appear to have varied greatly. A report on the Lake and River Service in 1919 recommended that for jams, jellies, preserves, and preserved vegetables the policy should be "to use the Okanagan brands. . . . In fact we might make a specialty of using these goods, which are excellent, on all our steamers."

An interesting feature of early menus was the inclusion of wild fowl and game. A December 1904 menu from the Kootenay Lake steamer *Moyie* noted Stuffed Goose (Wild), and a New Year's dinner on the sternwheeler *Kokanee* in 1898 featured braised venison cutlets, roast canvasback duck, and broiled snipe. The 1920 instruction guide to dining-car staff provided information on preparing roast or broiled wild duck, roast haunch or saddle of venison, and venison steak.

Most of the cooking and service was based on English culinary traditions. Dishes such as roast beef and Yorkshire pudding, steak and kidney pie, plum pudding, and rice and raisin pudding were featured frequently. While the influences of other European traditions were also apparent in, for example, spaghetti and Macaroni Milanaise, Spanish omelette, fruit compotes, or French sauces, non-English dishes were infrequent.

Opportunities to experience the late 1885–1930 era of railway and steamship dining services are very limited. Of the CPR's dining cars, only the *Argyle*, preserved at the Canadian Museum of Rail Travel at Cranbrook, British Columbia, has been restored to its original elegance. The *Argyle* is part of the 1929 *Trans-Canada Limited*, the only complete, restored, first-class passenger train in North America from the pre-Second World War "heavyweight era," which is generally recognized as the zenith of rail travel in North America. Tea and light meals are served in the car regularly and special events highlight dining in the finest traditions of the CPR service. Two interior steam vessels, the *Moyie* (1898) and the *Sicamous* (1914), are being restored and their dining saloons will be fully refurbished.

Fortunately, most of the great railway hotels survive. The smaller facilities, including those at North Bend, Revelstoke, Glacier, and Field, have all been demolished, but the Empress, the Hotel Vancouver, the Banff Springs Hotel, Chateau Lake Louise, the Palliser, and—at the other end of the western transcontinental train services in Toronto—the Royal York, survive and prosper. Several of these magnificent hotels have undergone major renovations, and their original elegance has not only been restored, but enhanced.

The Canadian Pacific, through its dining cars, hotels, and steamships, established a level of service, food quality, and variety of offerings that set an early standard across Western Canada. No other organization was able to do this. While individual hotels, restaurants, inns, or roadhouses might offer fine cuisine, sometimes exceeding in quality the CPR's, no restaurant or hotel company had the number of outlets or the geographical diversity of places offering food to the general public. In consequence, the CPR's standard, which was a high, consistent standard, became a benchmark from the late 1800s through the mid-1900s.

Canadian Pacific cuisine and service standards helped define an era in Canada's first century as a country in a time when the frontier was still very much a part of Western Canada. Later, cultural influences from other traditions would broaden perspectives and tastes in Western Canada, and these preferences would be reflected in the surviving railway food services. For many years, the food services of the CPR were without doubt the most dependable standard of high-quality foods available in the Canadian West.

Until the 1950s, the great trains were the major means of travel throughout North America, and, the Canadian Pacific was very much a part of this highly competitive market. In the words of Robert Louis Stevenson, "to travel hopefully is better than to arrive." For the customer, during this formative period of our railway history, to "travel hopefully" and enjoy the journey was often as important as the destination. Meals became a hallmark of fine service. However, by the 1960s, despite the introduction of luxury trains such as *The Canadian,* rail travel was in serious decline. The advent of mass air travel, private automobiles, and high-speed roads changed the way most Canadians travelled and thought about time and distance. For some, train travel remained essential to the "Canadian experience," but for others it had become an expensive luxury that was largely irrelevant and needed to be discontinued. Today, VIA, through its reconditioned *Canadian* equipment has brought back much of the elegance from this era in its first-class services.

Acknowledgements

Special thanks are extended to Tom Barnes, who worked on CPR dining cars; Bill Curran, for his recollections of the Lake and River Service; the late David Webster, chief steward on the B.C. Lake and River Service; Isabella E. Turner, for her memories of travel during the 1920s; Gary Anderson and Mike Westren of the Canadian Museum of Rail Travel, for their insights into the dining-car services; Canadian Pacific Corporate Archives; the National Archives of Canada; Canadian Pacfic Hotels and Resorts; VIA, and the Royal British Columbia Museum.

Robert Turner is the author of eleven books on railroad and steamship history in Western Canada. He has also written many articles and reviews in magazines and journals and given numerous lectures. His photographs have been widely published. After many years with the Royal British Columbia Museum, where he was chief of Historical Collections, he is now a curator emeritus. He works independently as a heritage consultant and writer, based in Victoria. His newest books are *The Skyline Limited*; *The Kasloo and Slocan Railway*, co-authored with David Wilkie; and *The Sicamous and the Naramata: Steamboat Days in the Okanagan.* Two of his most recent major books, *West of the Great Divide* and *Logging by Rail*, each won the Canadian Railroad Historical Association's Book Award. He has also received the Award of Merit from the American Association for State and Local History for his books.

THE REGIONAL CUISINE OF ONTARIO

ELIZABETH BAIRD

The Future of Ontario's Fruit Industry

ONTARIO CUISINE is rich in fruit. Rhubarb, strawberries, blueberries, raspberries, cherries, peaches, pears, apples, and pumpkin are made into pies, single crust, double crust, or the specialty of Perth and Waterloo counties, Dutch apple pies dotted with brown sugar, cream, cinnamon, and just enough flour to rein in the thick wedges of fruit. There are coffee cakes, topped with a good layer of apples or rhubarb and dappled with crumble, peach crisps, apple pandowdies, apple tortes, apple dumplings, or big Northern Spy apples bundled into flaky pastry, baked golden brown and served drenched with caramel sauce.

In the past, cider and apple butter both came from the mills situated in most villages. Apple butter became the makings of puddings, loaves, and pies and topped numberless slices of bread. What was not baked into a sweet finale or eaten fresh with juices running down your chin was preserved or stored for the fruitless winters. Peaches, pears, berries, rhubarb, and applesauce went into screwtop sealers and old blue granite boilers steamed up kitchens across the province. The jars of preserves lined the fruit cellar shelves where they beckoned like jewels: red, purple, blue, and gold.

In the north, wild low-bush blueberries became jam. It was an affront in this province to serve plain toast or biscuits. Marmalade was more likely to be peach, pear, or rhubarb with a touch of orange and lemon. Even savory relishes were fruited—chili sauce was enhanced with chunks of peaches, apples, or pears. Apples popped up in turkey stuffing, cabbage salads and condiments to serve with meats, especially pork. Peaches glazed hams and pears sweetened mashed rutabaga. Native Concord grapes were cooked, strained and took the place of wine at Protestant communion services. In short, the presence of this abundant fruit deliciously affected our way of life and our traditional home cooking.

It is difficult to believe that Ontario's fruit belt is in the same latitudinal band as the south of France and Florence, Italy. But, were it not for the Great Lakes there would be no fruit industry in Ontario. The Great Lakes act as a thermostat that tempers the winter cold and summer heat. These large bodies of water cool the area surrounding their shores in the spring, preventing fruit trees from blooming while there is still a danger of frost. During the summer the lakes store heat, warming the temperatures in the same area, letting fruit ripen before the first frost. Superior fruit is produced in specific areas, the result of suitable soil. But more important is the microclimate created at the western end of Lake Ontario where the shore of the lake runs parallel to the Niagara Escarpment. The Escarpment, thirty to fifty metres high, was the edge of an Ice Age lake and acts as a buffer for on-shore winds from the lake. The resulting convection effect ensures a continuous air flow, minimizing the risk of frost damage to blossoms and tender vine shoots. Where the Escarpment meets Lake Huron at Georgian Bay a similar microclimate can be found and excellent quality apples, especially cold-acclimatized McIntosh and Northern Spy are harvested. Similarly blessed fruit-producing areas of note in Ontario are Kent and Essex Counties along Lake Erie shores, Pelee Island, protected areas around Bowmanville and Brighton along Lake Ontario, and Prince Edward County at the eastern end of the lake.

Historically, the first raves from a gourmet travel writer came from plucky Mrs. Simcoe. In her diaries written two centuries ago, she recorded her reaction to the peaches growing in Niagara-on-the-Lake and noted that three peach trees provided enough for an eight-week supply of pies and desserts, plus enough to satisfy all the young men. Her share of peaches was trifling compared to theirs which was thirty peaches per day. Such an abundance of fruit, more exotic then, seems astonishing. In the same century, fruit-bearing orchards were described around the French fort of Detroit, and French missionaries established apple orchards around Georgian Bay to provide their usual drink, cider. John McIntosh is given credit for our most famous apple, but part was good fortune since he found the seedling growing on a farm abandoned by a French settler. Recognizing the value of this particularly juicy, bright red-skinned apple that seemed to thrive in cold climes, he promoted it to other growers.

It was not until the late nineteenth century that population and transportation came together to create an industry in fruit-growing areas. In 1880, seventy thousand baskets of peaches were shipped from Grimsby by rail, and local canning plants processed 150 bushels per day. In the same decade, peach cultivation reached commercial scale in Essex, Kent, Norfolk, and Huron Counties. By the turn of the century, a hundred different apple varieties were growing in Ontario.

But, today, the viability of Ontario fruit is precarious. The best fruit-growing areas of Ontario, within hauling distance of concentrated populations, are also the most desirable for land development. The aptly named town of Fruitland, for example, has been swallowed by the paved-over suburbanized Golden Horseshoe. Not many shopping at the Burlington Maple Ridge Mall today would have an inkling that Burlington was once famed for its strawberries. Closer to Niagara Falls, the Queen Elizabeth Way passes by fields where stark dead fruit trees and vines are the backdrop for billboards announcing applications for rezoning or the coming of a new development.

Global competition ranks high as another concern. Cheap imports and changing tastes impacted the canning industry decades ago. Canned fruit, generally packed in syrup, fell victim to the sugar scare of the 1960s. When fresh became available, why would consumers buy canned peaches or pears? As everybody believed, fresh was better. Today, if you live in an Ontario city, fresh fruit is available in numerous varieties year round. Moreover, the province has become a market for fruit harvested from the Eastern seaboard, Florida, California, Mexico, Central America, and increasingly, the southern hemisphere, especially South America and New Zealand. For twelve months of the year we have the choice of kiwi on cereal, fresh-squeezed orange juice, a slice of melon with prosciutto to start dinner, or a fresh mango chopped into a salad for its beta carotene.

There is no contest, however, when it comes to taste. A peach imported from points south doesn't smell like a peach, doesn't peel like a peach, and doesn't cook like a peach. Worst of all, it doesn't taste like a peach. Why anyone would buy one of these faux fruits is a mystery, but they do. Unfortunately, by the time Ontario peaches arrive late in the season, many people are no longer interested and miss the deliciousness of our local fresh peaches.

You might say that at least we grow good apples. But visit any supermarket and look at the apples on display, piled high in glossy technicolour: green Granny Smiths, garnet Red Delicious, burnished Goldens, striped Galas, to name a few of the regulars. And where are the Ontario apples among these gems? On occasion, there are some British Columbia baubles, but more often than not, Ontario apples are smaller, bagged to guarantee bruises, and certainly less impressive than imports. Retailers claim they choose these apples to ensure a year-round supply. Consumers interested in different varieties and homegrown products must trek to the country or to farmers' markets for them.

Free trade has added to the challenge with the influx of even cheaper imports, and the flight of the fruit processing industry to points south. Labour is cheaper, the weather is more indulgent, and there is appreciable investment in research. As well, economies of scale are already in place.

To paint this gloomy picture of our local fruit industry ignores the advantage Ontario fruit producers have with lower transportation costs and a cheaper dollar. Orchardists, governments and entrepreneurs are taking important steps to keep their industry not only alive, but vibrant and growing.

A first step is recognition of quality and branding of fruit. The juice factories, cider mills, apple butter and pie filling factories that take smaller or poorly coloured fruit are few and far between. Growers producing inferior fruit will not be in business long. Programs such as Orchard Crisp, organized by Ontario apple growers, give their brand name "Orchard Crisp" to apples, whether they are Empire or Ida Red varieties. Brands are perceived as a guarantee of quality, fighting the image that Ontario fruit is a shabby sister to imported fruits. Improving quality by research is ongoing. At the Simcoe Research Station, for example, Dr. Adam Dale is experimenting with thousands of strawberry plants to develop disease-resistant plants that produce the bountiful, colourful berries consumers want. Consumers perceived locally grown and naturally dark port-red berries as overripe, preferring the lighter red imports. Produce managers, understandably concerned with their bottom line, were reluctant to stock the darker Ontario berries. The research station developed the clearer red Governor Simcoe strawberry, and produce managers and customers alike were willing to pay a premium for them. (As luck would have it, the Governor Simcoe berries taste good, too.)

With government research cuts and university budgets slimming, orchardists are seeking solutions among themselves, looking to the most successful to share their knowledge, and more importantly, forming groups such as the Norfolk Fruit Growers Association to improve the processing, storing, and marketing of their fruits.

Close to cities and towns, many growers have switched to "Pick-Your-Own," offering city folk an opportunity to harvest without planting. For the harvesters they offer facilities such as on-site cherry pitting, baskets to pick with, wagon rides, picnic tables, and of course, lots to buy. Cold drinks, home baking, and preserving supplies are offered, and for the rushed visitor, already-picked fruit. Good fruit lands don't go out of production when locals and tourists alike come out for fruit and watch bubbling fruit pies emerge from the oven and sniff the aroma of strawberry jam simmering in the pot.

Varieties are changing, too. Standing in his orchard in Norfolk County, Tom Heskett pointed to mature Northern Spy trees growing on one side, "These are the apples of yesterday," and to the dwarf Empire across the path, "those, the apples of tomorrow." "Spies," as every pie baker lovingly calls them, just don't redden as other varieties and in storage their thin skins are easily pierced and bruised. Empire apples, on the other hand, store well and look appealing. Orchardists are also taking their cues from consumers who want a sweeter apple and varieties new to Canada such as the Gala. Case Droogers, growing apples north of Simcoe, finds that his sweeter Jonagold and Crispin apples are popular. Customers drive up to his orchard and load up their trunks with these apples.

Even packaging has changed. Large families of the past loved heaping baskets of summer fruit, but the two-person household today acquires fruit fatigue trying to figure out ways to eat it before it becomes mouldy and mushy. The solution was smaller baskets and one-layer boxes that show off the fruit while preventing bruising.

The location of principal fruit areas has again become significant for the survival of the industry. Niagara is but an hour's drive from Toronto, less from Hamilton or Brantford. The Erie shores are a destination for the population of southwestern Ontario. Fruit purchased where it is grown can be picked a little riper, hence juicier and certainly sweeter—and it brings locals and come-from-aways back. Experts call this "agri-tourism." Growers such as the Chattens in Brighton have set up a country market with fresh cider, doughnuts, coffee to have with a slice of freshly baked pie, and fruit they're proud of. People out for a drive have a chance to do something more than just buy apples. Nicolette Novak and Phil Andrews of Lakeland Orchards provide the fun of Peach Days and corn boils. In the Niagara Peninsula there is the opportunity to buy Ontario wines, many not available in LCBO outlets. Vintners pour endless glasses of sample wines, and many provide lunches and dinners in their restaurants overlooking the vineyard.

The future of fruit in Ontario? An abundance of cheap home-grown fruit may not be the right of every Ontarian. But it looks optimistic at the moment as energetic growers initiate creative solutions for marketing their produce and keeping their customers coming back for more.

Elizabeth Baird is Food Director of *Canadian Living* magazine. Winner of the National Magazine Award and the Silver Ladle of the Toronto Culinary Guild, she is the editor of the single subject cookbook series, *Canadian Living's Best.* As well, she has edited other *Canadian Living* cookbooks including *Country Cooking, Desserts,* and *The Canadian Living Christmas Book.* Her first forays into the food world were *Classic Canadian Cooking, Apples, Peaches and Pears,* and *Summer Berries.* Baird is chairman of the Nutrition Education Committee of the Canadian Living Foundation, created to provide funds and nutrition information to breakfast programs across Canada.

EDNA STAEBLER

Faith, Family, and Food:

The Old-Order Mennonites in Waterloo County

IN WATERLOO COUNTY in southwestern Ontario, every good local cook of pioneer stock has her own variations of Mennonite recipes. She substitutes an ingredient she likes for one that she doesn't. She improvises, adapts, and invents with daring and zest, sometimes to suit an occasion, sometimes to use up leftovers or a surplus, or simply to see how a mixture will taste. Mennonites *love* cooking and they make wonderful food. This jolly creativity is their heritage from the Mennonite pioneers who, in 1800, came in their Conestoga wagons from Pennsylvania to Waterloo County. Using the cherished little handwritten recipe books they had copied from the similar books of their forebears (who came to America from Switzerland, Alsace, and the Rhineland), they devised palatable ways to cook whatever they found in the wilderness or could grow on the land they were clearing. Almost a century later, other Mennonites came from Russia, and their cuisine reflects that of the Ukraine.

Mennonite cooking in Waterloo County is plain, but divinely flavoured and different from any other. Some is similar to the Mennonite food you might get in Pennsylvania, but it's a "little bit different yet," as they would say. You don't have to belong to the Mennonite faith to enjoy it. Everyone who has grown up in Waterloo County is devoted to sour-cream salads and apple schnitz pies. Visitors and newcomers beg for recipes that have passed from generation to generation of Mennonite housewives. Anyone who tastes drepsly soup, schnippled bean salad, and apple fritters wants to know how to prepare them. All the villages in Waterloo County have festivals that attract tourists: the Wellesley Apple Butter and Cheese Festival, the Elmira Maple Syrup Festival, and the New Hamburg Mennonite Relief Sale and Quilt Auction. The most popular food is found at the booths where the ladies stand and make apple fritters all day. There is always a long lineup of people waiting to get at them.

Simplicity and economy and experience are the keynotes of Mennonite cookery. Recipes are invented to make use of everything that is grown on Waterloo County farms. All the growing season is spent in preserving and processing food. Surplus fresh fruits are canned and pickled or made into juicy pies. Ham is cured with maple smoke. Pork scraps become well-seasoned sausages. Sour milk is made into cook cheese and *schmierkase* (cottage cheese)—you may have to be brought up in Waterloo County to like them as I do. Sour cream is used in cakes and salads. Stale bread is crumbled and browned with butter to give zest to vegetables, noodles, and dumplings. Nothing is ever wasted and every meal is a feast.

Years ago I stayed for a week with the Martin family, who belong to a splinter sect of Old-Order Mennonites. Many will remember Bevvy Martin, the mother, from my book *Food that Really Schmecks.* One day Bevvy and her family were talking about their favourite pies. Bevvy's little boy said he liked the pie made with peach peelings best. Bevvy was a little embarrassed. "Well, you know we don't throw anything out," she explained.

The Mennonite farm housewife seldom has to go shopping for food. She makes meals with what she has in her garden, kitchen, or cellar. In a dark pantry stand crocks of cheese and apple butter; bags full of *schnitz* (dried apple pieces), dried corn and beans, rolled oats, herbs and spices; jars of maple and apple syrup; sacks of sugar and flour.

Eva Martin is another Old-Order Mennonite friend, who lives about a mile from me. Eva's cellar—or any Mennonite cellar—is a wonderful sight. It has floor-to-ceiling shelves filled with shiny half-gallon jars of fruit, vegetables, jam, and pickled things. These big jars are always so shiny! I asked Eva, "Do you come down and dust them all the time?"

There are crocks of head cheese, jars of canned chicken, gravy beef, and pork sausage sealed in with lard. In a cold room smoked meats and sausages hang from the ceiling—the room smells so nice. There are great bins of potatoes and turnips. Root vegetables are stored in boxes of dried leaves, next to barrels full of apples. Meat, bread, doughnuts, cookies, and ice cream fill several freezers if the house has electricity.

No directions for cooking meat are given in the handwritten recipe cookbooks of my Old-Order Mennonite friends. Meat is eaten three times a day in some Mennonite homes and women naturally know how to prepare it. They make pot pies of pigeons, rabbits, and veal. They roast beef, pork, and lamb, which they serve with gravies that are brown and shiny. They fry chicken in butter. Trout caught in the Grand and Conestoga rivers are dipped in egg and breadcrumbs and fried crisp. In an iron pot they make stew and pot roast browned with onions and bay leaves. Sometimes they have duck or roast goose bursting with savory dressing, and always the flavours are magnificent. Leftover meats are jellied, pickled, warmed over, or combined with vegetables or homemade noodles to make nourishing suppers. Hot gravy is delicious on bread. Beef drippings make the best-flavoured shortening for frying potatoes, onions, or steak. Chicken fat, pure and mild, gives cookies a delicate crispness. Bacon drippings are the preferred base for warm sour-cream salads. Goose grease is saved and rubbed on sore throats and chests when the children have colds, I've been told, or for waterproofing boots. Fat that can't be used in these ways is poured into a kettle with lye to make soap.

The treasured notebook does contain recipes for all those magical baked things that need more or less definite measurements—cakes, cookies, squares, doughnuts, breads, biscuits, coffee cakes, muffins, and fritters. There's always a plate full of something delicious on the table three meals a day, for lunch during a quilting, or with a cup of tea in the afternoon when a visitor drops in.

Whenever I go to Eva's place she says, "Have you time for a cup of tea?" She then puts the kettle on and we have mint tea or lemon balm tea and a piece of pie or some cookies or muffins, or something—always something.

My Old-Order Mennonite friends are the most generous people I know. Though they don't mingle or seem to know much about the many other Mennonite sects, they cooperate in the Mennonite Central Committee, which sends help anywhere in the world it is needed when an earthquake or some other disaster occurs. In our area the Old-Order Mennonites rebuild barns that have been burned or destroyed, and they are always the first to shovel mud after a flood. Some of the women have several sewing machines in their basements and they come together to make or remake clothes for people in need. When the Central Committee gives help it always reaches the people who need it.

The Mennonites speak Pennsylvania Dutch, a Germanic dialect, interspersed with English words. Some children do not learn how to speak English until they begin school. The children attend parochial schools, which the Mennonites pay for, though they also pay taxes for public schools. Children leave school when they are fourteen years old or have finished grade eight. "That is when their real education begins," Eva has told me. The boys learn as they work with their fathers in the fields, the barn, and the sugar bush. Just as the girls learn from working with their mothers. At fourteen, the girls are happy to pin up their hair instead of wearing long childish braids. They are taught by their mothers to plan, plant, cultivate, and harvest the large vegetable gardens and to prepare and preserve what is grown there. They learn baking, milking, sewing, caring for the animals and younger children—all the responsibilities of running an efficient household. If there is enough help at home young men and women hire out to other Old-Order farmers, where they continue learning Mennonite ways.

Old-Order Mennonites don't take old-age pensions and family allowances, and they don't have OHIP. Since they are given the right to be pacifists by the Canadian government, they feel they should not take social benefits.

Instead, the Mennonites look to one another for any help they might need. Years ago when Eva and Melvin were going to be married she said, "Soon we won't live very far from you. Please come and see us." When I went to call, she showed me a brick house with seven bedrooms—and they were adding to the front of it! I thought, Why do they need so much room? Eva told me. "That's going to be the doddy house. We're taking over the farm from Eli and Lovina, who have no children. When they get old we'll look after them as if we were their children." This is their way of caring for their elders. The main house has a big kitchen but the grandmother normally makes her own meals in the doddy house. A connecting door to the main house is built so that if the older folk need help the young people are there. In the event they become sick, they take food in to them. In return, the older folk are convenient babysitters, and they teach the young their traditions.

The old people are highly respected and what they say goes. Several years ago Eva and Hannah, her sister, were anxious to have a telephone because of their cows. If a cow got sick at night they couldn't call the vet, even though an obliging neighbour at the end of their lane let them use their phone. They really needed a telephone, but it took a long time before the church elders allowed them to have one. The phone had to be black and attached to the wall, so that telephoning would be uncomfortable and they wouldn't spend too much time talking. When I visited Nancy, Eva's friend, the other day, I noticed her wall phone had a very long cord that reached right across the room—there are ways around these things.

Faith, family, and food dominate the close-knit Old-Order community. Social life is almost exclusively restricted to church services, family gatherings, quiltings, singings, funerals, and weddings. Members attend no public entertainment, have no television or radio to distract them from their work, which keeps them busy all year long.

In the winter when the garden is frozen, they sew clothes, knit, embroider, and make maple syrup. Eva keeps a quilt in a frame in the parlour, where it can be worked on at odd moments. In the spare room upstairs, a hope chest stands at the foot of the bed, with two more chests in front of the windows. They are for Eva's three daughters, who will have twelve quilts each when they are married. The quilts are made of scraps of prints from their dresses. The scraps are blended so beautifully that the quilts are truly works of art.

Quiltings are a favourite social event filled with friends or relations. Eva invites six step aunts, who are great fun. Her maternal grandfather, a widower, married a woman whose husband had died and left her with six little girls and not much money. Eva told me her grandfather married the woman to look after her and her children.

One day Sylvanus, Eva's brother-in-law, phoned me from a neighbour's house.

"Hannah wants you to come to a quilting," he told me.

"But, Sylvanus, I can't quilt."

"YOU CAN'T QUILT?" His surprise to me meant, "What kind of a woman are you?"

After a pause he added, "Well, I guess she'd want you to come anyway—you can bring your knitting."

I didn't go to Hannah's until two o'clock in the afternoon; the quilters had come at nine. Hannah had all the threads cut and ready so they could quickly thread their needles. They didn't waste any time, and finished a whole quilt in one day. While they worked they chatted and laughed.

At noon they had dinner around the long kitchen table, and at about three o'clock Hannah served chiffon cake, homemade ice cream, and tea. At another quilting at Eva's, she served Easter cheese, a solid, custardy cheese with maple syrup poured over it.

The one and only exciting event of the week for the young and unmarried is the Sunday-evening "Singing." Here one to two hundred people gather at someone's farm to meet one another and sing hymns. I don't know if they also sing old favourites like "A Bicycle Built for Two." They're rather secretive about singings. I've asked questions, but they seem to put me off.

Eva has four daughters (one's only five; the other three are older) and she wouldn't let the older girls go to the singings until they were sixteen. The singing is where something magical takes place when a boy asks a girl if he can drive her home in his buggy. Before Joanna was married, Hannah whispered to me, "Joanna's got a boyfriend." And I said, "Do you like him?" She said, "Oh, yes, he's real nice." One day I heard Hannah ask Eva, "What time did Joanna get home last night?" She said, "Oh, about two o'clock." That may be late for a sixteen-year-old, but it can take two or three hours to drive home with a horse and buggy.

When Eva's younger sister Mary got married and moved to Mount Forest, her mother told us, "Mary had sixty-two for dinner on Sunday and twenty-one for supper." Sixty-two people! "If that many people dropped in on me I'd jump in the lake!" I said. The Mennonites attend church in a different district each Sunday. It can take them a couple of hours to get there by horse and buggy and the service is from nine a.m. to noon. After that they're hungry, so they just "drop in" at somebody's house and have dinner.

Recently Eva said, "We've got church in our district this week." I wondered how they would have enough food for an unknown number of people. She explained that they prepare what they can, and if not many turn up they eat the food that's left during the rest of the week. They may bake twenty pies on Friday, their baking day, and store them in the cellar. When Sunday comes, all the women pitch in. If the food that was prepared is insufficient, they go down to the cellar and bring up a jar or more of meat, vegetables, or fruit. As Eva says, "We can always count on our jars."

Funerals are large gatherings. The black-clad men and women come many miles in their buggies. A few years ago Eva's little niece Violet drowned in a pond. I went over to the house the day before the funeral. Several ladies were there getting ready for it; they were peeling potatoes, slicing summer sausage, large bologna and ham, bread and cheese. Fifteen hundred people came to the funeral at the white clapboard church, and most of them were fed at the house after the service. The church lends boxes of dishes and cutlery for all special occasions and the women are so well organized that they can do things quickly and easily.

Weddings are the greatest of all Old-Order celebrations. Bevvy's daughter Salome was married at the end of September some years ago (anyone who owns a copy of my book *Schmecks* knows Salome). Bevvy said they'd like to invite me to the wedding, but the guests could only be their own people. So they said, "Come up the day after and you can see what we had to eat." I drove to the farm the next day and there was Salome! Surprised to see her, I said, "Salome, aren't you on your honeymoon?"

"Oh, no, we don't have a honeymoon. You see, we're going to live in the house his [her husband's] mother and father lived in. They're going to retire to Elmira, and when they move out I'll move in."

I don't know why they and Salome couldn't live in the house at the same time, but maybe the young couple were going to move into the parents' bedroom and it might have been embarrassing for her. She waited two weeks before she went to live with her husband.

"Why didn't they just postpone the wedding for a couple of weeks?" I asked Bevvy later.

"Well, if we'd waited until November it would have been too cold for the horses to stand outside so long—our weddings last all day."

When Eva's eldest daughter, Joanna, was married I was honoured to be the only non-Mennonite invited to the wedding. Invitations were delivered to 150 people. They listed the bishop, the preachers, the guests, eight bridal attendants, children, the young women who would serve the dinner, and the young men who would look after the horses.

Joanna's wedding took place at Eva's house on a cool, sunny day in October. I went into the kitchen, as I always do, and Eva greeted me joyously. "Would you like to go down to the cellar and see what we're having to eat?" she asked.

Grouped on tables were salads, *crudités*, pickles, relishes, and butter moulded into roses—all numbered so the waitresses could whip them up to the correspondingly numbered dinner tables upstairs later. And there were ten high chiffon wedding cakes the bride herself had made, using dozens of eggs from the family's own chickens and icing made with lots of home-churned butter and not too much sugar.

Throughout the main floor of the house stood rows of chairs, and if anyone had had to go to the bathroom I don't know what they would have done, because there was no aisle down the middle. All the women wore long, plain, navy-blue dresses identical in style. The bride had on navy blue, too, but in a fancier material. She looked shy and sweet as she and the groom and their attendants came down the stairs and sat in the front row in the parlour.

I was in the dining room and couldn't see the preachers who conducted the service. The preaching was in Pennsylvania Dutch and I didn't understand it, but occasionally the bishop would interject some English. I heard that the husband must be the head of the household and the wife must never cut her hair. (I've never seen evidence of male domination in the homes of any of my Old-Order friends. The men are hard-working, fun-loving husbands, who have hard-working wives who do as they please.)

During the wedding the guests would stand up, face their chairs, and kneel on the floor to pray. Then they'd get up again, and led by a male voice, they'd sing verse after verse of a hymn, with no instrumental accompaniment.

After the ceremony, which lasted two and a half hours, the chairs were rearranged, while people in groups had conversations all over the house. The youngsters had a whale of a time running up the front stairs, through the long hall, and down the back steps. As Joanna and her groom opened their presents in an upstairs bedroom the children stuck sticky bows all over the back of Joanna's dress, while she laughed happily and looked unusually festive.

When it was time to eat, tables were set up throughout the main floor. In a large room where Eva does her laundry, makes soap, and cans maple syrup, a long table was arranged for the children. The bride's table was in the kitchen, and there were two tables with fourteen guests each in the dining room, a similar table in the parlour, and another in the kitchen of the doddy house.

Soon we were seated, our heads bowed in a long silent prayer, before we devoured the scalloped potatoes, canned corn and peas, veal schnitzel, and the salads I'd viewed in the cellar. For dessert there were nappies of fresh fruit and cookies, deliciously smooth butterscotch pudding, the high wedding cakes, tea, and coffee.

Once we'd eaten, all the used dishes were stacked at the end of the tables and huge bowls of hot water were brought in. The women, guests included, washed and dried all the dishes, then reset the tables for the second sitting. The organization was amazing.

After all the dishes and extra tables were cleared away people gathered around the dining-room table and sang hymns lustily for almost two hours. The children came around with decorated baskets full of oranges and apples that they gave to each of us. Lastly, the bride passed around a tray with little packages of hard candies wrapped in cellophane. The groom followed her, carrying a tray full of chocolate bars, which he distributed to all.

About nine o'clock some of the older women put on their shawls and black bonnets, while the men hitched up the horses.

I got into my car and drove home. May they all live happily ever after.

Edna Staebler is one of Canada's most-loved women authors. This paper was written twenty-five years after she wrote her now-famous *Food that Really Schmecks*, which is not only a cookbook, but a book about Old-Order Mennonites and their lives. Her career as a writer began with the article she did about a trip to Neil's Harbour, Cape Breton, in 1945. Since then she has written about Canadians for magazines such as *Maclean's, Chatelaine, The Star Weekly*, and *Reader's Digest*. Many of her essays have been reprinted in school texts and anthologies, as well as in her book *Places I've Been and People I've Known*. She is currently putting together a collection of letters written by her sister, Ruby, about her family in the 1950s. More than forty years ago, Edna was awarded the Canadian Women's Press Club Award, and she is still being honoured. She received the Canadian National Magazine Award in 1987 for her article about the "Cookie War" and was recently given the Silver Ladle Award of the Toronto Culinary Guild. As well, in 1984 she received a doctor of letters from Wilfred Laurier University. She lives with her chubby kitten, Mally (so named after Edna found her in with a carton of kittens in a shopping mall), in a cosy, warm home overlooking Sunfish Lake in Waterloo County.

ROB McLAUGHLIN
OWEN ROBERTS
SHERRY MACKAY

A Vision for Agriculture

AGRICULTURE is facing monumental changes. Some are inevitable, some are desirable, others are essential. But they are all reaching a critical point. Domestically, the country is confronting relentless farm debt, urban sprawl, and pressure from cheap imports. The population is growing, yet rural communities are in decay. Public sympathy for farm support is ebbing, yet Canadian farmers face huge and costly environmental challenges. Issues of food safety are continually surfacing. Internationally, Canada must deal with competition from other exporting nations, the global dictates of the General Agreement on Tariffs and Trade (GATT), and free trade under the Canada–U.S. Trade Agreement. Additional challenges come from the North American Free Trade Agreement and an increasingly powerful European Community.

As a nation, we are reacting to these situations instead of anticipating them, addressing them in an ad hoc way instead of with forethought as a team of consumers, industry and government representatives, and academicians.

The Canadian agri-food sector must be proactive, responsive, and allied in the face of these unprecedented challenges. Canadian farmers must rise above the turbulence, fulfil food requirements at home and abroad, and make a financially sound, environmentally responsible living simultaneously. A vision is needed to permit farmers to make a living while protecting and sustaining the environment.

The first step in the process is to recognize the changes that have taken place in Canadian agriculture. Over time, two distinct types of farms have developed: high output farms and low output farms, each with unique needs. Traditional government programs based on one kind of farm and farmer are no longer valid.

Canadians want affordable, wholesome food produced in an environmentally friendly fashion. They also want to take leisurely drives through the countryside where foods are grown and enjoy the fields, barns, hamlets, villages, woodlots, and clean streams. As well, they want to retain their country's lofty standing as the best place in the world to live—due in part to the prosperity created by the agri-food industry. We consider this part of our heritage. But the leadership and the vision needed to meet these wants are lacking. Federally, consultation with the stakeholders has slowed and priorities have shifted. We're doing well when it comes to self-policing the industry and serving as a watchdog for food quality and safety, but when it comes to policies and programs, we're mainly putting out fires.

It's clear now that farmers need support to balance their roles as food producers on the one hand and countryside stewards and environmentalists on the other. The roles are actually inseparable—you won't last long as a farmer unless you look after your land and animals, and you can't farm if you don't make a reasonable return on labour and investment. Yet, despite this inherent truth, two distinct groups of farmers have emerged, as we've said: those who are globally competitive full-time farmers on high-output farms and those who maintain "lifestyle" farms, with low output.

The globally competitive group is small in numbers—encompassing about one-quarter of Canada's 200,000 farmers—but it supplies 75 percent of all the food produced in this country. Members of this group run the biggest farms in Canada, each producing well beyond $50,000 worth of farm products each year.

They need specific programs, policies, and strategies to help them produce food sustainably and competitively and provide the raw goods that keep Canada's food processing industry active and healthy.

The other group is significantly larger, comprising nearly 150,000 farmers. They produce appreciably less food (less than $50,000 worth of sales annually) on smaller tracts of land than their counterparts. Most derive the majority of their income from jobs held off the farm; many maintain an agricultural operation because they like the lifestyle that farming represents.

This group also plays a distinct role in the agri-food system. It's their patchwork of forests, barns, pastures, hedgerows, and streambanks that urbanites fondly recall after a drive through the country and that Canadians in general have come to expect in the countryside.

Like Canada's large-scale farmers, members of this group need government policies uniquely suited to help them steward their land, preserve the fabric of rural Canada, and fill local niche markets. They also need support to help them be as efficient as they can be and produce the commodities most suited to their operations.

But, despite the clear trend toward larger, globally competitive farms and smaller enterprises that emphasize lifestyle farming, governments basically treat all farmers the same. A minority of our producers grow the majority of our food, yet many farm programs are used heavily by lifestyle farmers, too. To what extent can resources be distributed evenly? New and current initiatives fail to recognize that while all farmers share some common ground, significant differences exist between globally minded enterprises and lifestyle farms.

Why do we need to be concerned about agriculture in Canada? Because agriculture means food, and food is a necessity of life. Unlike many consumer commodities, food is a day-to-day requirement. A constant supply is a must.

Without a domestic agriculture industry, food becomes a question mark. If a country chooses not to support its own food producers, it's taking a chance—a very big chance—that it may become dependent on foreign sources for food. Indeed, some argue that a secure food supply is a matter of national sovereignty.

Agriculture in Canada makes sense. Canada is a good country for producing food; the soil is rich and the weather is generally favourable. And food production has been good for Canada. Just consider these facts:

- Agri-food is the second largest industry in the Canadian economy, behind forestry.

- Agriculture employs one in five Canadians, directly and indirectly.
- Agricultural exports make up more than 11 percent of all Canada's exports.
- Today a single-farm family feeds 120 people, compared with forty-seven people just fifteen years ago.
- Canada's food supply is safer now than at any time in our history.

A vision for agriculture must include a coordinated effort by both the public and private sectors to promote the significance of the agri-food sector to Canadians.

Canada's population is approaching twenty-eight million. It has grown by nearly 8 percent in the past five years, and there are no signs of a slowdown. To meet Canada's future needs, we have several options. We can stop exporting, decrease our demand, or import more food. We can bring more land into production and improve the efficiency of current agricultural systems.

To stop exporting is not the solution. Trading agricultural products is a major source of foreign income for Canada. How would we maintain viable farms in provinces that rely heavily on export sales? For many, those exports are the future of agriculture. Bringing more land into production is inconsistent with many environmental concerns, particularly the need to leave marginal land uncultivated. Importing more food renders Canada susceptible to swings in international politics, which increasingly are threatening food supplies.

Reducing population growth and human demands on the Earth is the ultimate answer. But for now, improving efficiency is the best path to choose. Increased efficiency, driven by research that is focussed on the needs of farmers to be productive and competitive, has been taking place for decades. It's made a real difference in the amount of farmland we need. In Southern Ontario, for example, the total amount of land used for farming has been cut by almost 25 percent over the past thirty years. Most of this "lost" land has actually been retired as marginal farmland—unproductive and prone to erosion. To ensure that our agricultural industry has a secure future and that we don't inadvertently cut off our own food supply, we must strengthen existing programs and institute new ones that make certain enough good land is available to feed the growing population.

In Ontario, for example, the farmer-led Environmental Farm Plan Agenda is helping producers assess their farms for "ecosensitivities," potential environmental problems either natural or created by certain farming practices. This is a vital step toward safeguarding the future of a productive land base. Our vision for agriculture calls for capitalizing on this momentum by further enhancing the farmer's role as steward of the rural landscape. Farmers learn from the practical experiences of other farmers and this knowledge becomes a part of an information system that directs environmental programs to the areas of greatest need. Farm plans will enable farmers to qualify for publicly funded environmental programs.

But right now, financial returns to farmers are low. There's a real possibility that environmental programs may be more expensive to farmers than the market can bear, especially if the programs drive up production costs. We must address who pays for environmental programs and policies related to agriculture.

Agri-food research and education will be marked by greater private-sector involvement, more emphasis on developing technology and transferring this new knowledge to the agricultural industry.

The benefits of agricultural research are distributed throughout society. Investment in agricultural research is smart. Returns are high—on average nearly forty to one. Significant long-term investment in research is essential to maintain the creative energies of the Canadian research community in its effort to address problems and issues important to Canadians. Research should be driven by industry; focussed around strategic initiatives established by consumers, representatives from industry, government, and academia; and measured by specific identifiable milestones. Besides providing real leadership for sustainable agriculture research, universities must produce graduates who understand the entire agri-food system. Canadians must commit to long-term investment in agricultural research and education.

Farmers primarily grow food to feed urban Canadians and for export to other countries. But it's rural Canada that provides farmers with the necessities of life. A healthy rural climate includes a strong, diverse economic base as well as adequate and appropriate social, medical, and security services. Dynamic communities with effective local leadership make it possible for community members to choose their lifestyle rather than be trapped in one by default.

The prosperity of the agricultural industry and the well-being of rural communities are inseparable. That's highlighted when commodity prices are low and rural Canada falls into despair. There's a ripple effect: farmers are forced to look for jobs in towns or cities. Inevitably, the majority of their consumer purchases such as groceries and clothing are transferred there, too, if for nothing more than convenience. That takes dollars out of the rural economy, exacerbates already scant employment opportunities in smaller communities, and further erodes the stability of rural Canada.

With help, this could change. In Ontario, the increase in the non-farm population has altered the nature of many rural communities and brought in new members with resourceful ideas. Social programs and vehicles are needed to optimize this change. Rural revitalization and growth are necessary to bolster the foundation on which agriculture is built.

Essential sectors of Canadian society all have a plan. The economic sector, for example, has a Prosperity Initiative. Business and industry have the U.S. and North American trade agreements. The environmental sector has a Green Plan. But the agricultural sector has no plan.

There is no active, collective vision for the policies, programs, and strategies needed to keep Canada's agri-food industry competitive in the global race. In particular, there is no acknowledgement of the distinct emergence of "competitive" farms and "lifestyle" farms and the unique needs of each.

Previous attempts to achieve a national vision—most notably, the landmark Growing Together agri-food conference in Ottawa two years ago—have been sidelined by a multitude of distractions. At the top of the list: the international political wrangling surrounding the GATT negotiations, which has changed the agri-food industry forever.

Nationally, there's a ground swell of support for a united outlook. All over the country, participants in the food chain are trying to come together as never before to gain a competitive edge. We're at a crossroads. We can seize on this nationwide momentum and choose a common path to meet international challenges. Or we can wander haphazardly and face the consequences.

Rob McLaughlin is dean of the Ontario Agricultural College, University of Guelph. The college sponsors a student writing program called SPARK (Students Producing Articles on Research Knowledge), which is coordinated by Owen Roberts. Sherry MacKay is a SPARK participant.

DOROTHY DUNCAN

Ontario Cooking:

Cuisines in Transition

FOR CENTURIES cultural diversity has characterized this land we call Ontario today, but the recognition that other cultures may influence our own food preferences and daily diet is very much a twentieth-century phenomenon. Ontario, indeed all of Canada, is a land of immigrants or descendants of immigrants. Historians believe that even the First Nations crossed the land bridge from Asia about 15,000 years ago[1] and immediately began to adapt to this new environment to survive. As they dispersed across the continent those First Peoples became as diverse within their clans and tribes as we newcomers are within each of our cultures. Origins, history, geography, topography, distance, flora, fauna, habits, and attitudes have all influenced their daily life and food traditions, so that these traditions vary dramatically from tribe to tribe and nation to nation.

To add to this cultural diversity, newcomers began to arrive from the Old World, and although the majority were from France and Great Britain, many other cultures were represented, as well. As early as 1824, William Lyon Mackenzie described an election crowd at Niagara:

> There were Christians and Heathens, Menonists and Dunkards, Quakers and Universalists, Presbyterians and Baptists, Roman Catholics and American Methodists; there were Frenchmen and Yankees, Irishmen and Mulattoes, Scotchmen and Indians, Englishmen, Canadians, Americans and Negroes, Dutchmen and Germans, Welshmen and Swedes. Highlanders and Lowlanders,

> poetical as well as most prosaical phises, horsemen and footmen, fiddlers and dancers, honourables and reverends, captains and colonels, beaux and belles, waggons and bilburies, coaches and chaises, gigs and carts; in short, Europe, Asia, Africa and America had there each its representative among the loyal subjects and servants of our good King George, the fourth of the name.[2]

Despite the diversity of their backgrounds all of these newcomers were united in one common purpose: to survive and prosper in a frontier society. They brought with them memories of the ingredients, recipes, and food traditions of their homelands, but the hope that this culinary heritage could be transplanted to Ontario soon vanished. They were all confronted with a harsh climate, new and often unknown vegetation, virgin forests, no roads, and the challenge of finding and planting seeds in the newly cultivated gardens and fields. Both residents and travellers have left us graphic descriptions of the challenges:

> In the backwoods education or refined tastes brought very little immediate profit. It was physically difficult for the rich as for the poor man to build his log cabin, clear his land, extract the first unwilling crop, and raise the children through the perils of childhood. There were few luxuries that money could buy in the form of either goods or service, and less leisure to enjoy these, even if within the reach of the settler. For all there was the prospect chiefly of grinding labour. The backwoods recognized no differences in station or rank because almost all were engaged in a similar type of work. There the son of a gentleman became a hewer of wood and a drawer of water. He studied the art of chopping trees, piling brush heaps, splitting rails for fences, attending fires during the burning season. Dressed in a coarse overgarment of hempen cloth, called a logging suit, with trousers to correspond a Yankee hat flopped over his eyes. To tend and drive oxen, plough, sow, plant Indian corn and pumpkins, and raise potatoes were among some of the emigrant's needful accomplishments. At the bees magistrates, counsellors and colonels might work side by side without any feeling of degradation. The fact that all men

laboured at the same occupation tended to give rise to a sense of equality.[3]

Events in Great Britain contributed to the growing number of immigrants to Ontario in the nineteenth century. The potato famine in Ireland caused the most momentous shift of population in the first half of the century.[4] Although there were many Irish artisans and small farmers among the immigrants, there were also thousands of single adults with other occupations—young women ready to go into service in servantless cities like Toronto and Hamilton and young men who found employment in construction projects such as the building of the Rideau Canal. Their love of potatoes in soups, stews, bread, scones, pancakes, cakes, and puddings was easily satisfied, for this was one crop that thrived in Ontario.

Another large cultural group that arrived in the nineteenth century were the Scots, who tended to stick together, forming communities and networks of mutual support and assistance, such as those in Glengarry, Wellington, and Grey counties.[5] Bannock, shortbread, oatmeal porridge, Black Bun, and haggis were only a tiny part of the cultural baggage that they brought with them and have protected and promoted as vigorously as the Scots in the homeland.

As the nineteenth century progressed and the frontier was pushed farther north and west, dramatic differences became apparent between the well-established towns and cities in Southern Ontario and the relatively unknown, sparsely settled areas in the north. In larger communities, entertaining at home was very popular, with food an important component of every occasion. Dinner parties, ball suppers, afternoon teas, at home teas, five o'clock teas, six o'clock teas, picnics, garden parties, soirees, and kettledrums were all part of the social scene and all patterned after the traditions of Great Britain. Opportunities for dining out were limited: you could be invited by those within your social circle or those who shared your religious affiliation to dine in their homes, or you could go to a local hotel. The menus there were often in both French and English in an attempt to persuade clientele that a French chef oversaw the kitchen.

The 1901 census tells us that as the new century began, Ontario was still British, Christian and white, with 79 percent of the population

British in origin, 7 percent French, 9 percent German, 1 percent Dutch, and 1 percent First Nations. The cookbooks of the day, such as the *Dominion Cook Book*[6] or *The New Galt Cook Book*,[7] were filled with the favourite dishes of the dominant British population: game, beef, fowl for the main course; pies and puddings (both savoury and sweet) for dessert; soups with a vegetable base; and scores of breads, rolls, scones, cookies, and cakes with a simple glaze or frosting. A few rare recipes reflected the wider world—Lapland Cakes, Russian Taffy, *Kaoka* (a hot beverage), Spanish Puffed Fritters, and Mango Chutney.

Even as the census was taken, forces were at work to bring about dramatic changes. The Liberals under Wilfred Laurier came to power in 1896, and Clifford Sifton, minister of the interior, inherited a disaster. Decades of promoting settlement had yielded nothing except a persistent drain of pioneers to the United States. Sifton began to aggressively recruit peasants from central and eastern Europe. Here is a description of the kind of "foreigners," as they were called, Sifton wanted to attract: a "stalwart peasant in a sheepskin coat, born on the soil, whose forefathers have been farmers for ten generations, with a stout wife and a half-dozen children."[8] This new recruitment policy was to change the face of Ontario forever.

Over three million people responded to the campaign and entered the country between the beginning of the century and World War I.[9] In many cases men came alone, leaving their wives and families at home in the Old Country, to be looked after by kinfolk. A great many of them stayed in Ontario and found employment in the newly discovered silver and gold mines in Northern Ontario, the forest industries, or construction of the expanding railway system. These men had been migratory workers for the most part in the Old World and they expected to be sojourners here, not settlers. They worked long hours, daylight to dark, and ate four meals a day. Mike Giroux describes the cook, who would have been assisted by a "cookie," at his camp as a "pretty good cook, a Frenchman. His helper was Six Nations Indian from down at Bala. The old fellow used to make nice raised bread."[10] The owners and the foremen were anxious to keep good workers, and when the workers demanded "the kind of food we had at home" the camp cooks turned to catering companies that provided "pea soup for French Canadians, macaroni with parmesan cheese for Italians, roast mutton and tripe for Englishmen, caraway-seed bread for Finns, and so forth."[11]

In some camps, workers had the freedom to choose their own provisions, thus satisfying their own tastes, while saving them more money to send home to the Old Country or for their own future. One track worker recalled: "We used to go out in groups of four or five to buy our food. If there wasn't a store where we were, there would be one within a few miles. It wasn't a barren desert. There were little villages.... There just wasn't any [Italian food] in those stores of the little villages. So we ate meat instead, veal and steak. At that time steak was only 25 cents a pound. We ate well."[12]

There were many young, ambitious, and resourceful men among those early-twentieth-century immigrants. Once they saw the opportunities for advancement, they gave up the idea of retiring to the homeland and brought their families to settle here. One such group was the Japanese. Before 1910, the immigrants were men, but after 1910 a crucial change occurred and the majority were women. Some were brought by husbands who had returned to Japan for a wife, but many were brides of men they had never seen, legally married by proxy in Japan. Marriage, children, and family life made them permanent settlers, farmers, and fishermen.[13]

Among the family groups that arrived, some made restaurant-keeping a specialty from an early date. The Greeks were one of these groups, and by 1910 had established many restaurants and cafés both in cities and in small towns. The restaurateurs were enterprising, working-class immigrants who seized a business opportunity that demanded little capital, few skills, and utilized the labour of all members of the family.[14]

The Chinese also changed the restaurant business significantly as they opened establishments in cities and towns, bringing their dry ingredients from Asia eastward on the railway. The Chinese restaurant owner did not escape the discrimination meted out to other Chinese. It was believed by many that the Chinese had a lower standard of living, and created unfair competition because they accepted lower wages. People also believed that the Chinese were a threat to white women because of their supposed connection with opium dens and the white slave trade.[15] In the early 1920s, Ontario, along with

Saskatchewan, Manitoba, and British Columbia, passed laws forbidding white women to work in Chinese restaurants. However, with the decline of the Chinese population resulting from passage of the Chinese Immigration Act in 1923, that law was no longer enforced.[16]

Jewish merchants and businessmen were among the first settlers in Ontario, and their numbers steadily increased. By 1901, there were 3,000 living in Toronto in "The Ward" (the area bounded by Yonge Street, University Avenue, and Queen and College streets).[17] By 1912, that number had grown to 19,000. There were ten Jewish bakeries in the area producing bread and rolls, combining the small business tradition with their tremendous respect for bakers.

Early bakeries were family affairs. The baker and his wife and children lived above the shop. If they could not do all the work, the first people hired to help were relatives who needed jobs. If nonrelatives were taken on, they were absorbed into the family and shared its woes and delights, scolding its wayward younger members and the like. Regular customers were also treated as family, and given highly personalized service.[18]

By 1914, foreign-born Canadians made up 22 percent of the population, but many of these newcomers still showed little evidence of being "Canadianized," or of sharing their culture with their neighbours. Critics pointed to the ethnic ghettos of Toronto and Thunder Bay, where the newest arrivals clung to their traditional dress, religious beliefs, educational patterns, and food ways. Within these communities, such as Little Italy in Toronto, bounded by College, Crawford, and Dundas streets and Manning Avenue, daily life was patterned after the homeland and based on the unity of the family, who worked together to improve their economy.

> Along with their husbands, women tended their gardens in which familiar vegetables—tomatoes, beans, lettuce, peppers, and such—as well as herbs, and sometimes fruit trees, were grown. Even those with tiny plots (some scarcely covering a dozen square feet), by making use of every inch of available soil, were able to meet most of their fresh vegetable needs for much of the summer and sometimes beyond. While this provided for traditional tastes, people recognized the benefits of gardens for the family budget.

In addition to gardening, every autumn, paesani women had responsibility for supplying the family with traditional preserves that would see it through the year. Chief of these tasks was the making of the tomato purée used in so much of Southern cooking. This involved boiling the produce into a pulp in large cauldrons, after which it was passed through a sieve, bottled and then boiled again to pasteurize the preserve. Eggplants and peppers were likewise preserved, as were pears and peaches. Moreover, Toronto women worked alongside their husbands in the annual production of preserved meats (sausage, salami, ham, bacon) and wine. Women alone, however, were responsible for making blood pudding, jellied pork hocks, and the like.

Moreover, the meats and vegetables needed for preserving could be bought from small Italian farmers on the outskirts of the city. It was common for families to travel to nearby farms to pick bushels of tomatoes for the year's stock of purée, which required more produce than their gardens could supply. In buying direct from the farmer, villagers were able to save substantially over retail prices in the city. In addition to this activity, paesani women would search the nearby parks, fields, and railroad rights-of-way gathering wild greens such as chicory, orach and dandelion. Hunting for mushrooms, which often involved treks beyond the city, was undertaken with their husbands.[19]

The First World War slowed down immigration, accelerated food production, and raised concerns about the Germans living in Ontario, many of whose ancestors had come more than a century earlier. The town of Berlin, for example, was forced to change its name to Kitchener. Women, by this time, were finally able to vote. The Prohibition Act was passed in 1919, removing the demon whiskey, rum, and all other spirits, save for medicinal purposes, from the homes, hotels, inns, taverns, and restaurants of the land. The Great Depression struck in 1929 and spawned the slogan "Make it do, make it over, use it up!" Many Ontarians depended on some form of government assistance, called "pogey," to survive. Farm families saw the best and the worst of the Depression. They had some degree of self-sufficiency because of their gardens and livestock. But they also had to cope with the sudden return of family members who had left years earlier for high-paying city jobs and, having lost those jobs, had come back to the farm to survive. As well, there were the "tramps," that steady stream of men knocking on their doors, looking for a handout and willing to do anything to pay for it. Tales were told of the marks the tramps put on gateposts if they had been treated kindly and fed before being sent on their way, so that other homeless men would know that particular farm was a refuge—for a few hours at least.

From the desperation of the Depression, many positive things emerged—credit unions, turkey pools, cooperatives, a revival of beef rings and the barter system, and many other enterprises that helped thousands to earn a living through their own efforts. In kitchens, cooks learned how to make something out of nothing, or next to nothing. Recipes for Economy Cake, Save All Pie, and Economical Chicken Salad, which required only one cup of chicken to feed a family of ten, were used whenever a family was fortunate enough to have the ingredients to make them. Those still eating three meals a day could expect to have porridge for breakfast, bread fried in lard or drippings at noon, and macaroni for supper, all washed down with strong, hot tea.

Enterprising and innovative cooks developed new recipes for macaroni and cheese, macaroni and tomatoes, fried bread, bread pudding, bread sauce, casseroles of bread stuffing, and every conceivable form of baked and steamed bread, biscuits, dumplings and puddings. Using up leftovers by combining them with other leftovers and perhaps adding a new ingredient was honed to a fine art, and many families discovered that popcorn was a wonderful way to fill an empty stomach.[20]

The Second World War, well named the Global War, brought us food rationing, conscription, munitions factories, instant towns like Ajax that covered some of Ontario's best farmland, and a booming economy. "War brides" arrived after the war, with food traditions from all over the world. The postwar years also brought new waves of immigrants, who influenced farming, agriculture, and taste, for well-spiced, international cuisine had great attraction for Canadians after the blandness of wartime food.[21]

Pretending to be very good at cooking international fare, we made things like Polynesian chicken with coconut or Hawaiian shrimp with pineapple. In restaurants from coast to coast, Canadians ate North

American versions of Chinese food. A sweet-and-sour dish, whether pork or chicken, was one of the first ventures into Asian cooking at home.[22]

Many of the new cultural groups made great contributions to Ontario's food production and availability. For example, Dutch immigrants bought land in what is today called Holland Marsh, reclaimed it, and turned it into one of the best vegetable-growing areas in Canada.

The 1960s saw changes in our immigration policies. Those who are termed visible minorities began to enter in considerable numbers: blacks, South Asians, and Chinese.

Caravan was launched in Toronto in the 1960s. People purchased "passports" to visit the many pavilions highlighting the foods and beverages, music, dress, and everyday life of different cultural groups. The festival was obviously a positive turn of events in raising public awareness about the rich and varied culinary traditions that exist in Ontario. Later, Ugandan, Asian, Indochinese, and South and Central American refugees became part of the mix. Most settled in Toronto, but virtually every town and city in the province received a share of newcomers and benefited from their dynamism.

Nowhere was the impact of the changes in immigration more apparent than in the food industries. Ethnic groups previously too small and too poor to support their own butchers, bakers, and restaurateurs could now do so. New minorities quickly attained the size and affluence necessary to support shops of their own. People with experience and skill emerged to take advantage of the opportunities, and if the labour they required was not at hand, they summoned trained people from their homelands.[23]

Ontario's economy was booming, a mood of optimism prevailed, unemployment was virtually unknown, and many families enjoyed two pay cheques and annual paid vacations. Free to travel, to eat out regularly (for both lunch and dinner, and yes, sometimes breakfast, too) Ontarians wanted to explore new gustatory sensations. Businessmen were quick to exploit this dramatically changed attitude to new foods, different foods, prepared foods, food fads, and food snobberies. An excellent example of this is Peter Spiros Goudas, who could not speak or read English when he arrived in Toronto from Greece in May 1967 with

$100 in his pocket. He recognized the need for ingredients for ethnic foods, and as he moved up the economic ladder, he developed more and more diverse products, until today Goudas Foods markets more than 350 items from around the world. The company also owns plants in the Dominican Republic, Sri Lanka, Greece, and Trinidad.[24]

What does the future hold? There are a multitude of answers to that question. Obviously traditional foods and beverages, enjoyed for generations, still make up the daily diet in many homes. In others, ease of preparation, more attention to likes and dislikes, cultural and religious intermarriages, and our fluctuating economy are changing eating patterns. In addition, many Ontario communities claim very large cultural communities such as Thunder Bay's Finnish population and Toronto's five Chinatowns, which are home to more residents of Chinese descent than any other North American city except San Francisco. There is no doubt that cultural groups such as these will have enormous influence in the future.

New concerns are being raised about the substances being added directly to our food by manufacturers—colour, vitamins, iodine, salt, and other minerals, to improve freshness, taste, or texture—or indirectly through animal diets, plant pesticides, and chemicals from wrapping materials. Allergies to modern prepared food and beverages, plus our increasing sophistication, have brought strong support for health foods such as goat's milk, tofu, oat bran, seaweed, and kelp. The First Nations and newcomers to Ontario have shown a renewed interest in herbal medicines.

There has been a growing demand from Ontarians of all cultural backgrounds to revive food traditions. In response, organizations like the Ontario Historical Society and many of Ontario's museum villages are attempting to teach people how to make their own bread, churn butter, steam a carrot pudding, bake bannock and blueberry grunt, and revive food traditions only vaguely described by older family members.

As we approach the twenty-first century few of us are willing to predict what the future holds for Ontario cooking. Will curiosity, affluence, mobility, and pride of birth continue to affect us? Will import shops, markets, specialty stores, restaurants, and training courses continue to grow? Will cookbooks and food writers continue to expand their horizons with success? Or will each of us revert to our own cultural traditions?

Dorothy Duncan, a former elementary school teacher, has worked in the heritage field for many years, as curator of Black Creek Pioneer Village in Toronto and as museums advisor for the Province of Ontario. She has served as chair of the Ontario Heritage Foundation, and as a board member of Heritage Canada and the American Association for State and Local History. At present, she is the executive director of the Ontario Historical Society and Country Fare editor for *Century Home* magazine, published in Port Hope, Ontario.

BERTHA SKYE

Traditional Cree and Iroquois Foods

WHEN we were children in Northern Saskatchewan we were taught to be dependable. We had chores to do, including some cooking. I could bake bannock by the time I was ten years old. If I found the bread box empty, it was my duty to make bannock for the rest of my ten brothers and sisters. Even as a very young child, I can remember asking my father to let me catch rabbits for dinner. My father said, "You may have three rabbit snares, but you must be responsible for them." Alone on a wintery day 40 degrees below zero, I hiked through the woods until I found rabbit tracks where I could set my snares. The following day I proudly brought home my first rabbit, and my mother skinned and cooked it for dinner. Today children are not often given this kind of responsibility.

We ate a lot differently in those days, too. Many of our foods were boiled rather than fried. We had nourishing porridge for breakfast every morning. In the wintertime my mother would put a handful of sun-dried saskatoon berries into our porridge. They would puff up just as if they were fresh, and the porridge would taste much better. My father never did like bacon and eggs, so we always had just porridge and bannock for breakfast. And my mother and father, married for sixty-three years, lived until they were ninety and ninety-one years old. They must have been doing something right!

It was my mother who taught me how to make her traditional Cree recipes. From her I learned how to bake bannock and how to dry berries in the sun. We would go on berry-picking expeditions or tag along with my father when he went hunting in the bush. It was there that I learned how to cook over an open fire. We would make the bannock, roll it into a thick rope, and twist it around a stick. Then we'd turn it slowly over the fire until it was baked. (Young people today still enjoy making bannock this way.) Partridge and rabbits were also roasted over the fire. For both we would skin and clean them, then cut them down the middle and wash them well with saltwater. For roasting, we would open them flat and attach them to a Y-shaped stick, which we would then secure with another stick so that it could be suspended over the fire. The roasting meat was turned occasionally and the fat would drip on the rocks—that was a healthy way to eat meat. My mother also taught me how to dry meat for the winter and how to cook wild game like venison and moose. Our "caviar" was moose muzzle, boiled and sliced thinly.

I began cooking professionally at the age of seventeen, when I was first hired to work in the dining room of a residential school for 500 children in Prince Albert, Saskatchewan. In the beginning my job was to clean the dining room. But after finishing my work I'd assist the cook in the kitchen. The cook, observing my abilities, decided that my talents would be put to much better use in the kitchen. During my time in the school kitchen, I was quite happy, and native dishes and desserts, especially pies and pastries, became my specialties.

My next job was in Norway House, also a residential school, in Manitoba. A friend who was a schoolteacher there told me that they needed a cook and she had recommended my cooking. At the age of twenty-three I was hired as head cook. I flew into Norway House, since this was the only way to travel to this remote area. The menus at school contained a lot of freshly caught fish and wild game, which was good for the children coming from the north—it was the food they were used to. Fortunately, my cooking abilities have always enabled me to find employment. When my school's vice-principal was transferred to Moose Factory, he said, "We need Fraser." [My maiden name.] I was single, unattached, and wanted to travel. After visiting my parents for a week, I went by train to my new job. How well I remember that long train ride! The train went from Saskatchewan to North Bay. Then I had to transfer to the Polar Bear Express, which went to Moose Factory. It was a tremendous adventure. The weather in Moose Factory was surprisingly enjoyable, despite the cold. The native people made mukluks for me and warm clothes from fox fur. Soon after arriving in Moose Factory I met my husband, and two years later we were married. He taught school there and he must have liked my cooking! We moved to the Six Nations Reserve in Ontario thirty-five years ago.

The Six Nations' Iroquois culture was much different from the Cree culture in Saskatchewan. The Iroquois culture was much richer, and they had retained their language, their traditions, and their longhouse ceremonies. The Crees, on the other hand, had lost everything—their heritage, values, language, even their religion. The nagging question of why this had happened led me to begin to study my husband's people. In my research I found that even though the Iroquois' survival was threatened, they had always had plenty of food to eat. Because they were an agricultural people, they had corn, beans, and squash to sustain them. They fished the Great Lakes, they caught all kinds of wild game in the bush. When the Europeans came to this country the Iroquois were not starving. In the West, however, the Cree and the Blackfoot were virtually wiped out when the buffalo herds disappeared. They starved because the buffalo was their only means of survival—they depended on it for food, clothing, and shelter—everything. When residential schools were built for them, they lost their language, their traditions—all because they had had no food and needed help to survive.

The Six Nations Reserve is a small reserve, only fifteen miles long and seven miles wide, and is home to about 10,000 people. The reserve also has about ten acres of land in Brantford, where the Woodland Cultural Centre is situated. That is now the location of my cooking school.

It was my mother-in-law who taught me how to cook Iroquois foods. She showed me the many ways to prepare corn, which is sacred to the Iroquois. When the Creator gave the native people white corn it was the most important of his gifts. The Iroquois use it in casseroles, stews, porridge, but most important, in soups. We make flint corn soup, yellow corn soup, white corn soup, or dried corn soup. The process is very simple—just boil any of these kinds of corn with kidney beans, fresh pork, and a little salt. In olden days, the Iroquois used venison instead of pork, which the native people still prefer to use when it is available.

Three Sisters Soup is my favourite and was the soup I entered in the Culinary Olympics in Frankfurt, Germany, in 1992. I never expected it would be awarded a gold medal! The Three Sisters are corn, beans, and squash. Nutritionally, the combination of corn, beans, and squash contains everything that our bodies need. In the past the Iroquois planted these vegetables together in hills. The beans would twine around the corn stalks and the large squash leaves would keep the grasses from growing, so that less weeding was required. The older people still plant them this way. My recipe for the Three Sisters Soup came from my mother-in-law, who learned it from her mother. Corn, beans, and squash are cooked together with finely cut-up pork or venison in a large pot. Once I made Three Sisters Soup for 600 people in Saskatoon for a big conference. The chef was surprised to see that onions were not a part of the recipe. But by simmering the corn, beans, and squash for a long time, the flavours come together beautifully and create a delicious soup.

When I was chosen to be in the Culinary Olympics at first I thought someone was playing a joke at my expense. Held every four years in Frankfurt, the Culinary Olympics attracts 14,000 chefs from around the world. Native chefs were selected from across Canada to form a native chef team. The final team consisted of Andrew George from British Columbia, Arnold Olson from Saskatchewan, David Wolfman from Toronto, Brian Sappier from the East Coast, and me from Southern Ontario. The team started meeting and planning, each one of us submitting several native menus. For one day of the five-day competition we cooked Iroquois foods. We began preparing the food at two in the morning to have it ready by seven a.m. In addition to Three Sisters Soup, some of the other Iroquois foods we made were corn soup, bannock, and corn bread.

Years ago, in my catering business, I created hors d'oeuvres made from bannock and served them with berry juice, our traditional drink. Bannock hors d'oeuvres were one of the special foods we prepared for the Culinary Olympics. Bannock is an excellent base for hors d'oeuvres because it doesn't crumble. We put whatever is available on the bannock. Since the Iroquois people use beans a lot, I purée beans, season them, and spread them on tiny bannock. For weddings and other parties I've catered, I've used ham, pheasant, buffalo, or anything that we had. One learns to be creative. For the Olympics we used salmon, Arctic char, muskox, caviar, even dandelions, on the bannock.

Bannock is a favourite of both the Cree and the Iroquois, and there are different ways of preparing it. The Cree make a flat bannock—which is the kind we had when I was a young girl in Saskatchewan. When my father went hunting my mother would make about ten of them and put them into a bag. All my father would take with him was tea and bannock, then he'd add venison or rabbit or whatever he had caught. Fry bread is a lot like bannock, but it is a little thicker and is fried in a bit of oil. We also make a pan bread that uses the same dough as bannock, but it is cooked in a skillet either over an open fire or on top of the stove. One of our favourite dishes is Indian tacos. To make an Indian taco you start with a fry bread about six to eight inches in diameter. You cover it with beans or meat, top it with chopped onions, tomatoes, and cheese, and serve it with hot sauce. It is always served at our powwows.

Most people have heard of the powwow, but the Indian people have many ceremonies during the year. The Iroquois never lost these ceremonies, and outsiders are rarely invited to them. The first one in the winter is the maple syrup ceremony. It is a two-day event to "open up the trees." The entire family comes, bringing with them a basket of food for the feast. Tobacco is burned and the smoke from the tobacco is the prayer that goes to the Creator. At the ceremony we drink the maple sap. After the tapping of the trees another ceremony is held to give thanks to the Creator.

In May we have our "cleaning of the graves" ceremony, which takes place over two days. Families bring feast foods, eat together, and put some food aside for the dead—we believe we are eating with our ancesters. When I lost my mother-in-law, I looked forward to this ceremony—I wanted to do a little for her because she had done so much for me, and it helped me, too.

We also have a strawberry ceremony when the wild berries ripen, and we make a juice from the strawberries that is used in the ceremony. For the growing season, there is the planting ceremony, the green corn dance, then the harvest ceremony. All the services are held in the longhouse and thanks are given to the Creator for his gifts of food to us. The rituals are said in our native language and only the elders speak.

All the ceremonies involve food—everybody brings some and it is placed by the stove in the longhouse; sweet grass is burned and the food is blessed. We learn how to protect the earth and the trees so that the animals in the forest will survive.

After the Culinary Olympics there was so much publicity that the many demands on my time became difficult. Finally I decided to stay home and be a grandmother. But everyone said, "Oh, no, Bertha, you're our role model. You can't quit on us now." I told them that I didn't go to the Culinary Olympics to be rich, famous, or greedy. I've been given hands to work and I'll keep working as long as I can. But one day I was ready to quit. The chief came to me and said, "Bertha, you can't quit now. We'll fund you to train three people and they can assist you when you have a speaking engagement." That is how I began a chef's training program in the Woodland Cultural Centre. It was formerly a residential school built in the last century, and although it's quite old, it has everything a cook would want. We had to do many repairs because the equipment was old, but we now have stainless-steel counters, a potato peeler, steam cookers, walk-in freezers, and a bakery department. Tours come to the centre and we cook a hot lunch of native foods. I find it very exciting to be teaching others about my native foods and letting others taste our cuisine.

And the future? I am very interested in native cooking and teaching native people about our traditional foods. Native people are not eating properly and diabetes has increased in our community. It's not unusual for our people to be diabetic by the time they are thirty years old. I travel to Saskatchewan about three times a year to give workshops on nutrition and to teach workshops for people who want to learn to cook native foods in restaurants. Niagara College, Cambrian College, George Brown College, and the University of Guelph Hotel School are starting to teach native cuisine and this is very exciting. It is needed, and not only in the native community. People in general can learn from us—eating natural foods and soups that can be easily cooked. This makes me optimistic about our eating habits in the future.

Bertha Skye was a member of the Culinary Olympics team in 1992, which came back to Canada with seven gold medals, two silver, and two bronze. Moreover, this team was the first aboriginal team to enter the Culinary Olympics. Although born a Cree, she became interested in the Iroquois after marrying and moving to the Six Nations Reserve in Brantford, Ontario. She operates a cooking school in the Woodland Cultural Centre in Brantford, teaching about native foods and traditional cooking. Her recipes have been widely published in newspapers and magazines such as *Canadian Living* and *Foodservice and Hospitality.* She is frequently called upon to speak to children in schools, to church groups, and to others about her foods and the Iroquois culture. She lives on the Six Nations Reserve with her husband, who is a schoolteacher. They have five children and four grandchildren.

ELEANOR KANE

Taste, Quality, and Mass Culture

THERE ARE MANY within the restaurant industry who share an enduring commitment to excellence. Graduates of the Stratford Chefs School move out into the restaurant industry armed with a belief in quality, zealous in their commitment to good food and the pleasures of the table. But I keep hearing their voices after they have been working awhile. Students have often become discouraged by the realities of the workplace. How can we sustain their aspirations and encourage restaurants to allow newcomers sufficient time for skill and talent to develop?

I believe that relentless pressures exist in every area of the food industry to step back from high standards, to compromise quality, to use shortcut methods. For me, this reality comes to the fore whenever I take the time to examine the contents of shopping carts at the supermarkets. What has the consumer been convinced to buy this time? What messages has he or she responded to, and why? How will those mass-market products nourish body and spirit? Is it possible that in the past few decades quality in effort and product have become vanishing features of our civilization?

"Taste, quality, and mass culture" is a weighty topic indeed! Let me begin by defining what I mean by taste and quality. It may seem logical to start with a definition of the term *taste* from a sensory point of view, but the meaning intended here is a more general one. It has to do with discernment. In searching for understanding, we often look back in time to examine the links to our past in order to better understand where we are today. Doing so, we reach a clear understanding of the term, surprisingly, in the eighteenth century.

Taste then was concerned with the ability to discern and appreciate the beautiful in nature and art. At that time more than at any other, there was a more or less general consensus as to what constituted good taste. Privileged classes had the wealth, power, and resources to commission the finest in workmanship, materials, and design.

In the cooking world, this was also true. Haute cuisine reigned in the houses of the nobility, where classical influences in taste were obvious in table plans and tableware, as well as in the design of the dishes themselves. Gastronomical literature flourished. Grimod de la Reynière set in place the *Almanachs des gourmands*, which is considered to be the precursor of the *Guide Michelin.* His "tasting jury" met for five-hour sessions, sampling dishes and remarking on their qualities. These remarks then became the substance of an issue of the *Almanach.* Certificates were awarded by the jury to the approved food shops and restaurants of the day.

Brillat-Savarin, another French writer, contributed that wonderful piece of gastronomical literature *The Physiology of Taste,* wherein he declares that man's refined capacity to taste ensured him supremacy over the animal kingdom. A detailed, often amusing analysis of the tongue and its taste capacities follows. Interestingly, Brillat-Savarin notes that good-tasting food prevailed beyond Europe's borders. Contrary to the popular view that North American settlers survived on nothing but bark and corn husks, Brillat-Savarin remarked on the quality of food during his sojourn in New York State in 1794. Dinner, he writes, was "a superb piece of corned beef, stewed goose, a magnificent leg of mutton, then all manners of root vegetables, and at both ends of the table two enormous pots of excellent cider of which I couldn't get enough."

Times have changed, however. Today, regardless of wealth, social standing, or power, it appears that few of us are able to eat as well as people could a century ago. Money cannot buy many of the pleasures of the middle-class table of the eighteenth and nineteenth centuries, or the skilled and loving cookery that enhanced them. Good food, food that tastes of what it is, is now outside the mainstream of our culture.

This historic disaster has been obscured by great gains in productivity and wages, which have elevated a large section of people into the affluent middle-class. We have a level of comfort in living that, granted, no one would want to replace. Nevertheless, it is my feeling that we are a nation that has been convinced by skilled advertisers that industrial food tastes good. Despite the clamour in recent years for a return to "natural foods," most people have grown so accustomed to mass-produced, artificially flavoured foods that anything else tastes peculiar. Tests have shown that fresh fruit juices taste odd, and hence unpleasant, to people raised on processed and imitation juices. Fresh flavour, believe it or not, has become unfamiliar.

In today's world, pop food is designed to appeal to our eyes rather than to our stomachs. Never has food looked better and tasted worse. Subtle advertisements summon our instincts but fail to satisfy our longings. Modern food technology has triumphed in pairing our ancestral hungers with fast food, frozen food, chemically treated food, and out-of-season food. Our supermarkets abound with "fresh" foods, and preach the fantasy that tomatoes are always ripe, that strawberries grow in the dead of winter. We have forgotten the connection between our food and the earth and its seasons.

What seems lacking then in mass-produced, mass-marketed food is quality—quality of ingredients and quality of purpose, which should lead us to a heightened enjoyment in our daily lives.

I like the definition of quality proposed by the American historian Barbara Tuchman, who calls it "investment of the best skill and effort possible to produce the finest and most admirable result possible." The presence or absence of quality in some degree characterizes every man-made object, service, labour. You do a job well, or you do it half-well. Materials are sound and durable, or they are second-rate. Method is painstaking or whatever is easiest.

In almost every field of human endeavour, alarms are sounding about the erosion of standards—in our schools, in the workplace, in the arts, in politics, and in public life. If we are increasingly surrounded, almost swallowed up, by the second-rate, what has changed in this modern age to bring us to this point?

Historically, the age of privilege referred to earlier is over, and civilization has passed into the age of the masses. Our culture has been taken over by commercialism directed to the mass market and, necessarily, to mass taste. The public is now the consumer, and the criterion for the goods and services and arts that society produces is the pleasure and purchasing power of the greatest number, not the most discerning. When the dominant culture is mass-directed, we have to consider whether popular appeal will become the governing criterion and gradually submerge all but isolated islands of quality.

Quality cannot be put down altogether—it keeps breaking in. We come across quality here and there, from a symphony orchestra to a well-run grocery store. It appears in the crafts movement that expanded throughout the eighties, producing fine hand-woven fabrics and ornaments of glass, pottery, and wood. I believe that it exists within our food-service industry; for example, with the small pockets of organic farmers striving to restore produce to some level of decency, or with the chefs who believe in sustainable agriculture and are helping the independent farmer to survive. We feel encouraged, yet we have to recognize that the prevailing tendency is toward mediocrity.

We come across the same problem within our educational system. Schoolchildren are not prepared to work. The idea has grown that learning must be fun; students must study what they like; therefore courses have largely become elective. Some highly motivated students do learn because they cannot be stopped, but generally, many students do not acquire the coping skills that society needs.

Educators almost universally agree now that the public education system has to change. The question is how. Change is elusive because, in part, change requires that schools try to do what has not been done for decades: hold every student to high standards. In the past, only a relatively small elite excelled in school, but even those who dropped out could find well-paying unskilled jobs. In the high-tech economy of this decade and beyond, those who fail in school are more likely to remain unemployed or in dead-end jobs.

One educational model that encourages initiative and high standards is that of the Stratford Chefs School. The school's philosophy of training embodies the principles of excellence: excellence in program concept and direction, in candidates selected, in teaching methods, in products and materials, in practical work experiences.

When the school was formed its philosophy was in part inspired by a gentleman in the local community college, Aubrey Hagar. He championed the notion of the alternate apex of training, wherein the principles of selection, thoroughness of training, and excellence of mentor that apply in university professional education would equally apply in trades and craft training. The question for Aubrey was always why would we, or should we, expect any less from an electrician than from an engineer, from a chef than from an architect? And doesn't our society require the finest from the skilled trades as from the professionals?

At the core of the school's training is the very traditional master-apprentice relationship that has existed for centuries in trades and crafts training. This very unmodern relationship is not at all democratic or egalitarian. It would not fit inside the covers of most management-theory textbooks. It is an old-fashioned, almost authoritarian relationship. Yet, when imbued with a generosity of talent and a respect for the learner, it is still a most powerful tool for developing real skill and creativity.

Add to this the apprentice's exposure to quality ingredients, painstaking methods, and tenacity of vision, and we come to what continues to distinguish the training at the Stratford Chefs School. Part of the school's mandate is to urge our country's political and social institutions to embrace the values of initiative, merit, and achievement and allow distinction to occur where it begs to.

The public must be educated enough to appreciate excellence of craftsmanship in the food-service industry, so that we will value perfection in cuisine as much as we value the fine tunings of the Rolls-Royce engine. Standards in the industry need to be articulated and communicated. Our age cries out for what Brillat-Savarin called "the heroes of gastronomy"—people who are able and willing to support the development of cuisine.

In 1977, **Eleanor Kane** combined her interest in human relations with a lifelong interest in hospitality by opening the Old Prune restaurant in Stratford. In 1983, she was instrumental in founding the Stratford Chefs School (with partners Jim Morris and Joseph Mandel). As its co-director, she has guided the school through a decade of growth, to the point where today it is considered the leading training institute of its kind in Canada. To celebrate the school's tenth anniversary, the Stratford Chefs School sponsored Northern Bounty, the conference, in 1994, which was the genesis of the papers in this book. Prior to her work in the hospitality industry, Eleanor earned a master's degree in psychology at the University of Alberta and directed one of the first multidisciplinary treatment teams in this field at the Constance Lethbridge Rehabilitation Centre in Montreal.

DONALD ZIRALDO

Founding the Vintners Quality Alliance (VQA)

EVERY wine-growing region has a body of regulations that set standards for its finest products. Based on years of trial and error, these laws define the geographical areas where grapes can grow and specify how the wine is made. The Vintners Quality Alliance (VQA) is to Canada what the Appellation d'origine contrôllée (AOC) is to France, the Denominazione di Origine Controllata (DOC) is to Italy, and the Qualitätswein mit Pradikät (QMP) is to Germany.

The VQA was founded for several reasons. In the early 1980s, Canadian wine makers blended their grapes with those harvested from vineyards around the globe. The resulting wines were sold as "Canadian." There was an obvious need to differentiate these blends from those vintages that were indeed 100 percent Canadian grown and vinified.

In Europe the concept of "appellation of origin" had evolved to identify wines by where the grapes were grown and to define the buyers' specific geographic appellation. For wines to be sold in countries in the European Economic Community today, the EEC must recognize the wine's "appellation of origin."

The first step in establishing the VQA, which was referred to in its infancy as the Niagara Vintners Alliance, was to create parameters to delineate those geographic areas being proposed. We followed the guidelines laid out by the Office international de la vigne et du vin (OIV) and adopted at their 1947 General Assembly, which state:

"A wine or spirit may only bear an appellation of origin if the latter is sanctioned by usage and is of acknowledged repute. This reputation must derive from qualitative features determined by the following factors:

1. natural factors that play a decisive part: the climate, the nature of the soil, the varieties, the exposure, and geographic distinction;
2. factors due to the intervention of man, playing a part of varying importance: growing methods, vinification methods."

To properly ascertain these Designated Viticultural Areas (DVA), I approached the late Dr. Peter Peach, professor of geological sciences at Brock University in St. Catharines. Dr. Peach assisted in determining three specific viticultural areas. Each has geographical and historical significance. In other words, each has defining geographical characteristics and a history of grape growing. Unlike some countries—the United States, for instance—the geographical features used in our definition are natural rather than man-made. We also insist, before granting an appellation, that there be a history of wine growing in the area. Under Canadian rules, merely throwing a few vines into the ground would never qualify for an appellation of origin.

The three viticultural areas are:

- The Niagara Peninsula, which is bounded by Lake Ontario, the Niagara River, and the Niagara Escarpment. It has significant glacial deposits layered over alluvial soil.
- Pelee Island, an island in the western extremity of Lake Erie, with a soil composed of clay, loam, and sand.
- Lake Erie North Shore, which is bordered by Lake Erie, the St. Clair River, and the Thames River. The soil here varies from gravelly loam to clay and sand.

A stringent code of regulations governs the right of the vintners to use these highly specific geographic regions on their labels.

In reading this label we know that:

- A minimum of 85 percent of the grapes used to vinify this wine have come from the named viticultural area.
- Only *Vitis vinifera*, the classic European "noble" grape varieties such as Chardonnay, Pinot Noir, Cabernet Sauvignon, and Riesling, has been used.
- For these varietals, 85 percent of the wine has been made from the variety named on the label and exhibits the predominant character of that variety.
- The wine has been produced from 100 percent Canadian-grown grapes.
- Because the wine is "Estate Bottled," 100 percent of the grapes have been grown and vinified on the property and have not left the winery prior to bottling.
- If the vintner has designated the vineyard where the wine was

made, the site is within a designated viticultural area and 100 percent of the grapes have come from that vineyard.

- Minimum sugar levels have been set for wines designated as "Estate Bottled," as well as dessert wines, and icewine.[1]

Wines are evaluated by a panel of experts. This panel, composed of the six senior consultants from the Liquor Control Board of Ontario, is autonomous from the wine industry. Panel members have honed their talents through years of rigorous tastings under controlled laboratory conditions. Given the stringency of VQA standards, panel members perform blind tastings for both faults and varietal characteristics. Only those wines that meet or exceed production and appellation standards are awarded the VQA designation. The top honour is the Gold VQA medallion. It is given to wines considered to be of exceptionally high quality, wines that perform exceedingly well as judged by the VQA tasting panel and laboratory analysis. The VQA Gold Medallion is not awarded lightly. It is the symbol of our wine makers' finest achievements.

Official commencement of the VQA was in 1988 in Ontario. The Ontario VQA then asked British Columbia to institute the same system. It officially began in 1990.[2] Each region has several rules and regulations that are unique to it, just as Burgundy and Bordeaux do under the French appellation of origin system, governed by the Institut national des appellations d'origine (INAO).

Experience has shown that certain vineyard areas, because of their favoured soils, exposure, and microclimate, produce the best wines year after year. By designating the appellations of origin on the label, vintners can provide wine lovers with a guide to their superior products.

Since Canada's wine regions are very young by world standards, many of the rules originally implemented by VQA were intended to form the basis for ongoing development. As in the centuries old winegrowing regions of Chianti and Burgundy, changes to our existing regulations continue to fine-tune every detail. A Canadian example of such ongoing development is the addition of Vin du Curé, a specialty dessert wine fashioned after Italy's Vin Santo, the amber-coloured "holy wine" of Tuscany. To qualify for VQA when produced in Ontario, this wine must be vinified using 100 percent Riesling grapes. At harvest, after pressing, the "must" (the crushed grapes and juices) has to have a Brix level of 18 (a measurement of the sugar content). After long, slow drying on frames or mats in a ventilated place, it has to measure 32 Brix.

Noble wines do not happen by accident. They are the result of fine grapes—generally the great European *Vitis vinifera* varietals—planted in the right soils, ripened in a nurturing climate, then selected and carefully vinified in strict accordance with the rules laid down by the VQA.

The future of Canada's VQA is full of great promise. There will be ongoing research to determine subappellations, such as the St. Davids' Bench, the Beamsville Bench, and so on, within existing regions. VQA standards will be harmonized nationally; within the OIV Sparkling wines, known as "champagne" in France, will be classified; and very soon we hope to include Quebec's growing number of wineries in our national network.

Donald Ziraldo was born in St. Catharines, Ontario, and received a bachelor of science in horticulture from the University of Guelph. He holds an honorary degree from Humber College. Presently he is the president of Inniskillin Wines Inc., Inniskillin Napa Vineyards Inc., and Ziraldo Farms and Nurseries. Since 1988, he has been chairman of the Vintners Quality Alliance. In 1991, his icewine won the Grand Prix d'Honneur at Vinexpo. He has been awarded numerous other honours, including the Citadelle d'Or Award in Bordeaux, France, and the Order of Ontario (together with his partner Karl Kaiser).

TONY ASPLER

Icewine

THE BEST KEPT SECRET in the wine world is Canadian icewine. When the Niagara Peninsula thermometer takes that first, prolonged plunge next winter, well-bundled volunteer pickers will harvest grapes frozen as hard as marbles. Hanging precariously from the vine, the grapes may look unappetizing to the untrained eye, but the lusciously sweet wine they produce is worth numb fingers and raw cheeks. Fortunately, vintners have machines to press the juice from the frozen berries—stomping the grapes with bare feet would be above the call of duty even if it were possible.

Canada is the world's largest producer of this vinous rarity, called *Eiswein* by the Germans who invented it. In the 1991 vintage, more than 80,000 half bottles were produced in Ontario. Small quantities are also made in British Columbia and Nova Scotia.

Canadian icewine first received global recognition in 1991, when Inniskillin's Vidal Icewine 1989 won the Grand Prix d'Honneur at Vinexpo in Bordeaux—one of nineteen medals awarded among 4,100 entries. In 1994, Stonechurch's 1991 Vidal Icewine received a Grand Gold Award at Vinitaly, in Verona, Italy. Today Canadian icewine is recognized and sold worldwide as a unique quality wine, fetching top prices, and vintners cannot keep up with the demand.

Like most great things in life, the discovery of icewine was accidental. In 1794, wine producers in Franconia, Germany, made virtue of necessity by pressing juice from frozen grapes. Up until that time they had achieved a sweet, concentrated juice by leaving the grapes to hang as long as possible in the hope they would be attacked by a natural infection called "noble rot"—*Botrytis cinerea*—a fungus that infects grapes in the autumn, attaching itself to the grapes, puncturing their skins, thus allowing the juice to evaporate.

The credit for Canada's recent and highly successful foray into icewine production goes to Walter Hainle in British Columbia's Okanagan Valley. In 1973, Hainle made icewine for his family and friends. His son, Tilman Hainle, has one bottle of the famous '73 vintage "in a glamorous Lowenbräu bottle, with matching cap and homemade label."

The uniqueness of icewine begins in the vineyard. During the fall harvest in September and October, vintners reserve a small area of the vineyard where the bunches of grapes are left unpicked. Only one or two acres at most are reserved, because farmers take a tremendous gamble leaving grapes on the vine. If birds and animals don't eat them, mildew or rot might destroy them, or a sudden storm could knock them off the vine. When the temperature drops to *minus* 7 degrees Celsius, the sugar-rich juice begins to freeze. The secret to making icewine is to pick the grapes and press them while they are still frozen. Grapes are actually 80 percent water, and when this water is frozen, the press extracts it as shards of ice, leaving a minuscule amount of juice. Intensely sweet and highly acidic, this juice is the perfect combination for making icewine, an ambrosia fit for Dionysus himself.

German Eiswein makers must harvest their grapes before dawn to ensure that the frozen grapes don't thaw. They have been known to connect outdoor thermometers to their alarm clocks to alert them if temperatures plunge during the night. But in Ontario there is no need for such theatrics. Wine makers can sleep secure in the knowledge that sometime between December and February there will be a stretch of subzero temperatures. Unlike Germany, the Ontario icewine harvest is an annual event as predictable as the turning maples. Sometimes the cold comes early, as it did on 29 October 1991 in British Columbia, when Hainle Vineyards, CedarCreek, and Gehringer Brothers picked frozen grapes in temperatures below minus 13 degrees Celsius.

A vineyard left for icewine is really a sorry sight. The mesh-covered vines are completely denuded of leaves and the grapes are brown and shrivelled, hanging like so many bats from the frozen canes. Yet the ugly, wrinkled berries taste wonderfully sweet, much like frozen raisins.

Harvesting icewine grapes is a torturous business. Invariably, snow combined with a high wind makes picking an experience similar to Scott's trek to Antarctica. The stems attaching the bunches to the vine are dried and brittle, and a twist of the wrist is all that is needed to pick them. A strong wind or an ice storm will easily knock them to the ground. When the wind howls through the vineyard, driving the snow before it, a temperature of "only" minus 10 degrees Celsius seems like minus 40. Pickers, fortified with tea and brandy, brave the elements for two hours at a time, before rushing back to the winery to warm up.

When the tractor delivers the precious boxes of grapes to the winery the hard work begins. Since the berries must remain frozen, the pressing is done al fresco or the winery doors are left open. The presses have to be worked slowly; otherwise the bunches will turn to solid blocks of ice, yielding nothing. Some producers throw rice husks into the press, which pierce the skins of the berries and create channels for the juice to flow through the mass of ice. Sometimes it takes two or three hours before the first drop of juice appears. This will be the sweetest juice, since grape sugars have a lower freezing point than water.

Roughly speaking, it takes about a kilogram of grapes to produce a bottle of wine—a kilo of icewine grapes will make, at most, one-fifth of that amount or less, depending on the degree of dehydration caused by wind and winter sunshine. The longer the grapes hang on the vine, the less juice there will be. Wine makers hope for a cold snap in December, which will yield more icewine than if they had to wait for a February harvest.

Once the oily, clear juice is extracted from the rock-hard berries, it is allowed to settle for three or four days before it is clarified by racking (siphoning) from one tank to another. The fermentation takes place in stainless-steel tanks. Since the juice is extremely high in sugar, it will not ferment without the addition of a special yeast. The fermentation is very slow and can take months. When bottled after clarification, the wine, which has become amber, fragrant, thick, and sweet, can be aged for a decade or more. Because of its better acid balance, Riesling will generally last longer than Vidal.

The very first commercial attempts at producing icewine in Canada were sabotaged by bird and man. Not all grapes can hold up to the rigorous treatment of winter freezing. Only the thick-skinned, late-maturing varieties such as Riesling and Vidal can survive such predators as gray rot, powdery mildew, unseasonal warmth, wind, rain, sugar-crazed starlings—and the occasional Ontario bureaucrat. In 1983, Inniskillin Winery lost its entire crop to hungry birds the day before picking was scheduled. Walter Strehn at Pelee Island Vineyards had taken the precaution of netting his vines to protect them from a feathered attack. But some persistent blue jays managed to break through the nets and were trapped in the mesh. A passing bird fancier reported this to the Ministry of Natural Resources, whose officials descended upon the vineyard and tore off the netting. Strehn quickly lost $25,000 worth of Riesling grapes to the rapacious flock. Then, to add insult to injury, he was charged with trapping birds out of season, using dried grapes as bait! Happily, the case was dropped. Strehn managed to make a small amount of Riesling icewine 1983 with the grapes he was able to salvage.

In spite of these setbacks, more and more Ontario wineries have begun to make icewine. Their products sell out the moment they reach the stores. To avoid disappointment, customers are encouraged to reserve their bottles while the grapes are still hanging on the vine. Ranging in price from $35 to $50 a half bottle and more, Canadian icewine is not something that you would drink every day. A small glass among friends at the end of a meal is sufficient. Its flavours of honey, peaches, apricots, orange, tea, and toffee—yes, you can find them all in a great icewine—will linger on your palate until the sun shines.

Tony Aspler is the most widely read wine writer in Canada. The author of eight books about wine, including *Aligoté to Zinfandel* and *Tony Aspler's Wine Lover's Companion*, he writes for numerous magazines and newspapers, and has been a wine columnist for the *Toronto Star* since 1980. As a consultant and wine judge, he makes frequent trips to the vineyards and wine fairs of the world. In the hospitality industry he is active as an educator and wine consultant for restaurants and hotels.

ROSANNA CAIRA

The Evolution of Canadian Cuisine in Restaurants

IN A MATTER OF A DECADE, restaurateurs across the country have learned to sing the culinary praises of Canada. A mere decade ago, the chances of a restaurant promoting *Canadian* cuisine would have been not only unlikely, but highly improbable. Most restaurants would never have thought to consider that a Canadian cuisine even existed. Was there more to Canadian cuisine than hamburgers and French fries—the quintessential North American fare—or roast beef and mashed potatoes, the old English favourite? Of course there was the usual reference to typically Canadian products like salmon, fiddleheads, and wild rice, but if Canadian cuisine existed beyond that, most people weren't aware of it.

Because Canada is a relatively young country that has opened its arms to various cultures from all over the world, a distinctly Canadian cuisine has never really emerged. Though initially much of our culinary heritage was shaped by British and French traditions, the influx of immigrants over the past four decades has left a strong culinary imprint.

Traditionally, restaurateurs across North America have been more concerned with French cuisine. In fact, in order to be considered serious, most restaurateurs and chefs believed they had to reproduce the dishes of France. But as Maurice O'Flynn, manager of the 1992 Team

Canada, which won the Culinary Olympics in Frankfurt, Germany, said in an article in 1993: "People often ask me what Canadian cuisine is and I respond by asking them to define French cuisine. They may answer that it's a café in Paris, the herbs of Provence, or that it's Paul Bocuse and truffles from Perigord—in others words, it's the totality of regional cuisine."

For Canadians, even that totality was hard to define. But a funny thing happened in the late eighties. A reawakening of our Canadian consciousness occurred, and all of a sudden everything from our wines to our foods began to grow in popularity. The impetus for this growth spilled over from a similar transformation occurring in the United States, where restaurateurs, chefs, and suppliers became intrigued by increasingly better food supplies suddenly available within their own regions. Whereas in the past it was natural for European-born chefs to look to Europe as the source of product, all of a sudden North American-born chefs began looking to their own backyards to meet demand for product. It was an adventurous culinary trait inherent in the new breed of Canadian chefs, who realized it wasn't necessary to invent something new, when in fact they could take old traditions, dress them in a new fashion, and create an entirely new approach to cooking.

No doubt France's three-star restaurants will continue to serve as the basis of comparison for many restaurateurs the world over. But the increasing trend to Mediterranean-style food and away from classical French cuisine has allowed regional cuisine to blossom even further.

The fact that more chefs are graduating from the Canadian system also bodes well for the continuing representation of regional cookery. Consider that in the late seventies many of Canada's chefs were European-born and male. By the mideighties, this started to change as many Canadian-born chefs began graduating from Canadian culinary programs. In Toronto, chefs like Christopher Boland, formerly of Trappers; the late Russell Cottam at Scaramouche; Jamie Kennedy of Palmerston; Christopher Klugman, founding chef of Bistro 990; and Mark Bussières, founding chef of Metropolis, were all part of the new breed of Canadian-born chefs responsible for laying the foundation upon which many other talented Canadians have built. In Quebec, chefs like Anne Desjardins and Louise Duhamel significantly shaped that province's regional movement.

These chefs worked diligently with local farmers and suppliers to cultivate and popularize fresh, local product. They then took that local product and used it creatively in dishes that were inspired by their cultural roots, their own interests, and their region's ethnicity. What they succeeded in accomplishing was the first sign that a Canadian cuisine, albeit a very regional cuisine, was even remotely possible. While some culinarians may argue that Canadian cuisine does not exist because they are unable to list dishes that are indigenously Canadian, the mere fact that Canadian-born chefs are using locally grown products to create wonderful new dishes proves otherwise.

One of the earliest restaurants in Toronto, perhaps Canada, to fly the Canadian flag was Trappers. Under the guidance of Chris Boland, a graduate of George Brown College, Trappers made its mark by promoting what Boland referred to as "contemporary continental North American with a Canadian flare." There Canadian products like smoked trout, maple-glazed Laurentian hams, and Ontario preserves were allowed to shine through in all their glory. "We don't import from Europe," explained Boland in an interview in *Foodservice and Hospitality* magazine in the mideighties, "We use indigenous North American products and highlight the Canadian."

A few years later in 1987, when Mark Bussières, a protégé of Chris Boland, opened Metropolis, he borrowed that philosophy. Even today, almost a decade later, Metropolis is a unique representation of what Canadian cuisine can be. "The background of most Canadians is European," explains Terry Kennedy, chef at Metropolis, "so you're taking a lot of food styles into consideration. Basically when we say Canadian, we are trying to use local ingredients, but then we'd get into things like Alberta beef, Manitoba or Saskatchewan wild rice, or Ontario Huron County lamb and rabbit." Located in mid-Toronto, Metropolis puts the culinary emphasis on recipes that look back to Canada's rural culinary heritage; some go as far back as Sir John A. Macdonald's era. Today, while neither Mark Bussières nor Christopher Boland is at their respective restaurants, their legacies live on as testaments to their creativity and their persistence.

Somewhat ironically, German-born Michael Stadtlander is one of the more famous advocates of Canadian cuisine. "Perhaps it takes someone who is not from Canada to recognize the beauty of our indigenous things, to zoom in on them and to present them in a different context," explained Jamie Kennedy to James Chatto in *Toronto Life* in 1992. "Michael was able to do that at Nekah. It was urban, cosmopolitan. It was art."

With the opening of Nekah in 1988, Stadtlander brought Canadian cuisine to a new pinnacle, using local product in ways that mirrored what Sinclair Philip was doing at the Sooke Harbour House in British Columbia. Nekah's motif was centred on nature, and the restaurant's very name was Indian for a wild goose. Buoyed by large, open spaces and the veritable bounty of unusual products, Stadtlander, who got his start in the restaurant business in Canada working with Kennedy at Scaramouche, has always been extremely keen on Canadian product. He was not afraid to develop a cuisine that borrowed from various traditions, but that capitalized on indigenous product. Unusual menu items included ocean eels from New Brunswick, Alberta buffalo, and prawn roe from British Columbia.

Today, though Nekah is long gone, Stadtlander is back doing what he does best—cooking in natural surroundings. Late last year, Stadtlander and his wife, Nobuyo, purchased the Eigensinn Farm, consisting of 100 acres of land and a five-bedroom farmhouse twenty minutes from Collingwood, Ontario. There, in addition to running a bed-and-breakfast, Stadtlander raises his own livestock and grows his own grain, vegetables, and fruit.

A restaurateur on the West Coast reputed to be the first to understand and effectively use local product is Sinclair Philip, owner and operator of Sooke Harbour House. Opened in 1979 by Philip and his French-born wife, Frederica, Sooke Harbour House has been referred to by Anne Hardy, author of *Where to Eat in Canada*, as sui generis. Understandably so. But for Sinclair and Frederica, the decision to promote local products was an easy one to make. Strategically situated a stone's throw from the Juan de Fuca Strait, Sooke Harbour House offers a bounty of distinctly Canadian fish and seafood, an abundance of fresh local fruits and produce, and a multitude of herbs, vegetables, and edible flowers that grow year-round in British Columbia's mild climate. Dishes include favourites such as octopus salad served on a bed of cabbage with caraway, hazelnuts, and mustard; and salmon baked with celery root, grey hubbard squash, white turnip, and kohlrabi. The wine list highlights British Columbia and Ontario vintages, as well as local ciders and beers.

Like Philip, Janice Lotskar is another West Coast native who has successfully married local product with a Pacific Northwest flair. Her restaurants the Raintree in Vancouver and, most recently, the Harvest Moon Café in Victoria, have built their respective markets by popularizing regional cuisine. Rebecca Dawson, the founding chef of the Raintree, established a reputation for using only fresh, local produce.

At the Raintree, pleasing the customer is accomplished via a menu that exclusively highlights the Pacific Northwest—a regional approach to cuisine that relies on a balance of fresh meat, fish, seafood, and vegetables. It's a philosophical approach to cooking made difficult during the winter months, when certain foods are not available locally. But during these months, the restaurant relies on root vegetables—carrots, turnips, potatoes—and does not use produce such as tomatoes or strawberries out of season.

As part of that philosophy, the Raintree also actively promotes its suppliers. "We promote the food product with its pedigree, be it farm produce from the Fraser Valley, Saltspring lamb, or B.C. wines," explains Barnaby. The restaurant features very few European wines, preferring to promote B.C. vintages."

Focussing on the regional niche has yielded positive results for the Raintree. In only four short years, the restaurant has established a loyal following. Since its opening, many other restaurants in British Columbia have jumped on the Canadian bandwagon. Barnaby explains why: "People will start celebrating indigenous foods of the area more. They'll want to discover what people ate in the past. There's going to be more regional cuisine because we've run out of countries to explore."

A province where Canadian cuisine has always been in existence is Quebec. Traditional foods like *tourtière, poutine,* and maple sugar pie have been favourites for many years. But like the rest of the country, the mass influx of immigrants in the fifties created many changes on the culinary front. According to Jacques Lacoursière, a historian and member of the Royal Society of Canada, writing in the June 1994 issue of *Foodservice and Hospitality* magazine, a 1985 survey taken in Quebec revealed that typical Quebec dishes like *tourtière, cipaille, poutine,* and pork and beans were chosen by only 3.25 percent of the respondents, while 42.9 percent chose Italian food, and ethnic food other than Italian claimed 13.4 percent.

Though today's Quebeckers may not choose the *tourtière*, the *cipaille*, or the sugar pie of their ancestors, there is still something markedly regional about the foods they do pick. Food items like duck, *pâté*, game, sweetbreads, and lamb, all part of the French tradition, are still being served, but the style and the influences have changed to represent a regional flavour. Like the rest of the country, today's Quebec chefs have been influenced by the burgeoning immigrant population and a dedicated coterie of chefs who saw great potential in local food supplies, and many Quebec chefs today have a special fondness for fresh, local produce cooked *à la minute*. One of the earliest proponents of Quebec cuisine was the late Serge Bruyère, who in 1990 used the culinary term *"la nouvelle cuisine Québécoise"*—a style of cooking that predominantly uses regional products.

Unlike Quebec, however, isolation from the rest of the country and a smaller influx of immigrants have allowed Newfoundlanders to maintain their culinary traditions. That explains why, on Canada's East Coast, Newfoundlanders continue their love affair with figgy duff, cod's tongues, and flipper pie.

Whether it be on the Prairies, where the Eastern European influences converged with wide-open spaces, or on Canada's East Coast, where the fishing industry shaped the primarily English and French ancestry, Canada is brimming with food traditions that are constantly evolving in a distinctly Canadian fashion. Though we may not be able to claim that we have invented foods like spaghetti or sushi, there is an underlying fabric of Canadiana that is woven into the fabric of many fine Canadian restaurants. Perhaps European-born chef Gerhard Pichler sums it up best: "You pick up the best from all over and adapt it into the Canadian." It's a sentiment echoed by Toronto chef Jamie Kennedy, who said in an interview in 1986: "I get really excited when I see something I haven't used before. It's there, so why not use it? You also think of the product's background, how it's used in the culture it comes from. Through all those processes you come up with something distinctly yours that maybe reflects a cosmopolitan reaction."

Isn't that what Canadian cuisine is truly all about?

Rosanna Caira is the editor of *Foodservice and Hospitality* and *Hotelier* magazines, Canadian trade publications circulated to more than 25,000 hospitality organizations. She is a past recipient of the Ontario Hostelry Institute's Gold Award, presented annually to those individuals who have contributed significantly to the hospitality industry in Ontario.

THE REGIONAL CUISINE OF QUEBEC

JULIAN ARMSTRONG

A Taste of Quebec

QUEBEC's cuisine has always had a regional flavour. Settlers carried their family culinary traditions with them into the wilderness and created versions of old favourites with the new foods they found in their new land. These dishes continue to characterize each region's cooking today.

The roots of Quebec cuisine lie in French country cooking, with its medieval influences. This medieval style is still evident today when Quebeckers prepare their traditional dishes for Christmas and other family gatherings. Many a *tourtière* (meat pie) is seasoned with cinnamon and cloves, spices traditionally paired in medieval cooking. These spices frequently flavour *cretons* (a country-style coarse pork pâté), *tête fromagée* (head cheese), and *cipaille* or *cipâte* (a layered meat pie). *Ragoût de pattes et de boulettes* (a stew of pigs' feet and meatballs in a gravy thickened and seasoned with spiced browned flour) begins with *lardons*, strips of salted pork that are fried to provide fat for browning the meat in the medieval fashion. Salted pork is added to humble baked beans, along with a sweetener, which in medieval Europe would likely have been honey, but in Quebec is traditionally sugar, molasses, or maple syrup. Even for dessert, Quebec cooks have the medieval habit of combining fresh and dried fruit in pies of apples and raisins or a spiced date cake.

Many traditional Quebec dishes can be traced to the northern provinces of France, the homeland of so many Quebec settlers. Game meats such as partridge baked in a bed of cabbage are still a specialty in Normandy. French country bread, like its medieval precursor, was coarse, shaped in big, round, flat loaves, and baked weekly in communal ovens. It was often stale, so trenchers, or slices, had to be softened with liquid to be eaten. The taste for dried bread soaked in various liquids is the origin of today's spiced bread pudding and French toast, called *pain perdu* in Louisiana. In Quebec City in August 1993, the medieval festival Les Médiévals de Québec featured a medieval hot dog—a sausage wrapped in a buckwheat crêpe. These crêpes, sold on the streets of Paris as *galettes,* are part of Quebec history. Quebec City founder, Samuel de Champlain, mentions *galettes* in his diary. The term is now applied to sugar cookies.

The first Quebec farmer, Louis Hébert, although sustained by foods imported from his homeland, no doubt grew foods he'd known in France, and enjoyed the lavish supplies of fish and game. He learned from the Indians about three hearty native vegetables—corn, beans, and squash. In the fall of each year, country roads in the province sport signs announcing *Blé d'Inde* and *Maïs sucre* (sweet corn). Both mean corn on the cob for sale. Beans are baked to make *fèves au lard,* frequently called *les binnes.* Pumpkin pie is an annual Thanksgiving dessert and some restaurants offer a spiced pumpkin soup.

The first settlers used the cooking techniques of their homeland and these classic methods still prevail. As a chef once told me, "The mother cuisine is French." Quebec cooks still brown meat in hot fat before stewing it with vegetables and seasonings; simmer a bouillon from leftover bones and vegetables; employ every scrap of meat in *pâtés, terrines,* and *galantines;* use salt to preserve pork and fish through the long, bitter winters; and make custard sauces as the basis for many desserts.

If you travel around the province today, you'll find certain core dishes, mainly pies and stews, but each of the twelve regions of the province has its own distinct cuisine.

Quebec City

The original settlers of Quebec City laid the foundation for Quebec cuisine. As their colony grew and gradually spread east and west along both banks of the St. Lawrence River, then north and south, too, the settlers adapted their cooking habits to the local foods.

Montreal has a United Nations of restaurants, but restaurants in

Quebec City still show their French roots. There's a charming restaurant just down the street from the Château Frontenac that takes pride in serving revived versions of earlier dishes. Called Aux Anciens Canadiens, it dates from the seventeenth century. On nearby Île d'Orléans in a farmhouse from the same seventeenth-century period is a rival restaurant called L'Âtre. Both places are run by women who have taken it upon themselves to bring alive the past by serving lighter versions of the earliest *tourtière*, *ragoût*, *cretons*, and sugar pie.

To visit the Île d'Orléans is to step back in time. Original stone and whitewashed seigniorial farmhouses still line the banks of the St. Lawrence, separated by long, thin strips of land that extend back from the water the way they did in the *Ancien Régime.* Here the original *tourtière* was made from white passenger pigeons called *tourtes.* They were so plentiful in New France that if grain was scattered on the ground, a flock would immediately appear. A wily settler could easily toss a net over dozens of these birds. They were baked in a shallow pie pan called a *tourtière*, and research shows that the name of the pie derives from this utensil, and not from the name of the bird.

Some *tourtières* in this region show the influence of the food habits of the English and Scottish soldiers who settled here and began growing the oats of their native land. Oats are used instead of potatoes to thicken the ground pork filling in some recipes.

Game is farmed on the island, making it possible for chefs and gastronomic cooks to obtain plumper, meatier birds that still have the same delicate flavour as their wild ancestors. One game farm, *Ferme d'Orléans*, produces such delicacies as the *pintadine*, a one-serving-size guinea hen, and quail *foie gras.*

But other foods are produced on the island, too. Late-season strawberries—ruby red and extra sweet—come into ripeness at the end of July after the regular Quebec strawberry crop has finished.

The island is one of the lushest agricultural regions in the province, and leeks grow happily in the rich soil. In fact, island farmers have long been nicknamed *les Poireaux.* Cooks like to substitute leeks for onions in a quiche that's a first cousin to the *Flamiche aux poireaux* of northern France. They put leeks instead of onions in their pea soup, in the boiled dinner called a *bouilli*, in a *pot-au-feu*, and in white sauce to serve with chicken or vegetables.

North of Quebec City, around Lac Beauport, onions rate first and farmers are called *les Oignons de Beauport* because of their big onion crop. The area farther north around St-Ubalde is a major potato-producing centre. It has spawned a local community cookbook devoted solely to the potato.

Montérégie

The seigniorial farms have largely disappeared in this long-settled region south of Montreal. Recipes from this early era are still popular here. The rich land has made this region a garden, with vast acreages of carrots, corn, spinach, strawberries, and apple orchards.

A host of Quebec's specialty foods—oyster mushrooms, white asparagus, artichokes, endive, and rabbits—are produced in this wide crescent of land. They turn up on the tables of many fine restaurants and inns in the region.

The founding families in this region take pride in keeping alive their heartier dishes, especially those made from pork, Quebec's favourite meat. At Christmas, many prepare *cretons* and *tourtières*, and a few still take the time to make the original *boudin* (blood pudding) or *saucisses en coiffe* (hand-made sausages).

Another Christmas favourite is oyster soup, even though the days when the St. Lawrence River was full of oysters have long gone.

Strawberry tarts are the dessert of June. The rest of the year, it's apples—in pies, cakes, applesauce, apple butter, and apple jelly. Traditional cooks also make *Tarte aux oeufs*, a spiced custard pie resembling the *Tarte à la crème* of northeastern France.

Côte du Sud

East of Quebec City, along the south shore of the St. Lawrence, is another long-settled area, where fish and game have always been popular. The river begins to widen here on its way to the sea and salty air wafts over hill and dale. In the Kamouraska region east of Montmagny, you'll see roofs on old clapboard houses that curve the way the fishing boats do—obviously the builders handled both structures. Fish was smoked here at least a century before Jacques Cartier claimed Quebec for France. Basque fishermen who fished in the river stopped on the islands off the Côte du Sud to smoke their catch.

Gibelotte of Sorel, a fish stew combining little catfish or perch with vegetables, is famous. The dish was invented in a small restaurant on one of the islands off the town of Sorel, and is celebrated each July with its own festival.

Low-priced family food is as distinctive as haute cuisine dishes around the province. *Chiard* is an economical hash fried up out of left-over meat, onions, and potatoes. Along the Côte du Sud, it's likely to be made of salt pork. Cooks knew that made this way, it would keep safely when fisherman took it out on a fishing trip. Savory, Quebec's favourite herb, often seasoned this *chiard blanc*, as it's sometimes called.

To flavour their cooking during the long winter, cooks mixed together fresh herbs and vegetables, layered them into jars with generous amounts of salt, and used spoonfuls of these *herbes sâlées* to season soups and stews. Now made commercially at Ste-Flavie on the lower south shore of the St. Lawrence, *herbes sâlées* sell in specialty shops all over Quebec.

Although Côte du Sud has major lamb farms, and progressive restaurants have lamb on their menus, the old families continue to reject this meat, which has never been popular in Quebec. Pork and beef are the choices for traditional dishes.

The classic French upside-down apple dessert, *tarte tatin*, originally from the Loire Valley, is made with maple syrup, rather than sugar, as the sweetener.

Charlevoix

Across the river, and one of Quebec's top resort areas, is Charlevoix. It has a distinctive family cuisine, and some of the finest restaurants in the province. Right after the British conquest, English and Scottish army officers were given tracts of land here, and they immediately started growing oats and potatoes, which influenced the original

French cuisine. Steaming puddings and the use of cream in cooking were other British contributions to the original French cuisine.

For no known reason, the Charlevoix *tourtière* often calls for cubed, rather than ground, meat. Family cooks prepare a miniature version of the *tourtière*—a pork turnover called *pâtés croches.* Originally made with game meats, it's a specialty on Île aux Coudres, the island off Baie-St-Paul.

Two little fish, smelt and caplin, have always been caught in "the sea," as the St. Lawrence is called here, although now, with massive water pollution, most fish come from farther downriver. Floured or battered and fried in butter or oil (or the original lard), these little fish are the basis for many a spring feast. Or they can be made into a pie, a traditional dish on Île aux Coudres.

Lambs graze on the grassy hills that are swept with salt air from the river. Eaten only occasionally, their meat has a natural tang and resembles the *pré-salé* lamb of Brittany—another region of France that was a homeland to many settlers.

The *gourgane,* a big, red-streaked bean whose seeds are made into a hearty soup, is almost as popular in Charlevoix as it is in the Saguenay-Lac-St-Jean region. That culinary link is easy to understand, because the Saguenay was settled from Charlevoix. Louis Hébert, the earliest Quebec farmer, is credited with being the first to grow this bean in New France, and it has been traced to the *fève des marais,* a bean grown centuries ago around Paris. Chefs in finer inns have been known to turn the lusty vegetable soup into a refined purée and top it with a dollop of whipped cream.

Murray Bay, now La Malbaie, has always attracted Americans, who come to spend their summers by "the sea." Americans are credited with introducing johnnycake. An elaborate Malbaie dessert is *Chaussons aux pommes,* a whole apple sweetened, spiced, and wrapped in pastry. Baked and served with maple syrup and whipped cream, it originated in Normandy, where it is called *Pomme en cage.*

Gaspé

The farther one goes off the beaten track, meaning away from the St. Lawrence River, the more distinct the original French cuisine. Gaspé, settled by the French, the Acadians, the English, and fishermen from the Channel Islands and the Basque coast, has also felt the culinary influence of the Indians.

Gaspesians have been nicknamed *Mangeurs de morue* (cod eaters) and they cook cod with variety and respect. In the Gaspé, their *bouillabaisse* of cod and other seafood resembles *Cotriade bretonne,* the fish stew of Brittany. This is natural, considering the many Breton fishermen who settled on the coast.

All parts of the cod are used. The whole fish, head included, makes a *cambuse* or *combuse,* an Acadian dish that treats the fish like a pot roast of beef or pork. The fish is simmered gently with *lardons* of salt pork and vegetables. Tiny cod tongues or cheeks or livers make hors d'oeuvres.

Salmon is prized, and the layered, pastry-topped pie called *cipâte,* which is normally based on game or domestic meats, is prepared with salmon in the Gaspé. The traditional Acadian salmon dish is made with a cream sauce that contains sliced, hard-boiled eggs.

Across the Gulf of St. Lawrence on the Îles de la Madeleine, what to us are luxury seafoods—scallops, lobster, and shrimp—are combined with vegetables in a creamy sauce and enclosed in pastry. It is now called *Pot-en-pot tante Yvonne,* after a feisty little island cook who once won a provincial cooking contest with the dish. Evaporated milk is still preferred for this luxury casserole, sugar pie, and other recipes, since the islands' dairy industry was started only in modern times.

For snacking in either the Gaspé or Îles de la Madeleine, seafood pizza, buttery chunks of lobster meat in a toasted bun, or fried shrimp "to go" are preferred, priced no higher than hamburgers are elsewhere.

Salt is used generously in all Gaspé cooking, a custom that began when European fishermen on the Gaspé coast salted fish. English fishermen, in particular those from the Channel Islands, made their mark on Gaspé cuisine with such dishes as Bubble and Squeak, the potato-and-cabbage dish. Puddings—rice, bread, lemon, and *Pouding du chômeur*, best translated as economy pudding—show the British influence. In the Gaspé, you make this dessert by putting the sugar syrup in the pan first, then dropping spoonfuls of batter into it to bake.

The Beauce

Maple syrup is a favoured ingredient in much of the cooking of this prosperous region south of Quebec City. The syrup is often stockpiled here in the millions of litres. Even before plastic hoses and evaporators streamlined the collecting and making of this exceptional sweetener, Beaucerons put it in and on almost everything they ate.

Pork and beans, baked chicken, cucumber pickles, apple desserts, and all the traditional spring favourites of the sugaring-off party are saturated with maple syrup. A type of salt pork called *viande boucanée* was originally smoked in the rafters of the maple sugar shack so that vapours rising from both the fire and the bubbling maple sap could flavour the meat. Another Beauceron favourite is eggs, beaten with milk and dropped by spoonfuls into bubbling hot maple syrup.

Salt pork and eggs pair off in the Beauce. An *Omelette beauceronne*, traced to the Loire River Valley in France, is filled with *lardons* (fried slivers of salt pork), tomatoes, and the mild cheddar cheese that's made in the Beauce.

Beaucerons take a little razzing in good spirit, even when they're nicknamed *Jarrets noirs*, or black hocks. That name dates back many decades to when farmers hauled their food to market along the muddy banks of the Chaudière River and their horses looked as if they wore thick, black boots.

One of Quebec's favourite packaged cakes is the Jos. Louis, a chocolate hockey puck of a snack invented some sixty-five years ago by the Vachon family of Ste-Marie in the Beauce. Advertised not long ago in a tongue-in-cheek campaign as a welcome relief from such nutritious foods as alfalfa sprouts or crunchy granola, the popular cake is a fixture in the province. Cooks of the Beauce even make versions of it at home.

The Mauricie

Across the St. Lawrence and stretching north from Trois-Rivières into lumbering and hunting country, the Mauricie shows an affection for traditional dishes, but with a regional twist. The *tourtière* is made with salmon. This dates from the era when the St-Maurice River was a thriving salmon river and not just a pulp-and-paper industry highway. The *bouillabaisse* in these parts can contain trout from inland streams that are not yet polluted. Perch turns up in the better restaurants, made into such chefs' specialties as mousse or *terrine.*

Each winter tommy cod are caught on lines lowered through the ice of the St. Lawrence off Ste-Anne de la Parade. These miniature cod, called *poissons des chenaux* (channel fish) make a fish pie layered with onions, carrots, and the ever-present diced salt pork.

This stretch of the St. Lawrence is wild-bird country and duck is on many menus. For a family dinner, though, roast pork with pan-browned potatoes is the number one dish.

Saguenay-Lac-St-Jean

A remote region of Quebec, Saguenay-Lac-St-Jean is often said to have Quebec's most distinctive cuisine. Old-time dishes are regularly served at family dinner tables. *Tourtière* here is not the shallow, ground-meat tart found throughout the province, but layers of cubed meat and potatoes in a deep casserole lined and topped with pastry.

Food historians compare this *tourtière* with the *cipaille* of other parts of Quebec. In the Saguenay, the shallow meat pie called *tourtière* elsewhere in Quebec is called *pâté à la viande.*

Another *tourtière* in this northern region is made with the now-scarce, land-locked salmon relative called the *ouananiche*, caught—if fishermen get lucky—in Lac St-Jean, also in Lac Mégantic in the Eastern Townships.

Other distinctive dishes of the region are *soupe aux gourganes*, a hearty bean, vegetable, and barley meal-in-one, and almost anything made with blueberries, the region's top fruit. In fact, residents of this region are nicknamed *les Bleuets.*

Pudding, spelled *pouding,* is often an upside-down blueberry dessert. The Saguenay style of *Pouding du chômeur,* the economical dessert, is to pour brown sugar syrup over the cake batter before baking, rather than the other way around, as in the Gaspé.

Indian cuisine has long been part of this region's cooking. The Montagnais Indians, who ranged over this area, have always considered a *cipaille* of game meats their festive dish. Here *cipaille* can also mean a layered dessert made of blueberries and raspberries. *Cipaille* was made by various northeastern Indian tribes in a clay pot. Flour made with wheat that arrived with white settlers had enough gluten in it to make a pastry topping for *cipaille.*

There are plenty of traces of English cooking, dating from the opening up of the area by large lumbering, pulp-and-paper, and aluminum companies. Baking in particular has an English flavour. It shows in a number of baked recipes, such as fruit crisp, in which blueberries, raspberries, or apples (or a combination) are topped with a mixture of rolled oats, butter, and brown sugar. Another dessert of English background is the blueberry upside-down pudding, and one of the popular cookies in the Saguenay-Lac-St-Jean region is made with ginger and molasses.

The Laurentians

The mountain region north of Montreal has a cuisine of contrasts. The ski hills and lakes have made the region a booming resort area, with some of the finest, most luxurious dining in the province. But the original family cooking was always the most economical in Quebec because the land was so poor for farming. Buckwheat was about the only grain that would grow in the Laurentians, and it is the basis for the traditional bread, cookies, pastry, and pancakes of the region. The short growing season meant a surplus of green tomatoes and their use in relish or ketchup.

In Quebec, the Roman Catholic Church's fasting regulations decreed that more than one-third of the days of the year had to be meatless. Meat was scarce in the Laurentians, and potato pie and buckwheat pancakes were the main dishes. Every scrap of meat, fish, vegetables, and fruit was used. Celery leaves, for example, flavour the Laurentian *tourtière.* Maple syrup was scarce and Laurentian sugar pie is traditionally made with brown sugar.

Wood-stove cooking influenced some Laurentian dishes. A stew would be placed in the oven as the fire died down at night, where it would bake slowly until the fire went out. A pot of baked beans would be put into a bread oven while it was still hot after the bread had been baked. The teapot on the back of the stove led to the use of tea in making gravy.

The Outaouais

Both the English and the French set up farms along the Ottawa River, so that culinary traditions in this region are mixed. The establishment of the lumbering industry on the Ottawa, Gatineau, and Petite Nation rivers meant lusty lumber-camp food to nourish woodcutters and log drivers. To this day, favourite dishes include ham braised with onions and beer, baked beans, thick soups and stews, and pancakes. Desserts are rich with molasses, pork, or suet, such as *Tarte à la ferlouche*, a molasses-and-raisin pie.

Vast tracts of hunting and fishing country north of Montebello still provide game and fish for families. Baked beans for a special occasion may have a partridge baked among the beans. Game and fish farms flourish in both the Outaouais and the Laurentian regions, providing chefs with pheasant, partridge, quail, rabbit, and trout.

Estrie

The Eastern Townships southeast of Montreal have a melting-pot cuisine today. Settled initially by United Empire Loyalists and then by the "great migrations" from the British Isles, the townships have a cuisine that includes lamb stew, mincemeat, oatmeal bread, tea biscuits, scones, and fruitcake. Across the border from the United States came corn and fish chowders, Boston baked beans, brown bread, pumpkin pie, and johnnycake. To this day, such foods are proudly presented at the many church suppers and bake sales in all the towns and villages.

Settlers found that the rolling hills and mountains provided abundant game—deer, hare, and wild birds, and there were plenty of trout in the streams. For the most part, these riches continue to this day. Deer in particular are an exploding population. But a duck farm at Knowlton supplies duck for most restaurant menus, and because of water pollution, the trout now come mostly from farms, too.

The end of the seigniorial system in the mid-nineteenth century meant that the French moved steadily into the townships, bringing with them their food traditions. The mixture of cuisines has become more complex during the past century with the arrival of Germans, Austrians, Swiss, and other Europeans, who found the mountains reminded them of home. Among the many European settlers to make their homes in the Eastern Townships are the Transylvanians. Their dishes include *rakot krumpli* (a sausage-and-potato dish) and *vadasz* (beef and vegetable stew flavoured with caraway). Koreans are the latest arrivals.

Quebec Cuisine Today

Unique new dishes are changing the face of Quebec regional cuisine today. Reform-minded, Quebec-born, Quebec-trained chefs started a movement that, like a pot of soup that begins at a simmer and gradually starts bubbling, has now reached a rolling boil.

In the early 1980s these chefs, the tourism department of the Quebec government, and the chefs' school, called the Institut de tourisme et d'hôtellerie du Québec, launched a project to track down early family recipes. More than 30,000 traditional Québécois dishes were found and tested, and a representative group published them in 1985 in a cookbook called *Cuisine du Québec.*

Following this venture, the chefs' organization, Le Société des chefs, cuisinières et pâtissiers du Québec, became involved in the movement called *Cuisine régionale du Québec.* Its purpose was to search out the foods native to each region, increase their production, create dishes using these ingredients in today's light and healthy style, and put them on restaurant menus. Both the 175 chefs who have joined this movement and independent chefs throughout the province are encouraging local producers to provide more of their specialties. Thanks to these young, progressive chefs, the historic differences in cooking from one area to another are being re-emphasized in the 1990s. Just as the province's political life is lively and changing, so is its cuisine.

Julian Armstrong is food editor of *The Gazette* of Montreal, Quebec's largest English daily newspaper, and is responsible for a weekly food section. She has been writing about food for newspapers and magazines for thirty-five years and has won a number of journalism awards in both Canada and the United States. Her book about regional Quebec cuisine, entitled *A Taste of Quebec*, was published in English in 1990, and in French in 1992. A graduate of the University of Toronto with a B.A. in modern history, she covers gastronomy, nutrition, supermarketing, and food safety for *The Gazette.*

RONALD MARCOTTE

La Cuisine régionale au Québec

FROM Nova Scotia to British Columbia, chefs are creating dishes for their clientele using unique products from their own corner of culinary Canada. In Quebec we call it *la cuisine régionale au Québec*, and it is now a formal association that nurtures a special relationship between local food producers, chefs, restaurateurs, hoteliers, and the Ministry of Agriculture.

For an inn or restaurant to qualify for membership, 70 percent of the food on its menu must be produced within the province of Quebec. Moreover, 50 percent of the food must be from the local region, one of twelve regions within the province. No more than 30 percent of the food may come from outside the province.

The members of the association are chefs, owners of restaurants, hotel operators, and culinary/hotel schools. For four years, I was the executive chef at the Auberge Godefroy in Bécancour, near Trois-Rivières, and the cuisine at the inn was chosen according to the guidelines of *la cuisine régionale au Québec*. My menu featured Quebec products such as pheasant from Oka, fiddleheads from St-Grégoire, asparagus from St-Étienne, and cranberries from Manseau. (Every year those small, juicy cranberries sell out—the area simply cannot produce enough!) I served goat cheese from Tournevent, rabbit from St-Pierre-des-Bacquets, and maple products from all around Trois-Rivières. To round off my menu, I used Atlantic salmon from outside the province.

La cuisine régionale au Québec began with a new generation of food producers and chefs. Proud of their products, young local food producers were searching for new markets, and they needed chefs, restaurateurs, and hoteliers. At the same time, chefs were having difficulty finding local ingredients. About five years ago, representatives from both groups met with the minister of agriculture to explore their options. *La cuisine régionale au Québec* was born.

Today food producers work together to meet the needs of restaurants. For example, yesterday a chef mentioned that she had trouble finding lamb locally. I told her that I get fresh lamb every week from Agnobec, near Trois-Rivières. I was able to reserve more than thirty strip loins for a sold-out gastronomic dinner.

One of the major problems our food producers face is price competition from countries who sell low cost—and generally low-quality—food in Quebec. Their prices are so low, in fact, that our producers cannot compete with them. Monsieur Charryère, a cheese maker in Champlain who produces fondue-style cheese, has difficulty selling his cheese because Swiss manufacturers sell their mass-produced cheese in the Quebec market at a low price. He simply cannot compete. In the past, his excellent cheese would slowly have disappeared. But now, thanks to *la cuisine régionale au Québec*, there are chefs who know about his cheese and buy it.

We must change the thinking of those who say, "Food is better when it comes from France, Switzerland, or Austria." I don't agree at all, and I'll hotly contest the statement (with all due respect to my wife, who is from France).

It took the French hundreds of years to develop a magnificent cuisine. We cannot expect to develop ours in a mere five. If we can share information, exchange recipes, and work together, it will happen in time.

All cuisine, both family style and gourmet, is good cuisine if you cook with your heart and use fresh products. In Canada and in Quebec, we can be very proud of what we are doing. Our culinary future is bright!

Born in Quebec, **Ronald Marcotte** began his work as a chef at the Ritz-Carlton Hotel in Montreal. He has been a chef at a number of restaurants, including the Café d'Opéra in Montreal, and opened the Auberge Godefroy in Bécancour. He has been given a number of awards for his culinary skills, including Le Grand Prix d'Excéllence, in Trois-Rivières. In 1993, he became director of La cuisine régionale du Québec, and the next year was made president of the Association des chefs cuisinières et pâtissiers du Québec. He currently does a daily cooking show, "Secrets de chef," for Quatre Saisons television in Montreal.

JOHANNA BURKHARD

Quebec Goes Country

FOR THE FOOD EXPLORER, Quebec is an odyssey of exciting new tastes, glorious scenery, and passionate people. Montreal and Quebec City's dazzling array of restaurants, open-air markets, and fine food shops may be where the heart of Quebec cuisine is, but its soul lies in the country.

The number of family farms is declining in Quebec, as in the rest of Canada, but there are dynamic changes to cheer about. Organic farming, for one thing, is booming. A 1992 survey conducted by the Ministère de l'Agriculture, des Pêcheries et de l'Alimentation du Québec (MAPAQ) asked Quebec's 40,000 farmers: "Do you practise organic agriculture?" The results were astounding. Over 11 percent said they totally or partially used organic farming methods.

Cottage and farm-gate businesses are also flourishing, thanks to support from neighbouring communities and a loyal city clientele willing to drive miles to buy the sweetest raspberries, the freshest organic bread, or the plumpest grain-fed chicken. Quebeckers are just two generations removed from the farm, which may help explain why there are such strong ties between city and farming communities.

The demand for high-quality fresh produce has encouraged farmers to set up attractive kiosks right at the farm gate. A 1992 survey by MAPAQ among market gardeners in the Montérégie region, the lush growing area in the St. Lawrence Valley referred to as Quebec's breadbasket, revealed that the number of produce stands in that area has doubled in the past three years. "Consumers are much more concerned about health and want the freshest market produce," says Louis Bernard, an agronomist with MAPAQ, "and they make a point of going to the country to get it."

Surprisingly, price isn't the deciding factor. The further removed we become from the farm and how the farm operates, the more and more impersonal the food system becomes. As people become more concerned about the quality of their foods, they want to re-establish that direct link to the farm. Howard Mussells of Dunany Farms in Lachute, a free-range pheasant farmer who sells at the farm gate, says: "People don't just come to the country to buy one of my birds. They come for the farm experience. The issue of price is secondary."

The momentum in the cottage and farm-gate industry is due to an adventurous group of entrepreneurs. Young people like Ginette Cadieux, who left Montreal to pursue a country life. She grows wildflowers and herbs in her one-acre garden in Georgeville and makes exquisite lavender jellies, herb pestos, and vinegars under the *Herborerie* label, which is sold in fine food shops.

These entrepreneurs also include business executives-turned-farmers like John Bastian of Morgan Highland Farms in Weir, who reclaimed land in the Laurentians and made it into a model organic farm. On weekends people come from all over to buy his organic beef, chickens, wild-boar sausages, and hearty German breads made from fresh-milled grains and baked in his farm bakery.

Some of the young entrepreneurs are from farming families. Like Pierre Gingras, a fourth-generation apple grower in Rougemont. He makes *artisanal* cider vinegar from freshly pressed apple juice that he ferments naturally in oak barrels. The sharp aroma of vinegar prickles your nose when you enter his *vinaigrerie,* which is open to the public year-round. Gingras sells the vinegar at the orchard and at Montreal's Jean Talon market in the summertime.

Culinary trends, too, are shaping Quebec's new cuisine.

Quebec is mad about maple syrup. Seventy percent of the world's maple syrup comes from here, and there are 11,000 maple-syrup producers in the province. At the first signs of spring, families and friends flock to Quebec's *cabanes à sucre* (sugar shacks) to feast on pancakes doused in maple syrup, maple baked beans, poached eggs in oodles of syrup, and sweet maple sugar pie. A bumper crop in recent years has resulted in a flurry of new maple products. Once there was just basic maple syrup and maple sugar; now roadside stands are brimming with "value added" products such as maple syrup pickles, jams, butters, lollipops, even maple wine.

You may have heard a rumour that we have a wine industry in Quebec. It's true! Just head to Dunham region in the Eastern Townships, where Quebec's modest but budding wine industry is located. There are seventeen cottage wine producers, though their total production is still small—only about 250,000 bottles a year of mainly white wine. These wineries are thriving, yet you won't find Quebec wine in liquor stores or on restaurant menus because of the barriers set up by the provincial liquor board permitting vintners to sell wines only at the farm gate. Quebeckers experience a kind of spiritual renewal when they visit these small wineries in Dunham, a spectacular vegetable- and fruit-growing region. An added plus is that the wineries have become a major tourist attraction.

Come fall, the sweet snap of a Quebec McIntosh apple is not to be missed. Apples are Quebec's largest fruit crop and the province boasts close to 1,000 orchards. From apples comes cider, not fresh-pressed apple juice but the alcoholic kind. We call the nonalcoholic variety *jus de pommes traditionnel* (traditional apple juice). Cider making, a home- or farm-based activity, was outlawed in the 1950s by the provincial liquor board to control the manufacturing and distribution of alcohol-based beverages. It was legalized again in 1970, and is making a comeback in the province. Licences were issued to mass producers, who still make low-quality cider sold in *dépanneurs* (convenience stores) and some supermarkets. If you want quality cider, go to the country and visit one of seventeen *artisanal* cider makers who have set up shop in the past decade. Like Quebec wines, sparkling ciders (made using tank or bottle-fermented methods) and still ciders can only be purchased at the farm gate. A lovely apple-producing region is Rougemont. Here Michel Jodoin and his family make a sparkling rosé cider using the traditional champagne method, in which the second fermentation occurs in the bottle. After a Sunday afternoon's drive, you can have lunch—with a bottle of cider—on the Jodoins' terrace and admire the surrounding orchards.

The home where the buffalo roam is not just the Canadian Prairies.

It's not unusual these days to take a drive in the country and spot a herd of buffalo grazing next to dairy cattle. A culinary phenomenon called the *mechoui* has emerged in the past five years, linked to Quebec's large Middle Eastern population (there are about 125,000 Lebanese in Montreal, for example). *Mechoui* is the Arabic word for barbecue. Adopting the *mechoui*, some game farmers have built banquet and catering facilities and barbecue whole sides of bison, wild boar, and venison over wood or charcoal on enormous motorized spits. Busloads and carloads of people come for family reunions or company parties. They eat, line-dance, and party. Or the *mechoui* operators will bring all their equipment to you for large backyard barbecues—a new concept in catering!

Quebec has become the largest producer of game birds in Canada. Quail is the most popular, but pheasant, partridge, and guinea hens are reared, also. Duck varieties such as Barbary and French Rouen-type duck, raised on the Île d'Orléans near Quebec City, are also some of the specialty birds you'll find featured on restaurant menus.

Most fine-food shops stock an array of birds, especially during the fall and for the Christmas season. The Semetin family in Mirabel run one of these specialty shops. It's located in the country, next to their hatchery and processing plant, and sells a variety of birds, *pâtés*, and fresh duck *foie gras*. If asked, they'll cook the birds for the uninitiated and provide recipes, too.

Dairy farming is Quebec's largest agricultural industry and cheese makers produce as many as fifty-three kinds of cheese. One prominent country cheese company is Fromagerie Clément in St-Damase. Claude Bonnet, a master cheese maker from the Brie region of France, arrived with his two sons less than a decade ago, and in that time, their company has become one of the most progressive in Canada. Not only do they produce wonderful traditional Brie, but they specialize in making first-rate low-fat aged cheeses and *fromage blanc*, a fresh-milk cheese.

Oka, of course, is our classic cheese, and it celebrated its centennial year in 1993. The abbey, at which the cheese was first made, is on a hill that slopes down to the Lake of Two Mountains and is a major tourist attraction in Quebec. In 1893, a French cheese maker, Brother Alfonse Juin, made Port Salut cheese the way he had learned in France. The French cheese develops a reddish brown mould on the outside as it ages, but a white mould grew over his Quebec cheese—the first Oka (sometimes called Trappist cheese), a new cheese variety. The monks sold the cheese-making facility when they grew older. It is now owned by Agropur, the largest dairy cooperative in Canada. The new owners still use the original curing rooms and have maintained the integrity of the cheese, which the monks still sell in a shop next to the plant.

Another specialty cheese maker is Fritz Kaiser of Noyan, Quebec, who recently moved to Canada from Switzerland. He loves our gently rolling hills, which remind him of the Alps. Kaiser makes twelve kinds of cheese and specializes in Raclette cheese, which traditionally the Swiss melt over small boiled potatoes.

Local goat cheese is also carving out a niche in Quebec's competitive cheese business. There are about fifteen goat cheese makers (the number varies by season), including several small farm-gate producers who make a variety of unripened, ripened, Camembert-, and cheddar-style cheeses.

One exceptional farm-gate producer is Danielle Parent of Chevrerie Les Trois Clochettes in St-Roch de l'Achigan, northeast of Montreal, who sells just about all the cheese from her herd of 100 goats at the small shop adjacent to the farm. She attributes her success to the large blue signs posted along the highway that attract visitors on their way to cottage country. To be eligible to advertise on these signs, you must be a member of your region's tourist association, offer guided tours, or allow people to explore your farm.

A good way to enjoy Quebec country-style dining is through the Tables Champêtres program that promotes regional agriculture. Run by the Fédération des Agricotours, the program began a decade ago and was adopted from France. Visitors can phone and reserve at any one of the thirty member families and enjoy a meal prepared by the farm host family. Seventy percent of the food served to you must be produced on the farm. The federation publishes a guidebook that lists bed-and-breakfasts, country inns, country houses and farmhouses, and farm excursions.

Country chefs usually deal directly with local producers, but Montreal chefs head to the city's open-air markets, which attract farmers from neighbouring regions. The largest public markets are Jean Talon and Atwater, and they operate year-round. Marché Jean Talon is the most colourful. Its best customers are chefs who arrive early in the morning to hand-pick and barter for the first white asparagus of the spring, the pungent garlic chives, the fat gourgane beans, or the globe artichokes, grown in Quebec and harvested in the fall, picked just hours before. Chefs also head to the Marché Centrale, the wholesale market, where Quebec-grown fruits and vegetables vie with fresh produce from around the world.

Organic farming is a viable enterprise in Quebec, and the province now has 550 certified organic growers. In fact, 65 percent of their products are exported to the United States and markets around the world, and Quebec organic foods are gaining a worldwide reputation for high quality. Organic farming is endorsed by MAPAQ, which assigns agronomists who specialize in organics to the various agricultural regions. With all that activity, surprisingly only a limited assortment of organic products are found in local markets. The government recently brought together certification groups, processors, retailers, and consumers to deal with problems facing the organic industry and to plot market strategy. "The most positive aspect [in organics] is that people are starting to work together and there's a team spirit emerging," says Robert Beauchemin, who hails from Milan, Quebec, and is past president of the Organic Group Improvement Association (OCIA). It's a farmer-run organization, with close to 20,000 members around the world, and it's active in Quebec.

The other major organic group in the province is part of a food certification program run by MAPAQ. Called Québec Vrai (the name is currently under review), this quality assurance and standards program overseeing foods from producers to retailers was initiated four years ago and is modelled after the French appellation system. It certifies that foods are produced within a specific region. Quebec Vrai products are identified by a green logo on packages. "There's not a program like it in Canada," says Pierre Daigle of MAPAQ. "The beauty of the program is that it is controlled by a third party not related to the industry, for the purpose of protecting consumers."

Vibrant changes are taking place in the countryside, altering the face of Quebec agriculture forever. The boom in organic farming and the increase in farm-gate producers have had a major impact. As a reporter, I've travelled in the country, spoken with the small farmers, seen their new products. I've tried to convey to you here what these farmers are doing—just how adaptable and inventive they are. Perhaps this will inspire others to strive to enrich our food community.

Johanna Burkhard is a weekly food columnist with the *Montreal Gazette* and freelance contributor to several Canadian magazines, including *Canadian Living, Foodservice and Hospitality*, and *Wine Tidings*. She is also a contributing writer to *Montreal and Quebec City Access*, a travel guide. A home economist by training, she has been a consultant and recipe developer for the food industry, and has appeared regularly on Montreal television and radio shows. In 1992, she was awarded the Nestlé Nutrition Writing Award, a competition for North American newspaper editors and writers. She was raised in Southern Ontario, lived in Calgary for several years, and for the past seventeen years has called Quebec home.

HÉLÈNE-ANDRÉ BIZIER

La Cabane à sucre

THERE isn't a springtime visitor to Quebec who escapes the temptation to visit one of the sugar shacks. They are generally situated in the middle of a sugar-maple grove, not far from the highway. Here the sugar-bush owners, often descendants of the original owners, carry on a Quebec tradition more than 200 years old and temporarily turn the sugar shack into a rudimentary restaurant.

Quebeckers themselves like to come. For many their annual visit to the sugar bush is a sacred rite. The enthusiastic hosts, transformed for the season from farmers to restaurateurs, enliven the rustic surroundings. Guests—the more the merrier—are seated on uncomfortable benches around a table. Of course there is only one menu. Whether you eat there during the week or on Sunday, at noon or in the evening; whether you are in the Beauce, l'Estrie, or les Laurentides, the rough wooden tables are invariably heaped with jugs of maple syrup; platters of omelettes, pancakes, crisp bacon, and golden sausages; and large bowls of *fèves au lard* (pork and beans) and boiled potatoes. You are expected to help yourself to the food and pour maple syrup over everything.

First-time visitors quickly feel they have had enough maple syrup. But custom demands that they continue to eat—eggs poached in syrup, more pancakes with syrup, until finally, outside the cabin, the inescapable climax: *la tire*—where hot maple syrup is poured onto the snow, turning it into sticky taffy that is then twirled around a wooden stick.

This wonderful ritual originated with the Amerindians, who tapped maple trees in the springtime to drink the sweet sap. They discovered that by evaporating the sap it became a syrup. But they didn't have metal containers in which to boil it. It was the French settlers in the St. Lawrence River Valley in the seventeenth century who developed modern techniques for harvesting the sap and turning it into syrup, taffy, butter, and sugar.

During the 1700s and into the next century, French settlers used the sugar for colds, sore throats, and other minor illnesses. They found that maple sugar agreed with the stomach better than cane sugar. Hospital records of the time indicate its heavy use, even though the general population did not have access to it because it was produced in such small amounts.

At the beginning of the eighteenth century, the sugar and not the syrup was popular—it was impossible to keep the syrup for more than a few months because of the lack of sterilized, airtight bottles. The sugarbush owners started to produce sugar not only for the hospitals and their own personal use, but also to sell to the public, who began to use it at meals. From that time on, production became more commercial.

The craze for maple sugar was a real blessing, since it allowed a farmer to augment his income during a season when there was nothing else to harvest. But he needed to modify his methods. Up until that time, he could tap a limited number of trees and do the boiling in his own house. More intensive production made it necessary to go deep into the maple woods, build a shack, and install a stove. The farmer would fashion large metal kettles and furnish the cabin with a table, benches, and a bed. Then he would live there for the entire maple season, often with the eldest of his children, who helped in all stages of the operation. Living conditions may have been difficult, but the group didn't suffer from the cold, because the sap and syrup boiled ceaselessly.

Several times throughout the season the farmer's wife and other family members would join the group at *la cabane à sucre*. Such times were festive occasions, particularly since they provided a break in the sober Lenten period. The basic living conditions, however, did limit the cook's creativity. Potatoes could be buried in the ashes beside the pot where the pork and beans were simmering in maple syrup. Otherwise, you could only cook in a frying pan or in a pot. Thus, in addition to ham and salt pork, which kept well, crêpes and omelettes became basics.

In the twentieth century, when industrialization pushed a large number of farmers into town, the sugaring-off times of old were remembered with nostalgia. Today at Eastertime, old-timers still gather at their father's, uncle's, or cousin's sugar shack to recreate the atmosphere of their youth.

Maple syrup production is highly commercialized across the province now, but *les cabanes à sucre* still signify warm hospitality and hearty menus.

Hélène-André Bizier is a historian and writer. Since 1974, she has written about the culinary history of Quebec and related it to contemporary practice. She is the author of many articles, published in *Perspectives La Presse* and *L'Actualité*, and she initiated the gastronomic section in *Elle—Québec*. Her interest in history has led her to explore many facets of Quebec. She has written six books about the history of crime in Quebec, and will shortly publish a book about Quebec missionaries in China.

YVON DESLOGES

Quebec's Culinary Traditions:

An Overview

As everyone knows, Quebec's motto is *Je me souviens*—I remember. In terms of culinary traditions, what collective memory do we have of the past? The typical answer is pork, pork, and more pork—in *ragoût de pattes, tourtière*, and *fèves au lard*. This is according to several historians from the 1960s, who found lard mentioned again and again in a few historical documents and jumped to the conclusion that eighteenth-century colonists ate mostly pork. But the historians forgot to ask how valid their documents were. Food ways should not be determined from a limited number of sources but from extensive documentation. Only meticulously researched and compared data—not just written documents, but archaeological faunal and floral remains, too—can give us an overview of the food ways of the settlers. Five major types of documents need to be looked at; each unveils part of the mystery: deeds made by a notary public; diaries and private correspondence; numbered sources, such as account books, newspaper ads, and clippings; and official correspondence and legislation. We can trace the culinary developments in Quebec chronologically.

By the seventeenth century, hunting game was rare in Europe. It was a leisure activity for the nobility, and had become a symbol of ostentation. Game was always a part of the menu on special occasions.[1]

To hunt meant one was on par with the nobility; and to eat game meant one dined royally.[2] Game, in other words, had become an extravagance at the table. The fauna of the New World, then, must have been a pleasant surprise for early settlers. Meat was available for all at a time when Europeans had less and less of it; this abundance in New France seemed to assure colonists that they could live like lords. But what exactly were their rights to hunt, and to what extent was game really available to them?

Archaeological evidence from the site of Champlain's *abitation* (the French living quarters in Quebec City) from 1608 until 1632 shows that moose meat was only a complementary food that filled in until the boats arrived from France with provisions. One must not be misled into thinking that game was a really important food in the settled areas of the St. Lawrence Valley. Reality was quite different, as the archaeological evidence shows.[3] Seeing and writing about fur-bearing game did not necessarily mean eating it!

The question then becomes, did the situation at the *abitation* reflect the scarcity of big game (as evidenced by the number of moose hides exported) or did the French just resort to big game only when they needed to. In actual fact, game was an essential part of the diet everywhere during the early decades of settlement. But as soon as domestic cattle herds were large enough, the reliance on it eased. Game then became a complementary food. It was not just a question of socioeconomics or a question of geography and biology; it was a matter of taste, since all ethnic communities on the eastern seaboard—the French, the English, the Dutch, the Germans, the Spanish, even the Swedes—fell back on domestic species after the first decades of settlement. In other words, it was a cultural decision.

As for wild fowl, early explorers, missionaries, settlers, soldiers, and travellers listed in great detail the various edible species. Contrary to the French peasants, all colonists were given the right to hunt and fish on their grants of land as early as 1652. But how many actually hunted? In 1681, one-third of the men in the colony had guns. By the mideighteenth century, only one home in five did.[4] Nevertheless, the hunt for passenger pigeons caused a major stir. In the St. Lawrence Valley, the hunt was a regular carnage.[5] The birds were consumed by everyone. Butchers in Quebec in 1710 complained to the Sovereign Council that when the pigeons appeared in the valley (May to September) they sold much less meat, and asked to have beef prices adjusted accordingly.[6] By the beginning of the nineteenth century, observers started mentioning a decrease in pigeon flocks.[7]

The situation for fowl was similar to that for large game: fowl were only a seasonal complement to the settlers' diet, although wild birds were predominant. By the middle of the eighteenth century, improved hatching technology, such as Réaumur's thermometer to control incubator temperatures in the hatchery, appeared.[8] This might explain why the consumption of wild birds decreased from nearly 98 percent of birds in the period 1608–1650 to 59 percent in the years 1750–1800.

At the end of the seventeenth century, the food ways of the French colonists changed dramatically: husbandry practices from the Old Country took over; the French chose to raise beef! A comparison of historical and zoo-archaeological data on game as food in New France provides an excellent case study for the debate about whether taste or culture is more important in making food choices.[9]

Even if the larders of the *habitants* or, for that matter, the town dwellers, did contain mostly lard one should not conclude that people ate mostly pork. The question of meat consumption in the seventeenth and eighteenth centuries is directly related to agricultural production and commerce.

In the eighteenth century, economics and war played a major role in changing food production. Following a major depression in Europe, wheat prices dropped. French colonists in Canada tried to cope with falling prices by producing more wheat, which caused further price drops. Two consecutive wars in the 1740s and 1750s struck a substantial blow to food production. The French colonists became more and more receptive to new crops like the potato. Potato crops thrived between 1763 and the end of the eighteenth century, and the surplus was fed to cattle.

By the beginning of the eighteenth century, beef was already the major component of the meat diet. Beef consumption rose roughly four times faster than the population in Quebec City in the first half of the eighteenth century, and the state-regulated price of beef was cheaper than pork by ten to fifteen percent.[10]

Table 1.
Number of domestic animal bones found in archaeological sites from 1608 to 1800.

Species	1608–1650	1650–1700	1700–1750	1750–1800	Total
Beef	80	445	3,754	5,452	9,731
Pork	249	309	2,701	2,311	5,570
Mutton	16	80	735	2,328	3,159
Total	345	834	7,190	10,091	18,460

Zoo-archaeological evidence (Table 1) shows that beef was important even at the time of the *abitation*, although Champlain and his companions relied more heavily on salted pork imported from France. By the second half of the seventeenth century, beef became predominant, and remained so until the end of the next century. Pork gradually fell in importance from the time of Champlain to the second half of the eighteenth century. Mutton was never that popular with the French, but the arrival of English merchants, soldiers, and Loyalists gave it a boost and its importance rose in the last fifty years of the eighteenth century.

In the eighteenth century, "good" cows produced only six litres of milk a day in the summer. Thus the production of butter was minimal and colonists had to resort to other fats; lard from pigs was the most accessible source. The *habitants* were reluctant to slaughter their swine before they could fatten them. They could dispense with their cattle more easily, since they lacked fodder to feed them. Zoo-archaeological remains confirm this, since nearly all the cattle examined were under age four.[11] These data indicate that the French colonists did not rely on a dairy industry, but chose to raise cattle for meat as early as the second half of the seventeenth century.

For grain, the French colonists chose to grow wheat. But what did they do with native ingredients such as corn? Even nowadays popular cuisine in Quebec does not have many recipes with corn, although corn is Quebec's main grain crop! French colonists had in fact rejected native ingredients by the end of the seventeenth century, feeding cattle corn and resorting to it only in a time of scarcity.[12]

Although French administrators tried to induce the *habitants* to diversify their crops and the potato was known in the colony, it was not successfully introduced until 1762–1763 by Governor Murray.[13] Unexpectedly, potato crops flourished. By the end of the eighteenth century, most French settlers were eating potatoes. The Montreal Agricultural Society reported that potato growing was "almost universal." According to one historian, the enormous yield of potatoes was the reason it became so popular so quickly.[14]

As for other vegetables, the colonists ate little squash (except for those colonists who lived near Indian missions), but they were fond of beans, although the cultivated variety came from Europe. By the end of the eighteenth century, turnips were popular; in fact, their yield exceeded that of the potato! Of course Canada was renowned for its peas, which were produced as early as 1608. Nevertheless, peas for soup are only mentioned for the first time in the middle of the eighteenth century.

By the end of the eighteenth century, agricultural and husbandry practices had changed, and were to be modified yet. The introduction of the potato and turnip meant that surpluses could be fed to cattle in accordance with "new agriculture" principles so that the cattle could last through the winter.[15] This meant that cows could be kept longer and that dairy products were readily available; pork was viewed as a fresh meat and lard no longer used mainly as a cooking fat. By the middle of the nineteenth century, Quebec agriculture was characterized as dairy producing, although there were fewer cows than in Ontario or the United States for the same period.[16] Only then was sufficient pork produced to provide the whole province with fresh meat. It was also by this time that the first French-Canadian cookbooks appeared, emphasizing dishes made with pork, and for the first time a "national" cuisine emerged.

In 1840, *La cuisinière canadienne* by Louis Perrault was published. It was not a work intended for professionals, but a cooking manual for the general public, in the tradition of French middle-class cookbooks and the English home economic cookery books. While recipes of regional origin were included, *La cuisinière canadienne* was not a repertory of what we refer to today as "traditional" Quebec cuisine. This book also contained recipes inspired by cookery practised in the rest of Canada and contained French, English, and even American recipes.

Influenced by the French middle-class cuisine of the eighteenth and early-nineteenth century, it borrowed several recipes from Menon's best seller *La cuisinière bourgeoise*, published in France. However, the English influence was also evident in what most differentiates the work from the French middle-class cuisine—"Canadianization." *La cuisinière canadienne* contained twenty-two recipes referred to as "Canadian-style," as well as several recipes for game or fish native to Canada (snow buntings, passenger pigeons, walleye, bass, whitefish) and other Quebec country-style dishes such as potato pie or fresh pork pie (the future *tourtières*), *ragoût* of pigs' feet, and fresh pork balls. The sauces accompanying these dishes were thickened not with a *roux*, but by sprinkling the meat with flour, in particular, browned flour.[17]

Later on, Mère Caron's manual *Les directions diverses données en 1878 . . .* was also designed to train good cooks. The majority of the recipes are even more rudimentary than those in *La cuisinière canadienne.* Many of the interesting recipes from French middle-class cuisine were no longer present. When Caron retained such recipes as civet of hare, she chose the least refined version: "Canadian-style." Recipes for soups, meat, fowl, game, fish, eggs, and vegetables are less numerous than in *La cuisinière canadienne*, and there is no section on sauces. On the other hand, there are more recipes for puddings, biscuits, cakes, and jams. Caron takes us further and further away from middle-class and professional French cuisine; the "Canadianization" process and English influence are more present in her book than ever.

Thus in three centuries, the French changed their food ways every fourth generation. In the first decades of settlement, they relied on salted pork and game mostly. But by the end of the seventeenth century, European husbandry practices had taken over. By the end of the eighteenth century, they ate beef, potatoes, and bread made from wheat flour. The introduction of the potato meant that they ate much less bread—in fact, they cut down from two pounds a day to only one pound. Furthermore, the potato, along with turnips, was fed to cattle. This meant that cows began to play a role as dairy producers by the middle of the nineteenth century. It is only then that *ragoût de pattes* and *tourtières* appear, as a direct consequence of agricultural practices and changes.

The French rejected Amerind food ways and customs. Their dependence on wild game and fowl, *tourte* in particular, was not that important as part of the subsistence scheme, and the taste for game fowl decreased as poultry became more and more available. The major innovations in the cuisine of the French settlers were those brought by the English.

But if ordinary eighteenth-century French colonists did not eat *tourtière* and *ragoût de pattes*, what was considered daily fare? Aside from the well-known *pot-au-feu*, marvellously described by John Joseph Henry,[18] they ate *boeuf à la daube*, with or without cabbage, accompanied by a green pea *purée*. Of course they had soup, either pea or bread soup. Dessert was not popular, but if they did eat it, it was fresh fruit such as berries—sometimes with fresh cream and maple sugar—or plums or apples.

Clearly tastes have changed since. The question then is, what is traditional cuisine? If we define tradition by purely statistical data from the past, we do not have much to go by. Nowadays Quebeckers have simply rejected *ragoût de pattes* and *tourtières* as daily fare unacceptable to the modern lifestyle. Traditions continue to change. Today Quebeckers still eat beef, less pork, and more and more poultry. Are we about to witness another major turnaround?

Yvon Desloges is a historian working in the Quebec regional office of Parks Canada. In 1982, he obtained his Ph.D. in history from Laval University. He is the author of several books and numerous articles, including *Goûter à l'histoire*. In 1989, Dr. Desloges and his colleague Dr. Marc Lafrance published a somewhat different recipe book, *Les origines de la gastronomie québécoise (A Taste of History: The Origins of Quebec's Gastronomy)* both in French and English. His research has focussed on the history of Quebec City; in particular the food ways of ordinary citizens in the province of Quebec. Dr. Desloges and Dr. Marc Lafrance continue to search through thousands of artifacts and old documents, and are compiling a history of the foods and food ways in Canada from the seventeenth to the end of the eighteenth century.

SUZANNE LECLERC

Quebec Cuisine in the Nineties

QUEBEC is famous for its traditional cuisine. Tourists always ask for *tourtière, ragoût de boulettes,* and maple sugar pie. To be honest, we're somewhat tired of this reputation. Of course we all love our traditional dishes, but we serve them mostly on holidays and special occasions, usually not more than two or three times a year.

So what kind of food do the Québécois eat? In the 1970s, Quebeckers were impressed by France's Nouvelle Cuisine. I'm sorry to admit it, but we copied it a lot. We put strawberries in our soup and ate it cold; we made beautiful designs on our plates. The result? Our men and women started to complain—they were hungry.

In the 1980s we tried California cuisine. Everything appeared *en vrac*—seemingly tossed onto a plate. It wasn't very appetizing. Besides, we ran out of jalopeño peppers. Like most people in North America, we avoided sugar, salt, and fat. We worried about cholesterol—or was it our heart? We exercised and ate healthy food. We were at a loss for a while, chewing our raw carrots and eating plenty of plain yogurt (the yogurt business boomed during those years). As many well know, the *Québécois* are people who love good food, good wine, good living, and lots of laughter. It was *very* boring! Although we agreed to be careful, we could not forget the good old days.

So what saved us? During this period bright young chefs graduated from chef-training programs across the province. They had to find jobs, but there wasn't enough work for them in Montreal and Quebec City. They moved around the province, and in doing so, they discovered new products—regional products. They experimented and succeeded in creating new regional dishes using local produce. This was the beginning of good, fresh, light, healthy cuisine. It was different—not French, not English, but ours: *québécoise*! It tasted good and it smelled good across Quebec. Eating in Quebec was fun again. We had found new flavours and different menus. Loving good food the way we do, we all fell for it. *La cuisine régionale* was born, and our chefs became proud of their regions. It has been very stimulating.

Our Department of Agriculture has helped them along the way. There are always many reasons for change—it does not happen overnight, as you know; it takes time. Consumers were changing. They knew and wanted better food. The food industry became aware that Quebeckers were not happy with the way food was in the 1970s and 1980s. They did their homework with the help of the Food Research Centre of Agriculture Canada, the Quebec Industrial Research Centre, and others. They began to create new food products, literally hundreds of innovative processed food items. Some were a disaster and disappeared overnight. Others, fortunately, were very successful. This new generation of food processors is scattered across the province.

In the meantime, farmers have worked hard to grow organic foods. Promoting organic food is more than just selling your products; it's promoting a new outlook on life. It's a social commitment. We want to protect not only the environment, but also our health. So the government has given the farmer a generous hand in realizing this new way of life. Furthermore, the provincial department of agriculture (MAPAQ) has put together a certification system to assure the quality and authenticity of organic products produced in our province. To reassure consumers and to encourage organic production, Quebec has a new certification logo controlled by the Quebec government. The logo is a marketing tool, especially for small producers who have no desire to become big.

In all fairness, I should add that Quebec consumers encourage innovation. They are curious, ready for change, and willing to taste new foods. The Quebec cooking shows on television have helped, too. They've shown people how to cook a little faster and not be ashamed to use processed food to make their cooking easier. The same can be said of the food magazines in Quebec—excellent recipes and beautiful pictures of appealing, easy-to-cook foods.

If you have a chance to travel across Quebec, you'll make one fascinating discovery after another. You'll see how proud the farmers are of our new products, as are the small entrepreneurs of their new specialty foods. The chefs, the food industry, the researchers, the new producers, the Department of Agriculture, and ultimately the consumers have been the instruments of change.

Suzanne Leclerc, a home economist and food specialist for the Ministère de l'Agriculture, des Pêcheries et de l'Alimentation du Québec, teaches and writes about the subject she loves more than any other: the cuisine of Quebec. She works closely with consumers and chefs and appears frequently on radio and television programs. She has developed recipes, published leaflets, and initiated recipe contests. Leclerc has been at the forefront in promoting Quebec's new and unique food products.

JAMES MACGUIRE

The Art and Science of Good Bread

BREAD is comfort food, with attributes more profound than size, weight, and texture. The spiritual and historical significance of bread in Judeo-Christian tradition clearly shows that the staff of life transcends the mere essence of flavour.

But what about the thing itself? "What is real bread?" And "How French is French-Canadian bread?" For example, some time ago it was found that Quebec's largest per capita consumption of a leading brand of sweet kosher wine was in Lac St-Jean, where French Canadians are a vast majority. In Montreal, the locally bottled Guinness beer is bought in great part by West Indians, and the city's best-known bread specialty is the bagel. Loss of tradition and borrowing from other cultures have clouded the contentious issue of defining bread. The baker who seeks the "real" bread must investigate not only its technical aspects (ingredients and recipes), but also the historical and philosophical aura that surrounds it. This should not eclipse bread's primary purpose: to be eaten.

Many who are resolutely modern and forward-thinking tend to treat "genuine" and "old-fashioned" as synonyms. Those who remember the bread of the 1950s with a certain fondness are probably justified in doing so for reasons that go beyond nostalgia. But there are catches to this: childhood memories are reflected in our minds through rose-coloured lenses, and who can say that someone else might not hold equal claim to another decade? How long ago is "old-fashioned," and when *were* the "good old days" of bread—the 1950s, 1850s, or 1750s?

Did it really *taste* better then, or does it seem so for reasons that are vague and unfathomable? We cannot taste the bread of each epoch, but the baker who seeks to make a truly French-Canadian bread should look into those questions, because whatever the ingredients, in most people's minds tradition (real or imagined) is often part of the formula.

Before wheat was first planted in New France in 1628, the settlers ground French wheat into flour and made loaves similar to those they had known in France. White bread, dark bread (containing bran and rye), and a compromise called *pain bis-blanc* were made. Edicts limiting the number of bakers, fixing the price and size of loaves, and dealing with dishonest millers or bakers were issued from time to time, as they had been in France. But there were significant differences between the Old Country and the New: the seigneurs had the right to impose the use of seigniorial flour mills and ovens. In New France, these ovens proved to be impractical because of the distances and intense winter cold (which caused the raw loaves to freeze in transit to the oven). From the outset the vastness of the New World affected bread and bakers, as it has so many other aspects of Canadian life.

Too little is said about bread itself in early documents from New France, perhaps because there seemed to be little point in noting the ordinary. In France, the first technical books on bread making appeared in the eighteenth century: Malhouin's book in 1767 on the art of bread making and Parmentier's *Le parfait boulanger* in 1778. The enlightened Parmentier did his best to ensure that science won out over superstition, debunking Malouin's claim, for example, that waters from different sources were more suitable or less suitable for bread making. He found it was purely a question of temperature. He describes the new *mouture économique* system of milling (which increased the yields and quality of flours, doing much to democratize white flours) and includes a clear description of working with sourdoughs. The use of beer yeast in bread was known, but it was considered suspect and not often employed; and salt did not come into general use until the end of the century. From Parmentier's time, bread making in France remained little-changed for a hundred years.

Even if we broaden the current definition of French bread—long and skinny, crispy and light (baguettes did not appear until after the

First World War), French bread was still far from being specifically "French" when Parmentier's book appeared. How French could French-Canadian bread have remained if we bear in mind that the English regime began eighteen years before the publication of Parmentier's book?

The beer yeast mentioned by Parmentier was, in his time, simply the foam skimmed from the top of a vat of fermenting beer. The face of bread making changed when baker's yeast, a form of beer yeast produced and compressed especially for the needs of bakers, was invented in Austro-Hungary in the beginning of the nineteenth century. Austrian bakers brought their method of yeast bread making to Paris in 1812 with the opening of a bakery by Baron Zang. *Pain viennois*, lighter, more delicate, and more quickly made than traditional bread, was well received.

Thereafter, yeast breads and yeast manufacture spread to the New World. Charles Fleischmann, who was born near Budapest in 1834, opened a yeast-making operation and distillery in Cincinnati in 1868 and operated a Viennese-style bakery at the 1876 Philadelphia Centennial Exposition in order to promote his product. "Vienna bread," a term still used, can be traced back to the Austro-Hungarian's yeast manufacture and the resulting bread.

Baker's (beer) yeast (*Saccharomyces cerevesiae*) and sourdough (*levain* in French) are entirely different cultures. In general, as researchers in the 1970s showed, sourdough is a combination of the wild yeast *Saccharomyces exigus* (or *Saccharomyces minor*) and a lactic culture. Sourdough ferments very slowly and yields dense loaves with pronounced acidic flavours. The changeover from sourdough to baker's yeast was gradual. In France, for example, there was a long period from the late 1800s to the end of the First World War when bread was made using a mixture of the two cultures (yeast was added to hasten and regulate fermentation periods). This method was called *levain de pâte*.

Bread recipes often began with a "sponge," a miniature dough made with a portion of the flour called for in a recipe. After a few hours of fermentation, the balance of the flour, water, and salt was added to make the main dough. Dough-consistency sponges made solely with baker's yeast were called *levains de levure*, imitating the sourdough method in its use of a small piece of dough to ferment the main dough.

Unfortunately, the words "*de levure*" have been dropped for expediency's sake, implying that yeast and sourdough are the same. In Quebec, things are further confused by the use of the word *levain* for any sort of bread fermentation method; in fact, the word has become synonymous with sourdough, sponge, even baker's yeast itself.

The intricacies of sourdoughs, which arguably have yet to be fully understood and require "feel" on the part of the baker, must be transmitted by "hands-on" demonstration. The greater dependability of baker's yeast made bread making more accessible to neophytes, but it also opened the doors to enormous influence from English Canada and the United States. Too many of today's treasured family recipes were in fact gleaned from commercial recipe booklets from the preceding generation. Yeast and flour companies tended to standardize both domestic and professional recipes, and companies in Quebec were no exception. The oldest French-language booklet in the Ogilvie-Five Roses ("The largest mill in the British Empire") archives in Montreal is dated 1907 and is obviously a translation from the English edition, with its recipes for Home Bread, Parker House Rolls, and Boston Brown Bread.

The Ogilvie and Five Roses booklets are among the oldest sources I found for bread recipes in Quebec. *La cuisinière canadienne* (1865) lists no recipes for bread at all. *La Mère Caron* (first published in 1878) includes bread recipes in its 1903 edition (the only one I have seen). Similar recipes exist in *The Bread Ovens of Quebec* and in the recent oral history *Le pain d'habitant.* They often begin with a type of sourdough made with boiled potatoes, water, and flour. Hops were added, and the mixture was set out to ferment for approximately two days before the main dough was made. In later versions, yeast was added to the mixture, resembling a *levain de pâte* (a mixture of sourdough and baker's yeast, both entirely different cultures). The addition of sugar and lard, and cooking in metal moulds, became almost universal.

The discussion thus far has been limited to household recipes. Most bread was made in rural Quebec homes until the 1930s, but from then on even modest towns had bakeries. The Gadoua family of Napierville was a typical bakery family: the grandfather of Marcel and Robert, who now operate the business with their sons, ran a small bakery. Most of the bread was delivered door to door, first by horse and carriage, then by truck. Friends and cousins had bakeries in nearby towns. A typical recipe might have called for one pound of sugar, eight ounces of lard, one pound of yeast, and two pounds of salt per hundred pounds of flour. In the great-grandfather's time, a potato starter (with or without the addition of yeast) was still common. The kneading was done with a slow-speed machine, and the rising times were relatively long. Weighing and shaping were done by hand, and most loaves were baked in moulds.

Mechanization and the arrival of supermarkets changed things. When giants like Weston began selling sliced bread, the Gadoua family had to follow suit. They remember the change to sliced bread as a downturn in quality because the texture was altered and additives became necessary to prevent moulding. However, this was unnoticed by their more affluent customers at that time, who flamboyantly paid an additional two or three cents a loaf for sliced bread. Gradually Gadoua bought out the bakeries in surrounding towns and became a regional bakery delivering to supermarkets. Today Gadoua delivers to Montreal, and Robert, who handles the technical side of the business, has on several occasions been summoned to France to consult on the making of hot dog and hamburger buns.

No French bread recipes or basic breadmaking techniques have survived from the days of Jacques Cartier. English words such as *yeast*, *muffins*, and *buns* (spelled "bonnes" in one contemporary, perhaps revisionist, reprint) appear repeatedly in even the older sources. More important still, moulded loaves containing fat, sugar, and potato starter have no French counterparts. (Parmentier *does* mention potato bread, but begins the recipe with a regular *levain* dough, using the potato as filler. His enthusiasm for the potato in general does not extend to potato bread.) In *English Bread and Yeast Cookery* (1977), Elizabeth David quotes several recipes dating from the 1800s that are based on potato/hop starters (with or without the addition of beer yeast) and that are virtually the same as those in Quebec at that time. France did not have a beer-drinking culture, and potatoes were not yet a staple (in spite of Parmentier's efforts).

French bread as we know it arrived in Montreal with the opening of bakeries such as *Cousin* (1921) and *Au Pain Doré* (1956). Cousin was actually a *charcutier*, who, suspecting there was a market for French bread, opened a bakery and began making the crusty French loaves. Claude Bouvet, whose father bought the business in 1947, is adamant that the local taste for French bread was (and remains) marginal, and that when Cousin opened, French bread was something brand-new.

The Gadouas dabbled in making French bread years ago, and they hope to start again in earnest one day. However, Marcel Gadoua cites market studies that invariably show consumers prefer moulded, sliced white bread, each slice a perfect square, with a maximum crumb and minimum crust.

While the history of bread may be interesting, it does not tell us what "real" French-Canadian bread is. Technical data, especially the influence of ingredients on taste and texture, should be *the* major concern for bakers (and eaters) in search of the real thing.

Raymond Calvel was professor of baking at the *École française de meunerie* for many years, and remains, during his busy retirement (he is eighty-two years old), France's foremost expert on bread. An outspoken critic of current French bread-making practices, Calvel, in lectures, magazine articles, and books, explains his point of view with tact, clarity, and patience. His immense technical prowess has not altered his belief that flavour and texture must remain the criteria for good bread. When pressed for his opinion on the use of certain additives, he will often simply state: "As a technician, I am fascinated, but as someone who eats bread, I cannot approve."

The simple Calvel message can be applied to all breads. It is based on a few principles governing basic flavours. These principles often provide justification and understanding of why things have always been done in a certain way.

One of these principles is that the nutty, wheaty flavour of the inside of a French loaf comes from the carotenoid pigments. These are destroyed by bleaching flours or by excessive mechanical kneading of bread dough at high speeds.

Another principle elaborated by Calvel is that French flours yielded sticky doughs that required long, cool fermentations. Organic acids, formed as a by-product of alcoholic fermentation, are natural dough conditioners that give doughs strength and body. This primary fermentation is the cornerstone of good bread, and management of these organic acids is the greatest measure of a baker's skill. The organic acids are responsible for the fermented, "yeasty" flavours in the finished loaf, as well as an agreeable chewiness and how well the bread will keep.

Calvel points out that careful attention to the dividing, shaping, and baking must follow to complete the process. Flavours from the caramelization and Maillard (browning) reaction of the crust migrate to the crumb, adding to its already complex flavours. Hearth breads require a proper oven and the addition of steam at the outset of baking to form a thinner, crispier crust. Insufficient baking is a very common fault found in all types of bread.

Last, Calvel reflects his origins and his generation in his distaste for whole grains. However, mixtures of flours and grains permit varying textures and flavours and, if the basic principles have been followed, can only lead to a good (albeit different) loaf of bread. Each baker must have his or her style, and each must make choices.

Having alluded to supermarket bread (the bread we love to hate), it seems only fair to quote the late Roger Corbeil, the great Canadian technical expert on flour and bread: "Supermarket bread has to be light, white, soft, virtually crustless and keep for two weeks without becoming mouldy. Now it has to contain added fibre yet retain its usual characteristics. People should be eating lentils and other sources of fibre as part of a balanced diet. It is unreasonable to expect two slices of bread to bear the whole burden." When I see someone shun well-made white bread (of the nonchemical variety), while buying white pasta for dinner, I wonder if reverse snobbery has become such that the vision of our ancestors eating white *pain mollet* from a silver platter rather than coarse black bread with sawdust in some hovel is too painful to ponder.

If we examine the technical history of bread in Quebec, a pattern emerges. Although roller milling and baker's yeast can be seen as positive, more recent developments raise an important question: at what point do technical advances begin to favour efficiency and production capacity over quality? Bleaching flour lengthens its shelf life but, in the process, loses the wheaty flavours; high-speed mixing produces an extremely light bread, but the resulting bread is flavourless; "instant flours" containing azodicarbonomide save time in fermentation, but again at the loss of flavour, and esterified fats (modified fats) are added to counteract the ill effects of other additives. The bread begins to resemble a sort of Frankenstein: to make things easy and foolproof, too many of its vital parts are tampered with or replaced.

Because most additives are put into flour at the mill, bakeries, bewildered by their intricacies, have become dependent upon the mills' technical departments for help. When a baker buys flour, the mill will provide a recipe and demonstrate its use. Thus, one can assume that many bakeries end up using the same flours and the same recipes to make virtually the same bread. Because of this, the diversity of breads has greatly diminished, and puffed-up bread is pervasive. Even ethnic breads are hard to tell apart. To know whether a loaf is Greek, French, Italian, or Portuguese, one must be told. Many bakers do not know that options exist. Canadian flour, with which Professor Calvel achieved superb results on recent trips to Canada, is often taken to task for problems that are not caused by the wheat but by the additives.

The French are in the process of legislating what they call *pain maison* and *pain traditionnel* to distance these breads from those that are factory produced. Also called *artisanal*, these breads reject the use of any additive, machine, or process that sacrifices authenticity or quality for ease and high yields. We have spoken about additives. What remains to be said is that the technical demands of automation are such that in many cases the texture of the dough, the time that it is allowed to ferment, and other factors are adjusted to suit the machine, relegating quality of the end result to a subordinate role.

Let's consider an extreme example. All over Quebec, stores have begun baking bread on the premises and hanging banners in the window that indicate *Pain cuit sur place.* The yeasty aromas bring people into the store and boost the sales of related food items such as cheeses and *charcuterie.* Most often, the loaves are bought from a factory in a raw, frozen state, thawed, then baked. The dough has been prepared with cold water to make sure it won't ferment, the additive-laden flour is bleached, and the bread is frequently inadequately baked, constituting a total departure from Calvel's basic principles.

A small bakery, equipped with a mixer, bags of flour, and a workshop is no guarantee of *artisanal* bread. Trips in recent years to three or four of the older Montreal bagel establishments found them all using bleached, instant flours. Despite wood-burning ovens, shaping by hand, and an air of authenticity, they are not *artisanal* as it has been defined. Most bakers end up using additives, which hurts the quality of their bread and compromises its *artisanal* status. Even a baker who works alone in a tiny bakery, if required to list all the additives (including those present in the flour used), might include virtually the same ones as those listed by a factory. This, unfortunately, is the case with a suburban Montreal bakery that uses a 1920s wood-fired oven and recipes from a Fleischmann's yeast booklet dating from the 1930s. Because of bleaching and additives, which have been around for long enough to put a fly into the "What is genuine, what is old-fashioned?" ointment, the promise implied by the old oven and wonderfully sincere baker remains unfulfilled.

French Canadians remain very attached to bread, and as quality has dropped and consumption has plummeted, mysticizing bread has taken up the slack. Poilâne, the well-known Parisian baker, wrote a book about bread (and not a little bit about Poilâne) in which symbolism, the wondrous qualities of the seemingly autonomous *levain*, and other intangibles play perhaps too great a part. This same tendency exists in Quebec. I am saddened when I see *cuit sur place* customers according "pretend" country loaves the status of a sort of edible historical artifact (in France, too, one sees balls of white commercial dough dusted with flour to give them an air of rusticity. These Professor Calvel calls "*travestis farinés*"). The cultural aspects of Catholicism remain strong, and one can still see Paterfamilias inscribe a cross on the bottom of a loaf before distributing a slice to each family member, often doing so with the nostalgic reminder that it wasn't that long ago that bread was still a large part of the diet and not a piece of superfluous fluff.

It has not been my intention to paint a pessimistic picture of bread in Quebec. French bakeries have done well. Cousin has expanded sales of brown-and-serve loaves to supermarkets and convenience stores. Idealists may turn up their noses, but the loaves are an option that did not exist before. Au Pain Doré has begun opening its own stores, and its bread is made with unbleached flour and at least some reference to Professor Calvel's teachings. Health-food stores, which sell organic, whole-grain bread to a different clientele, are another option. These have been joined by small bakeries such as La Fournée Bio and Le Fromentier, which have begun to demonstrate that whole grains, good technique, and good taste need not be at odds. Montreal and Quebec City have experienced a considerable growth in ethnic bakeries, and smaller cities and towns have started to benefit from this return to good bread.

History and authenticity have their place, but it is doubtful that many drinkers would welcome a return to the oxidized wines that were probably the norm before wine makers came to know better. Scottish distillers have been known to make dents in brand-new stills so they look exactly like the old ones they replaced, out of superstition or just in case it makes a difference. There is a school of bread thought that recoils from the idea of technical proficiency and views the perfect loaf with wariness, while eyeing a muddled effort with that special warmth and understanding usually reserved for the runt of a litter. If we don't know what bread was like in 1750, why would we assume the worst? It seems probable that Parmentier would have applauded any technical advance that permits making better bread, and it seems logical for bakers today to endeavour to make a given flour or recipe reach its potential. Quality-oriented methods (such as Calvel's) are there to be borrowed and adapted to the circumstances, with no qualms about "selling out." It is then up to the baker to use yeast or sourdough (or both) and whatever shape and mixture of flours seem right, making the result reflect regional and personal styles.

British and American techniques for making bread prevailed over those brought by the French settlers, and because bread's primary purpose is to be eaten (and not to be an edible artifact) the more effective techniques *should* prevail. The current effort all over North America to rediscover regional cuisines has at times led to excesses because the temptation exists to invent dishes that should have existed but didn't. This need not be the case with bread: a small bakery in Quebec that applies good technique to experiments with potato leavening could be onto something. Older bakers still remember forgotten shapes and sizes of loaves. These include Vienna and Mother, but also *fesses* (literally buttocks or buns) and *pain chinois* (a football-shaped loaf with a string of dough placed along its length, resembling the Burgundian *pain cordon.* The name *pain chinois,* like the French name for shepherd's pie—*pâte chinois*—reflects a whimsical exoticism. During my research, the term "Jack" appeared repeatedly to name a rectangular moulded loaf. I was dismayed at finding this Anglicism, but when Monsieur Bisaillon, who had once worked for Gadoua, said that "Jack" had originally been "Jacobin," it made my day.

James MacGuire is the owner and operator of Le Passe-Partout in Montreal with his wife, Suzanne Baron-Lafrenière. His bakery/restaurant is mentioned in guides such as *Where to Eat in Canada, Travel-Holiday, Distinguished Restaurants of America,* and other magazines. Born in New York City, he had an early interest in cooking, and worked in San Francisco, Los Angeles, Dallas, and other cities in the United States. He trained in France in Alsace, Lyon, Tours, and Chartes, and was the founding member and vice president of the Canadian branch of the Académie culinaire de France. He has received the Roger Champoux Award.

THE REGIONAL CUISINE OF THE ATLANTIC PROVINCES

JUDITH COMFORT

Some Good! The Maritime Harvest

WRITERS of cookbooks (me included) and editors of food magazines like to imagine that their publications have the following effect. . .

The innocent reader, savouring a cup of tea at her kitchen table, is suddenly inspired by the glossy food photos of an amazing recipe for preparing a humdrum dish in a new sexy way. Out comes the pad and paper to dash down the list of ingredients. Then it's a quick trip to the market, followed by a relaxing afternoon in the kitchen, and voilà—just like in the pictures.

As a resident of the rural Maritimes, I know from experience that menu planning is never like this. And I suspect this is true for much of the rest of rural Canada. My kitchen table, which happens to be fourteen miles from the nearest supermarket, is a good place for contemplating the waves of Medway Harbour or for enjoying a cup of coffee, but I know that there is no point in planning a special meal until I get to the store. I cannot drive the eighty-five miles to Halifax for a particular variety of vinegar or frozen phyllo dough.

In most cases the availability of ingredients pre-empts the recipe I choose to prepare. But I'm not complaining. My inspiration for cooking comes from what is on hand. And in the Maritimes, ingredients appear in the natural order of things.

When the smelts are running we eat smelts; when the apples are red we pick them; and when a generous, but anonymous, neighbour leaves a bushel (make that 35.23808 litres) of rhubarb on your back porch we have pie for the next few days and preserves for the rest of the year.

For the best, we have to be patient like our forebears, and eat what is in season and on hand. The real Maritime foods are gifts from the sea, forest, shoreline, and field.

The Maritime Harvest is a twelve-month event. It starts in January with a bloom of seed catalogues. There is no better antidote to the unceasing winter wind than perusing the pages of summer flowers in front of a fragrant maple fire.

February is the month that the tiny silver cousins of the salmon, the smelt, make their way up Maritime rivers. In spite of the cold, hundreds of people in parkas make their way down to the river to cut holes in the ice and fish for smelt. They build elaborate structures complete with the comforts of home—chairs, tables, even stoves—over each hole. There is an annual tournament on the Lahave River where a whole village of smelt shacks mushrooms overnight on the ice.

In February and March, warm sunny days and chilly nights combine to awaken the sap of the sugar maple. Maple suppers proliferate throughout the maple syrup areas of New Brunswick and Nova Scotia, and pancakes, sausages, baked beans, and brown bread are served to enthusiastic participants. Better still, there are sugaring-off parties, with tours of the woods and sugar houses. A blast of maple steam is an instant remedy for the winter blues and clogged sinuses.

When the weather finally breaks in April, the black flies are so thick you can breathe them. Trout fishermen will endure the worst conditions to catch their dinner. The passion for this sport defies all logic.

After the highest of the spring tides on the Bay of Fundy, a precious two-week period arrives when a leafless, but succulent and delicious, plant works its way through the cracks of clay. The *Salicornia europaea* (also known as samphire green, sandfire, glasswort, or crowfoot) has been picked by families on this shore for generations. Eaten raw, it is crisp and juicy, with a slightly salty taste. Traditionally it is cooked in quantity like spinach. The green is scraped off the inedible woody membrane in the middle of each stem, dotted with butter, vinegar, salt and pepper, and relished as the first green taste of spring.

Another green spring tonic, especially in New Brunwick, is the unfurling frond of the ostrich fern. Designed by nature, the fiddlehead is no less refined than the scroll at the head of a violin. Our ancestors spent a whole winter eating provisions from the root cellar: potatoes, carrots, potatoes, turnips, potatoes, salt cod, and salted corned beef, mixed with the odd bottle of mustard beans. When spring finally arrived, they watched patiently as the green shoots grew by the stream bed. When the shoots were about six inches high they were snapped off and rushed to the kitchen for that first taste of chlorophyl in months.

After a grey spring we look longingly at the trees for signs of life. One of the first is the fuzzy haze of white blossoms in every thicket alongside the road. The Indian pear is in bloom. It is also called saskatoon berry, serviceberry, and shadbush (because it presumably blossoms when the shad run), but we think that "Indian pear" aptly describes these seedy berries that taste like a juicy cross between a blueberry and a pear. The joy of Indian pear is in grabbing handfuls of it while cutting through the woods on the way to the beach. It is a delicious God-given fruit that is there for the picking.

In spring, we count on the old faithful of the garden, the elephant-eared, sassy, sour rhubarb. Rarely do Maritimers buy the stuff, because it grows everywhere, usually behind an old shed in a corner of the yard. Along with narcissi and peonies, we find it still flourishing next to the foundation holes of long-abandoned farmhouses. Rhubarb is served plain, just stewed with a little sugar. The first—and some would argue the best—pie of the season is a mixture of rhubarb and wild strawberries.

June is the month for the annual pilgrimage to the strawberry fields. People drive halfway across the province to the Annapolis Valley in Nova Scotia or to the Kingston Peninsula in New Brunswick to pick berries for jam. More than a third of the strawberry crop is set up in U-pick operations. You can't put a price on a day spent in the country with friends. And you'll never find a berry in the supermarket that tastes like the sun-kissed strawberry you just plucked off the plant and popped into your mouth.

There is a magic interlude when the spring rains stop, the sun warms our faces, and there's not a single black fly, mosquito, no-see-em, deer fly, or horse fly in the air. This is when Maritimers think about cleaning up the yard. But then they say to themselves, "Let's go clamming, instead." Digging clams is the best excuse for exploring a remote beach. The beaches that are accessible only by boat or by trek along a stretch of rocky coastline tend to remain more productive. We search for holes in the sand and are squirted with water by retreating bivalves. The trick is to get the shovel (or clam hoe, if you are a serious digger) in and out without crushing the soft-shelled creature. Sometimes we are lucky enough to get mussels on the same trip. We search under the air-filled bladders of rockweed-tressed, semisubmerged boulders. The blue shells are attached in clusters with their strong byssus threads, and can be gathered by the handful in good locations.

If the weather is good, we make a fire on the beach and steam the clams in a bed of seaweed. For more formal occasions, we take them home and steam them over a little wine and garlic. We strain the precious liquid from the bottom of the pot and freeze it for later use in fish chowders. The wild mussels that grow near sand have tiny pearls that crunch between the teeth if eaten too quickly. Children collect them as miniature jewels.

Although grabbing a net sack of cultivated mussels from the cooler at the store is not as adventurous as collecting them on the shore, the culinary results are the same. The spat of cultivated mussels are descendants of captured natives and are grown in long sock-shaped nets away from the bottom. They are tender and juicy and free from pearly grit.

Fishing the Bay of Fundy, where forty-foot tides are the norm, you will find your boat sitting high and dry on mud flats for a good portion of the day. When the tide is out, the flats may be covered with hundreds of tiny shelled caravans crossing the vast expanse. Periwinkles, called a poor man's escargot, are easy prey for the gourmet steam pot.

The special low tides from May to August give us access to sea plants that grow at the very edge and deeper—a reddish black seaweed called *Rhodymenia palmata* or dulse. Up to a foot long, with fingerlike projections, the best dulse is picked while it is still growing, then sun dried. A few days later it is at its peak flavor. It tastes like the North Atlantic, like salt and brine, and fish and sea air, and, well—dulse. You peel off a few layers and chew it and chew it and chew it.

Herring is an abundant seafood that, strangely enough, Maritimers have never developed much of a taste for. It is said that a herring skeleton is like a walrus's mustache. Perhaps the most inventive thing

Maritimers do with herring is to make the traditional Lunenburg County delicacy known as Solomon Gundy. The fish is soaked in a brine of salt, vinegar, sugar, and pickling spice long enough to make the bones irrelevant to the texture and flavour.

Atlantic salmon has always been a seasonal delicacy. We like to roast salmon the traditional Mi'kmaq way, planking it next to an open fire. This ingenious cooking method was developed before the introduction of metal cooking pots. While the old method was to use a flattened side of tree stump, on which the splayed open fish was lashed, we prefer a good thick hardwood board and a crisscross of alder twigs pinned with small nails. We prop the plank in front of our fireplace and the heat reflected by the fire wall sears the fish. The delectable juices are sealed in behind a golden smoky crust. We serve the fish on a bed of fresh dill and greens, lemon wedges and new potatoes. Scallops, which are harvested year-round, are also a delicacy over an open fire.

Oysters, thanks to aquaculture, are also available year-round. The native oyster, the *Crassotrea virginica*, traditionally prefers the warm waters of river estuaries such as Malpeque Bay, P.E.I., and New Brunswick's Acadian Coast. Oysters spawn only in warm water but will thrive in colder water, so aquaculturists set out immature spat generated by hatcheries.

In July we see the first of the new potatoes, sweet and tender. Along the shore, gardeners who have planted potatoes under a foot of seaweed can sneak a few tubers out from under the plant and still leave it growing.

Nova Scotians love their Hodge Podge, a medley of baby potatoes, immature peas, beans, and carrots immersed in cream and butter and served in a chowder bowl.

Potatoes are the lifeblood of farm communities in P.E.I. and the upper Saint John River Valley. This farmland is beautiful from spring through summer and fall when the perfectly parallel undulating furrows of soil transform into lines of white blossoms and finally a healthy greenery. Off to the side, the conveyor belt harvesters wait patiently. Varieties grown are mostly brown-skinned, white-fleshed descendants of Russet Burbank. New varieties have been developed to feed the maws of the huge potato processors: long ones for French fries, round ones for potato chips.

Yellow- and red-fleshed potatoes such as Bintjes, Yukon Gold, and Red Pontiacs are being grown on a small scale. The real variety in potatoes can be found in home gardens, where people save the *seed* from generation to generation. My neighbours grow *blues*, which are actually purple, and something they call a German potato, which is red skinned and yellow fleshed.

Summer means a lobster and corn boil to many people. The Shediac Lobster Festival, which culminates the season ending July 9, is quite an event. There are traffic jams in the centre of this town, whose town mascot is a truck-sized lobster sculpture. Everyone eats lobster—in the upscale restaurants, on the beaches, beside take-out stands, in picnic parks. True lobster gluttons participate in the lobster-eating contests. This is serious sport.

A large part of the traditional Maritime diet has always included the white-fleshed fish: cod, haddock, and halibut. Getting fresh fish—the bright-white, firm, sweet-smelling kind—has always been a challenge. Fish must be acquired at the source. Many Maritimers have a connection: a fisherman in the family, a neighbour, a friend. I've had halibut, mackerel, even squid, dropped off at the door. We sometimes get fish at the local plant (when it's operating) by watching for boats steaming by the house on their way to unload. We haunt the shopping mall parking lot and highway intersection for pickup-truck fish peddlers (whole mackerel, three for $1.00, guts and all).

Fish chowder is the generic dish here. Every cook has a variation on the same theme of fish, potatoes, onions, and milk. Some use butter or salt pork, striped bass or finnan haddie, heavy cream or canned milk.

Driving the backroads in August, you'll find people mysteriously crouched next to the road allowance. They're picking blueberries. It takes about an hour to collect the four cups required for a decent pie, so many choose an alternative, albeit more expensive, method of acquiring berries: buying them from a local child who has set up a roadside stand or taking advantage of a U-pick. These fields are not cultivated but are meadows where wild berry plants have been burned to encourage the plants to bear more fruit.

August begins the time of the true harvest. Travelling the Maritimes this month reveals a cornucopia of fruits and vegetables at roadside stands and farmers markets.

For our family, harvest time means a trip to the Annapolis Valley. This area was cultivated first by Acadians, then Loyalist Planters, and today by their descendants. In August we feel that surely the planets must have aligned to bring everything good there is to eat into the Annapolis Valley. On display are early or *August* apples—pale-yellow Russian emigrés called Transparent and other crosses developed at the Kentville research station down the road. Giant Atlantic squash, amorphous 300-pound deflated blobs developed by Windsor pumpkin farmer Howard Dill, lie around.

Peaches and Cream corn is sold by the cob or bushel sack. Boxes are full to the brim with red pears, sour pie cherries, yellow watermelon, high bush blueberries, pickling cukes, and every type of tomato: yellow and red, tiny Tims, and huge beefsteak. Prices are so reasonable that many people buy enough to fill their freezer and canning jars.

In late September, the wooden crates are filled to overflowing with apples. There are dozens of varieties: with exotic-sounding names like Cox's orange, Bishop's Pippin, and the jewel of the Nova Scotian crop—the Gravenstein. In Nova Scotia 30 percent of the apple crop is made up of historic varieties, not commercially viable on a large scale. Unusual and truly delicious apples, as well as precious genetic material, have been preserved for posterity.

One of the biggest thrills of the season is an invitation to a cider pressing. An old-fashioned hand-cranked press is set up right in the orchard. The apples are collected (preferably including some golden russet) and chopped into a heavy-hooped wooden basket. A screw press is turned down on the freshly ground pomace, and gallons of liquid apple gush down the wooden trough into a bucket. The pinkish greenish liquid instantly oxidizes into its characteristic brown colour. Pure ambrosia.

Thanksgiving in the Maritimes—fall rains permitting—can be a glorious time. We like to include in our festive meal as many homegrown and foraged foods as possible, starting with a turkey raised by a neighbour. We make a wild mushroom, fresh sage, and summer savory stuffing. We pull potatoes, carrots, and turnips out of the root cellar, and garden peas and bog cranberries from the freezer. We cook down and purée a pumpkin for pie.

Savouring our coffee and dessert, we sit at the kitchen table and contemplate the waves. We are grateful for the food that has been given to us. With beauty all around and the gifts of the sea and land, we have reason to give thanks.

Judith Comfort lives on the edge of beautiful Medway Harbour, on Nova Scotia's South Shore, with her husband, Alan, and three children. She is the author of five food books, including *Some Good!*, a regional best seller. Recently she published a travel book, *Country Roads of the Maritimes*, and is working on another travel book about Nova Scotia. As a volunteer she is active in economic development and health reform.

JULIE V. WATSON

Global Marketing of Lobster:

A Prince Edward Island Success Story

TO REALLY UNDERSTAND how Canadian lobster found its way to the dining tables of the world, let's begin with a look back in time.

Fishermen began "exporting" seafood from the waters of Atlantic Canada as early as 1497. The first to follow John Cabot to the New World (some even say they came before his famous voyage) were the fishermen of England, France, Holland, Spain, and Portugal. They came first to the Grand Banks, off the shores of Newfoundland; later they spread into other waters of the region. By 1608, fleets of 300 vessels were making the crossing. By 1634, crews on English ships alone totalled at least 18,000. The rich cargoes of fish provided food to feed the people of Europe. Catching, drying, and salting cod became Canada's first onshore industry.

Not only were those early fishermen the foundation of our culture, but they entered Atlantic Canadians into the earliest stages of global marketing, which continues to be vitally important to our economy today. As time passed we added other species of fish to our product list, and today we export all manner of seafoods, including lobster, mussels, oysters, scallops, sea urchins, and farmed salmon, as well as smoked seafoods such as eels, mussels, salmon, and scallops.

Canada produces volumes of fish and processed fish products far in excess of our domestic needs, with 80 percent of our fishery products exported to every corner of the world. And it is the world's largest producer and exporter of lobster. In 1992, total Canadian landings exceeded 46,000 tonnes, approximately 30 percent of total global landings. Almost 90 percent of Canadian production was exported, with a total value in excess of $300 million. The United States accounts for 70 percent of Canada's lobster exports, followed by Japan and the European Community. Lobster fishing is a major industry on Prince Edward Island, involving 11,000 lobster fishermen and 250 lobster processing establishments and exporters. However, fewer than a dozen of the firms account for the majority of our exports.

Canadian lobsters (*Homarus americanus*) are only found in the northeast waters of Canada and the United States. They compete in the global market with other species such as the European lobster, crayfish, and rock lobster. Not governed by marketing boards, lobster price levels are dictated by a worldwide supply and demand driven market.

Increasingly, consumers are concerned with product safety, health benefits, and environmental factors. The Canadian lobster industry is noted globally for its resource management, health and inspection services, and high-quality, hard-shelled product from pollution-free waters. The industry has an excellent reputation for maintaining rigorous standards through the federal government's Quality Management Program (QMP), a plant health-inspection system. As well, a testing system is in place that constantly monitors the waters where shellfish are harvested. At any sign of a problem, harvesting in that area is put on hold until the waters clear. Canada now has one of the best monitoring systems in the world. This, together with the Quality Management Program for processing, gives Canadian lobster a high reputation internationally.

The industry has identified the following factors in assessing the global marketing opportunities for Atlantic Canadian lobster:

- New technologies are becoming available that will improve the handling, packaging, transportation, and distribution of lobster products.

- The lobster industry, with the possible exception of the industry in P.E.I., does experience some cyclical variation in supply, but overall, landings have been fairly stable over the past three or four years.
- The industry has identified lobster as a product that would benefit from generic market promotion. To that end, CALPA, the Canadian Atlantic Lobster Promotion Association, is developing a generic export marketing plan.
- Seafood consumption is increasing worldwide with population growth and demand for alternative sources of protein. The consumption of luxury items, including lobster, especially in the hotel and restaurant industry, continues to grow.
- In Europe, consumption of lobster is closely linked to traditional events—for example, the Christmas and Easter holidays—while in northeast North America, live lobster demand is tied to summer vacations and tourist seasons.
- Supply is regulated by the harvesting season.

Lobsters are primarily exported live and frozen, but innovative products have been developed for niche markets. Because we have a broader range of lobster sizes than what is available in the U.S., our only competing supplier of *Homarus americanus*, we have more flexibility in serving niche markets. The Canadian lobster industry has introduced processed product innovations such as scored lobster claws, to compete with scored crab claws; and new packaging concepts and techniques such as the "Popsicle pack" favoured by the French. For this the lobster is cooked, placed in a plastic sleeve, topped with brine to prevent oxidation, and frozen. I'm constantly amazed at how lobster is packaged and sold. I've seen packs of claws all of a certain length; packages of walking-leg meat for sauces only; claw meat alone; tail meat; claws and tails; 11.3 ounce cans containing all the meat of four-to-six "canners"; broken meat for casseroles and sandwiches; portion packs of all sizes. In fact, if a retailer or restaurateur has a specific need or desires help in getting just the right product, CALPA directs him or her to the right processors.

Since lobster is an expensive luxury product and is perceived as being difficult to prepare, live and whole frozen lobster are mainly consumed in restaurants. To meet growing food-service demand for value-added, portion-controlled lobster meat, the industry has developed a vacuum-packed form of the product, which is replacing the more traditional canned product. This has caused a considerable boost in sales, particularly in the United States. Lobster meat offers opportunities for upscale menu items such as lobster sauces, bisques, salads, chowders, even casseroles, sandwiches, crêpes, or any recipe you would use chopped meat for, at a fraction of the cost. I know of one restaurant in Nova Scotia that makes a tremendous variety of seafood dishes, many of which feature lobster and scallop sauce, prepared with walking-leg meat and broken scallops. The restaurant's seafood sales have increased to 80 percent of their total sales.

Lobster is high in protein, has important trace elements and essential amino acids, is low in cholesterol or saturated fats, and low in calories, depending on how it is prepared. As such, it is attractive to a growing number of consumers concerned with the health benefits of food products, a fact that should be emphasized, particularly in Europe.

A well-managed fisheries regime in Canada, developed over many decades, holds the prospect of providing a stable supply of lobster on a sustainable basis. This contrasts with the situation in other parts of the world, where depletion of the resource is becoming evident. My personal opinion is that our lobster stock has thrived because it is strictly an inshore fishery, with no foreign trawlers destroying the habitat or wiping out entire "colonies" or, as happens with fish, schools at a time. The effective management of the Canadian lobster resource eliminates problems of "by-catch," associated with other fisheries, and is consistent with Canada's commitment to protecting the ecosystem in the lobster harvest. As a result of such management, lobster landings have actually increased 94 percent in the past decade.

Lobster is probably the best example of a wild harvest that is alive and, indeed, healthy. One of the strengths of the lobster industry is the regulated fishing that has been in effect for years. Our district system allows fishing for only four to eight weeks a year in any given district. Seasons are determined by the moult and breeding times. Wild harvest of the lobster is a noninvasive inshore fishery that does not destroy or even adversely affect the lobster's environment.

Yet the Canadian lobster industry has had its challenges. With its many small firms, it was vulnerable in the past to a lack of coordination in its marketing approach. The formation of CALPA and development of a generic marketing plan will make it possible to respond quickly to marketing challenges.

A tendency to market lobster simply as a commodity without more sophisticated marketing techniques (including packaging) undermines its appeal and, consequently, full profit potential. The subjects of upgrading and added value have been addressed by the lobster industry in its development of niche products.

How to maintain a strong Canadian identity at the consumer level in global markets has been another challenge. Canadian lobsters, for example, are often sold as "Maine" lobsters, with which consumers identify. Canadian hard-shell lobsters are sometimes mixed with American soft-shell varieties. There is also evidence that some U.S. brokers sell imported Canadian lobster as U.S. product. The Canadian lobster industry has responded with the use of distinctive claw bands or tags—Quebec uses a blue fleur-de-lis band, while Nova Scotia favours a maple leaf.

There is a perception that unstable prices, combined with fluctuations of supply, affect the growth of live lobster consumption in the restaurant and food-service trade. Again the Canadian lobster industry has responded. In the winter, even if fishermen could get through the ice they could not fish lobster. When it gets cold, lobsters back into a little hole or crevice and hibernate until the waters get warm again. This habit has allowed a company like Clearwater in Halifax to develop a huge holding system that puts each lobster in a private cubicle. The cubicles are in huge tanks that have a constant supply of fresh, cold sea water circulating through them. Chilled into a natural state of hibernation, the lobsters maintain their fresh flavour for months.

Newly developed shipping cartons mean that small quantities of live lobster can be shipped by air within twenty-four hours to most world centres. After they arrive they can be held in these specially designed containers for several days. This allows a chef in Paris, London, Amsterdam, New York, Miami, Seattle, or even Tokyo to feature live lobster on his or her menu as a special item, without having to carry inventory. With the coming of FAX machines, special handling and packaging, and airline connections, Canadian lobsters have gone worldwide.

Product substitution is of critical concern to the lobster industry. As lobster prices rise, consumers switch to alternative products such as salmon, snow crab, and shrimp. The lobster industry is challenging this situation by offering more market forms. It is also educating cooks and chefs on how to handle and use lobster for the best value. Most of this work is being done through CALPA, which develops "unique to you recipes," supplies promotional material such as tent cards and posters, and participates in joint promotions. CALPA also mounts an ongoing campaign to increase consumer awareness.

The future of the Canadian lobster industry looks bright as far as both availability of product and global markets are concerned. However, the volatile fishing industry has created some concerns for the processor. The demand, short fishing seasons, and high costs have led many processors to cut back on processing frozen product "to spec." In other words, they are hesitant to process product based on speculation of future market demand. Since lobster holds well as a live product, many processors seek orders before they process or freeze product. Part of their reasoning is that demand fluctuates for whole frozen products packed in brine, for canned meat, and for vacuum-packed speciality packs. Chefs and restaurateurs planning to feature lobster products are well advised to contact suppliers, discuss their needs, and place their orders between December and April. Since the major harvest begins in May, ordering early will ensure their supply of a product that is becoming more and more popular with consumers around the world.

Based in Charlottetown, Prince Edward Island, **Julie V. Watson** has been an active food writer for more than twelve years and now has numerous cookbooks to her credit including: *A Fine Catch Seafood Cookbook, Largely Lobster, Cultured Mussel Cookbook,* and *Seafood Cookery of Prince Edward Island.* She also writes articles for periodicals and government agencies. In her seafood consulting business, *Creative Connections,* with the Canadian Atlantic Lobster Promotion Association, she promotes lobster around the world and introduces chefs and the food media to the lobster industry through specialized tours.

MARIE NIGHTINGALE

The Enduring Influences on Today's East Coast Cooking

JOSEPH HOWE, Nova Scotia's great patriot, once said: "Next to himself, his wife, his children and his horse, the prettiest thing at which a man can look is his country." He didn't mention East Coast cooking. But we're going to add that to Howe's wise words.

The enduring influences on today's East Coast cooking are those of the Acadians, the British, and the Loyalists. It was these early settlers who combined the food traditions of their home countries with the ingredients available to them in their new land, and in doing so, established what we consider today to be down-home cooking.

I have two clear images of early Acadian life. The first is of the peace and contentment the Acadians lived in following their arrival in Acadie in the mid-1600s.

The men were farmers who were one with the soil. They understood it and willingly toiled long hours to clear, tame, and nurture it, so that the earth would respond and give back the barley required for the people's daily bread. Their needs were simple enough. As long as they had their families and their friends, with whom they gathered regularly, they were happy. These gatherings were fuelled by the music that was born of their souls and ran in their veins as surely as did their blood. Yet these men turned back the world's highest tides with dikes so strong that most are still intact today.

Inside the Acadian home, the women hustled through their own daily labours—from the hearth to the swift, from the kitchen garden to the table, and back to the hearth. Always back to the hearth, the centre of all activity. The heart of the home. The women sang as they bent to their tasks, stopping only long enough to answer the needs of one of their growing brood. Family, friends. The words from which contentment grows.

But then came the Expulsion, a time of confusion and sadness for the Acadians. For eight years, beginning in 1755, some 13,000 Acadians were uprooted and deported from their beloved Acadie. The song died. Yet for many, it was never completely forgotten. Acadie kept calling them home. Hardly a year separated the end of the deportation and the beginning of the Return.

They came back to find their lands being tilled by others, their chapels replaced by the meeting houses and churches of the New England Planters to whom their fertile meadows had been granted.

Now see the Acadians settled in new homes along the northwestern shore of Nova Scotia, in Digby and Yarmouth counties; around Cheticamp in Cape Breton and, more widely, along the south and eastern shores of New Brunswick. Other smaller settlements grew in Prince Edward Island and along Nova Scotia's Eastern Shore.

In these new homes, away from the fertile soil of Grand Pré, the Acadians picked up their lives, turning away from the harsher rocky ground to the sea. Though they gave up their ploughshares for gaffs, their tillage for fishing, this was still their home.

The work of the women changed little, except that fish was found more frequently in the pot that held sway over the hearth. Otherwise, the cooking traditions of Acadians endured—as they have these 300 years.

The rocky soil and harsher climate of settlements exposed to the sea permitted the growing of hardy vegetables like turnip, cabbage, and particularly potatoes, which the Acadians used in every possible way from the mundane to the imaginative. Buckwheat became the staple grain from which they made their bread and pancakes. Game, particularly wild rabbit or hare, added variety to meals based on the fruits of the sea, which were mainly cod, herring, and shellfish. Just as the British came to be beef eaters, the Acadians became known as fish eaters.

But forget the sauces on which Parisians and the Quebec French built their cuisines. Acadians preferred their fish simply prepared and unadorned. Boiled or, more properly, poached cod, seasoned with herbs, was the favourite dish. But there were two provisos: the fish must have same-day freshness, and it must never be overcooked.

Some Acadian dishes can be geographically located. Rappie pie, for instance, the favourite of Yarmouth County Acadians, is considered an atrocity in Cheticamp, where *fricot* is firmly established as the premiere dish. Even rabbit pies, still traditionally served on Christmas Eve after families return from midnight mass, have regional differences.

Between Digby and Yarmouth counties, you'll find a variation of the hamburger—the clamburger or quahog burger. Here and elsewhere, clams are king. Clam-pie suppers have long attracted tourists, though the pies have differed. Sometimes only clams and onions are baked in a two-crusted pie. Other variations call for potatoes to be layered with the clams and the inevitable onions, either under a single crust in a deep pie dish, or topped with biscuits. Where once salt pork, another Acadian essential, was rendered out and poured over the clams and onions, more often today margarine is dotted on the clams.

For pea soup, Acadians prefer a slab of salt pork over the traditional ham bone used in the Quebec version. The salt pork first has to be soaked overnight or boiled to remove the salt. But so much loved is the pork fat that it is often cut up and returned to the soup.

Poutine râpée is a traditional dumpling in which both grated and mashed potatoes are combined to form balls about the size of a snowball. A hole is punched into the centre so that a cube of freshened salt pork can be enclosed. They are then dropped into boiling water and cooked for two to three hours. They're eaten hot as a main course or side dish, or served with molasses for dessert.

Many Acadian dishes were born of frugality. Rappie pie and grated potato stew were actually spinoffs of starch making.

For rappie pie, potatoes are grated and squeezed through a cloth bag until all water and starch are removed. The liquid is then measured and replaced with the same amount of chicken broth, which is added to the grated potatoes. This potato mixture is cooked to a jellylike consistency, after which it is layered with cooked chicken and onions in a roasting pan. Pork fat or bacon is laid on top and the pie is baked for a couple of hours, until a golden crust forms.

This is only one version of rappie pie. Some have no meat at all; some have pork—fatty pork, both fresh and salt. Others have rabbit or seafood, particularly clams. And there are many Acadians who insist that molasses must be poured over rappie pie for the best possible taste treat.

Buttermilk pie is another Acadian delicacy that must be tasted to be believed. Here again we see Acadian ingenuity. The pie was a by-product of butter making. With so much buttermilk to use up, some thrifty cook decided to try to bake it in pastry, with egg yolks, sugar, butter, and a little flour to thicken it. The pie can be covered with meringue or not, according to regional preferences.

In 1860, when Cunard steamships crossed regularly between England and Nova Scotia, the town of Halifax was rich with contrasts. Gracious country estates lined the shores of the Northwest Arm, but the downtown waterfront area, where many of the estate owners did their business, was crowded and rowdy. West Indians, Yankees, coopers, shipwrights, hawkers, and tradesmen filled the narrow streets. At night, the infamous grog shops and brothels, just under the slopes of Citadel Hill, came into their own.

If we had been invited to dine at one of those gracious and elaborate homes, perhaps the one belonging to Samuel S. Cunard of steamship fame, we would have arrived a little before the fashionable dinner hour of 8 p.m. The menu that night might have featured Cornish hen, with a subtly spiced Osborne (rice) stuffing, Potatoes Melbourne (baked potatoes stuffed with cheese), green beans, and cauliflower. As starters, we might have enjoyed a parslied pâté and a light vegetable soup. In harmony with the reigning Queen Victoria's love for sweets, there would have been a variety of desserts, possibly Royal Blueberry Tarts, Strawberry Chantilly, or Crème Caramel Custard (despite its name, Crème Caramel had English origins).

Here we are, 130 years later, and nothing has changed. That menu could be offered at one of Halifax's better hotels or restaurants today, or even prepared at home to serve to guests.

Even as the elite were enjoying their Cornish hens, the soldiers would be dining in their own fine style. They might start with Hotch Potch, a delicious Scottish soup with a chicken base and fresh vegetables. The second course might be poor man's meat or potato pie (although, if judged by the amount of meat, it might today pass for Rich Man's Pie). And, always loyal, the Queen's servants would sweetly end their repast with a selection of pastries, including Edinburgh Tarts, Coburg Cakes, and Petticoat Tails.

Today the tradition continues, not in the barracks, but in the pubs of greater Halifax, where meat pies and more particularly fish and chips are ongoing favourites.

While youngsters of my day may have enjoyed a hot dog at the Sunday-school or Arbour Day picnic, it was at the corner fish-and-chip shop that we left most of our dimes. In exchange for that little coin, we could either walk out with a small cooked lobster or a brown paper cone of piping hot chips (today we call them fries). These would be topped with a good-sized piece of battered deep-fried fish.

With the onset of the 1950s, however, two completely diverse trends were under way and growing. One was the displacement of the little fish-and-chip shops by the large fast-food chains, most of which were flogging that upstart, the hamburger. The other was the health-food craze that placed fried foods at the top of a long list of no-nos.

Today another message is in the air: "Enough is enough! Give us back our fish and chips, our sausage rolls, our comfort foods of a generation ago." As if in answer to these pleas, fish-and-chip shops are opening again. What's more, that lowly Cockney fare is probably the most popular choice in upscale O'Carroll's Restaurant in downtown Halifax.

Other British specialties are available, both in restaurants and in the frozen-food sections of some supermarkets. This is because of one part-time baker who wanted his children to know and love true Scottish fare. Martin Coyle, a first-generation Scot Canadian, turns out authentic Scottish pies (having exchanged the original mutton for today's tender Nova Scotia lamb). He also makes Melton Mowbray or raised pork pies, Forfar Bridies, Wee Bridies, and, for Burns Night only, that "chief of the puddin' race," haggis. The tradition continues.

Looking back again, this time to the middle-class homes of mid-nineteenth century Halifax, we see that women planned their meals according to Isabella Beeton's *Book of Household Management.* Roast beef and Yorkshire pudding reigned over the Sunday dining table. The next day shepherd's pie followed. Trifle, or Tipsy Cake, and Charlotte

Russe—the more fruit, cake, and wine in it the better—might be the Sunday special dessert, while on other days Maids of Honour, lemon cheese tarts, and puddings soothed the perennial sweet tooth.

Today roast beef is still worthy of being called sir(loin) or even king. And trifle continues to hold sway at the Sunday buffets of leading hotels and private clubs, as well as in the dining rooms of British war brides, who have done much to perpetuate the cooking styles of home.

Lavinia Parrish Zwicker, though more of a baby boomer than a war bride, has built a successful business on the recipe for Olde English Pudding that her grandmother brought with her from England. "She served her culinary creation like a true artist, with grace and pride, delighting all those who sat at her table," Lavinia proudly says of her grandmother. The tradition carried on through Lavinia's mother, then was ceremonially passed on to the third Canadian generation, along with a pudding pot and cloth bag, when Lavinia came of age.

Among the wealthy and influential of Halifax were shipowners, merchants, bankers, and lawyers, who had emigrated from New England soon after the town was founded in 1749. Miles away, on the fertile farms left vacant when the Acadians were expelled, Puritan Planters were arriving to rebuild the lives they had lived in New England. Starting in 1760, and for ten years after, they established sixteen new townships, several of which were in the Annapolis Valley. By then, half the population of Nova Scotia had New England origins.

Having carried with them their colonial habits, both religious and culinary, they sowed seeds in these townships whose harvest has remained constant through two centuries. It was the Planters who brought the seedlings for the apple orchards that eventually became the basis of one of Nova Scotia's leading industries. When the best of the apples, the old-fashioned Gravenstein, comes into season, the time is ripe in Nova Scotia for luscious apple pies. Once you've had the taste of Gravenstein apple pie, you'll shudder as I do to see people slicing Granny Smiths into a pastry shell.

The New England element was further enhanced by the influx of the United Empire Loyalists, many of whom were educated men of generous means. More than 20,000 Loyalists came around 1783 to settle in mainland Nova Scotia. Again the population doubled. But all at once! And without provisions. There were so many mouths to feed.

The main difference between the Planters and the Loyalists was that the Planters arrived in small numbers and settled on cleared lands, while the Loyalists, with their vast numbers, had to carve their farms from the forests. The Planters were soon harvesting vegetables and fruits, occasionally killing a hen or butchering a pig for meat. But many of the Loyalists had long to depend on the government rations of cornmeal, salt fish, hard biscuit, and molasses, with only an occasional taste of salt pork and dried apples. These they augmented with what could be obtained from the forests, the sea, lakes, and rivers.

Both groups of New Englanders, as well as those Loyalists who came from farther down the eastern coast, as far south as the Carolinas, have left a strong legacy to the Maritimes. Down-home cooking, pure and simple, is the food on which later generations cut their teeth.

It is difficult to separate Maritime cooking from that of New England, since much of it is from the same chowder pot. Later, when Fanny Farmer came of age, it was her cookbook over any other that rural women turned to. The "Boston States" were so much closer and more familiar than Britain.

So it is that the perfect fish, seafood, or clam chowder becomes a matter of individual or regional taste. One tiny, unpretentious roadside dockside café in Chester Basin has developed a large clientele who come just for the seafood chowder. It's piled to the top with lobster pieces big enough to see and bite into, whole scallops, shrimp, mussels, and white-fish fillets. It's not an appetizer—it's a meal. Many first-timers make the mistake of ordering an entree, as well.

Corn, fresh from the cob or ground into meal for breads, puddings, johnnycakes (only the cornmeal mush is passé), is closely associated with those of New England background. Once declared the "chief food of man and beast," corn continues to be a major crop in the Annapolis Valley. Corn also sweetens the Nova Scotia chowder pot.

Anadama Bread, often called Yankee Bread, contains cornmeal. But this loaf comes in second to Porridge or Rolled Oats Bread. It, more than any other recipe, in my opinion, represents the Province of Nova Scotia.

Those other New England staples, baked beans and brown bread, became in Nova Scotia, as in the American colonies, the traditional Saturday-evening meal. Enough would be made to serve again for

Sunday breakfast. A renewed interest in dried beans and legumes is bringing them back.

To the New Englanders we owe the tradition of Thanksgiving. Sometimes called Harvest Home, it was a time for gathering the family together, attending the special thanksgiving service, and feasting around a table laden with the fruits of the field. Then, as now, turkey, cranberry sauce, and pumpkin figured prominently in this festive meal.

Perhaps more than any other food, Nova Scotians of New England ancestry are generous with desserts. I loved to have breakfast at my Aunt Helen's. Country-fresh eggs and pan-fried potatoes, toast and homemade jam, and anything left from the Saturday baking: doughnuts, Fat Archies, ginger snaps, Boston cream pie, and the seasonal fruit pie—rhubarb, strawberry, peach, blueberry, apple, pumpkin, mincemeat. Aunt Helen's, in the Valley, was a good place to be.

Eastern down-home cooking cannot be covered in a single paper. Even more impossible would be the documentation of Canadian cuisine in one volume. Our cooking heritage, endowed by our forebears, is as wide and varied as the country itself. But, whether it be Wee Bridies or perogies, rappie pie or cabbage rolls, sour dough or porridge bread, saskatoon pie or blueberry grunt, it all boils down to Canadian cuisine.

Marie Nightingale has been the food writer for the *Chronicle-Herald* and the *Mail-Star*, Halifax's leading newspapers, for the past twelve years. A passionate Nova Scotian, she spearheaded the Joseph Howe Festival, and is the author of two cookbooks. Her first, *Out of Old Nova Scotia Kitchens*, was an all-time best seller. In 1993, she published her second cookbook, *Marie Nightingale's Favourite Recipes*, a collection of comfort-food recipes that represent Nova Scotian cooking at its best.

DAVID LEWIS
MIKE WARREN

The Groundfish Crisis in Atlantic Canada

FISHING the bounty of the sea has been a traditional—and in many cases the sole—means of sustenance for coastal communities in Atlantic Canada. In Newfoundland, for hundreds of years, the harvesting of codfish has been the backbone of the economy and the lore of Newfoundland culture. The largest stock of cod in Atlantic Canada is northern cod, and Newfoundland fishermen have harvested on average 250,000 to 300,000 metric tonnes annually since the early 1800s. However, the catastrophic decline of the northern cod stock during the 1980s culminated in a fishing moratorium imposed in July of 1992. For the first time in Newfoundland's history, fishermen could not participate in the fishery industry that had been established in hundreds of communities in Newfoundland and Labrador.

The most recent scientific assessment of all species of Atlantic groundfish paints a disheartening picture. The general designation "groundfish" refers to fish that inhabit the bottom feeding areas of the ocean banks and shelves. In large part the life cycle of these fishes (that is, feeding, nursing, resting, spawning, growth, and migration) tends to occur near the bottom. Common groundfish species are cod, redfish, haddock, pollock, and such flatfishes as American plaice, yellowtail flounder, witch flounder, and Greenland halibut (turbot).

In the southern Gulf of St. Lawrence, cod stocks are at their lowest observed levels. The spawning stock biomass (the total weight of all sexually mature fish, usually seven years of age) in that area dropped from 249,000 tonnes in 1986 to 63,000 tonnes in 1993. The spawning cod biomass on the Scotian Shelf off southeast Nova Scotia declined from 100,000 tonnes in 1986 to a mere 14,000 tonnes in 1993. Southern Scotian Shelf stocks of cod and haddock have been subjected to such intense fishing that the federal government's Fisheries Resource Conservation Council (FRCC) stated that "less than 50 percent of the fish alive at the beginning of the year are still alive at the end of the year." The status reports presented by the Fisheries Resource Conservation Council in June 1994 revealed that all fish stocks either remain at low levels or continue to decline.

Of the Atlantic provinces, Newfoundland has been the most severely affected by the recent declines in fish stocks. Newfoundland fishermen have on average harvested more than 50 percent of all the groundfish landed in the Atlantic region. To put the present resource crisis in perspective, in 1982 some 302,000 tonnes of cod were landed in Newfoundland (192,000 tonnes of northern cod), with total groundfish landings of 418,000 tonnes—this compared with total Atlantic Canada groundfish landings of 694,000 tonnes. In 1993, however, only 37,000 tonnes of cod were landed (no northern cod), and Newfoundland groundfish landings totalled 97,000 tonnes. The entire Atlantic Canada groundfish landings in 1993 amounted to 240,000 tonnes. Moreover, in 1960 the spawning stock biomass of northern cod was estimated at 1.8 million tonnes. In the latest scientific advice released in June of 1994, that biomass has continued to decline from the low of 22,000 tonnes in 1993. This is less than 1.5 percent of the 1960 estimate!

The question now being asked is whether the northern cod stock is biologically capable of regenerating given natural mortality (estimated to be 20 percent), predation, and the negative influence of cold water. A similar situation exists for American plaice on the southern Grand Banks. In 1981, the spawning stock biomass for this fish was near 180,000 tonnes. In 1993, it was reduced to approximately 25,000 tonnes. Parallels can be drawn for a number of other groundfish stocks throughout Atlantic Canada. These statistics make it painfully obvious that there has been a precipitous and catastrophic decline in the groundfish stocks traditionally harvested by Newfoundland and other Atlantic fishermen.

To understand the dynamics of the fisheries, one must have a general appreciation of the oceanography and physical features of the region. Most of Newfoundland's fisheries occur on fishing banks, and the most productive is the Grand Banks. Other important banks include the Hamilton Bank off Labrador, the St. Pierre Bank off Newfoundland's south coast, and Funk Island Bank and Belle Isle Bank off the province's east-northeast coast. Physically these banks are underwater plateaus that are extensions of Canada's continental shelf, a term given to the relatively shallow area of the ocean that extends from the land. This area varies in size from country to country, and is a good habitat for fish, especially for groundfish. The shelf drops off to the ocean depths and this is called the "continental slope." The Grand Banks of Newfoundland extend outward to the continental slope.

In 1977, Canada, along with other coastal states, adopted a 200-mile Exclusive Economic Zone (EEZ) through the Law of the Sea process. Within the 200-mile EEZ, Canada controls the fisheries and is responsible for managing the fish stocks in that zone. If other countries wish to fish in the EEZ, they must obtain approval from the Canadian government. If this approval is given, there are numerous restrictions—when they can fish, the type and number of nets they can use, and how long they can fish. Thus, the moratorium on fishing within the EEZ applies to foreign fishing boats and fleets.

Two prominent extrusions of the Grand Banks, the "Nose" and "Tail," occur beyond the 200-mile zone (figure 1). Fishing in these regions is regulated by the Northwest Atlantic Fisheries Organization (NAFO).

The range of the northern cod extends from the Grand Banks, north to the Hamilton Banks off Labrador, and encompasses the Funk Island Bank and Belle Isle Bank. This is an enormous geographical area of some 385,000 square kilometres. The water masses that influence the fisheries in the Newfoundland region are the cold (-1 to 3 degrees Celsius), nutrient-rich Labrador Current and the warm Gulf Stream (10+ degrees Celsius), originating in equatorial regions. These two water masses converge on the Grand Banks to produce the ingredients for exceptional fish production and the famous fog banks.

Cod biologists and oceanographers with the federal Department of Fisheries and Oceans have recently begun to analyse bottom and surface water temperatures in the region. It has been determined that the Cold Intermediate Layer, that layer of the ocean water less than zero degrees Celsius, has cooled somewhat over the past several years and its area has increased. The influence of cold water is hypothesized to cause fish to migrate to deeper water or entirely out of their normal distribution range. It is also hypothesized that the cold water may increase mortality on larval stages, increase physiological stress in adults, and impair spawning. Recruitment, which refers to the number of young fish (three to five years in age for cod) that are mature enough to be fished, may also be reduced. While there is much debate and scepticism within the scientific community on the part played by cold water in the decline of fish stocks, it has been determined that it is a factor in the recovery of fish stocks.

The scientific community, the fishing industry, and environmentalists have put forward many and varied positions in an attempt to identify the cause of the alarming reductions in fish stocks. There is general agreement that the main contributing factors are:

- foreign and domestic overfishing
- discarding small fish
- destructive technology
- overestimation of stock biomass leading to excessive Total Allowable Catches (TACs)
- the predatory and competitive influences of expanding seal herds
- poor science

While arguments are regularly presented for all of these, there is a consensus that foreign overfishing is a major contributing factor to the present declines in the cod and flatfish stocks on the Grand Banks. Between 1986 and 1993, foreign vessels caught approximately 850,000 tonnes more fish than they were permitted to by NAFO. On any day there are approximately seventy-five to a hundred large foreign factory trawlers fishing on the Nose and Tail of the Grand Banks and the Flemish Cap. In recent years, as many as 137 foreign vessels have been fishing in the area at any given time. Undertakings by Canada to rectify the present crisis through conservation measures such as the moratorium on the northern cod fishery, and drastic reductions in quotas for other Atlantic groundfish stocks, are in vain if foreign overfishing on the Nose and Tail of the Grand Banks is not curtailed.

The principal culprit in this ongoing activity is the European Union, specifically Spain and Portugal. In the past, these countries have consistently disregarded the fish quotas established by NAFO, as well as other conservation measures such as regulated mesh sizes in fishing gear. Another element of the foreign overfishing problem is fishing by countries who are not members of NAFO. This problem is further compounded by the reflagging of existing vessels to fly flags of convenience; once again, the main culprits are Spain and Portugal. These vessels are not obliged to comply with the terms of the NAFO convention and their harvesting is now a substantial component of the overall overfishing effort.

The Achilles' heel of Canada's 200-mile EEZ is that it creates an arbitrary line that does not encompass the bounds of the ecosystems, and is not respected by migrating fish. While the 200-mile EEZ does encompass the bulk of the Grand Banks and the major fish stocks located therein, it is fundamentally flawed because it excludes the Nose and Tail. These two relatively small protrusions of the Grand Banks, comprising an area of approximately 45,000 square kilometres, occur outside the 200-mile limit and serve as the spawning and nursing grounds for a variety of groundfish. In the case of northern cod, during certain times of the year large aggregations of prespawning northern cod concentrate on the Nose and have been subjected to intensive fishing pressure by foreign fleets. While only approximately 5 percent of the northern cod stock, on average, is confined to this region during spawning, the stock has experienced high fishing mortality.

Continued overfishing by foreign fleets, and the harvesting and discarding of undersized fish, can only lead to the ultimate extinction of the stocks that straddle the 200-mile limit. This will have serious implications for fisheries within the Canadian zone.

In order to bring about change in the time frame necessary to ensure the long-term health of the straddling stocks, it is evident that a different strategy must be adopted. Canada has begun to bring the problem of overfishing to the international arena. During the Earth Summit, sponsored by the United Nations in 1992, Canada pressed for—and got—recognition of the problem and the measures necessary to address foreign overfishing. In response to the negative media attention that was anticipated by Spain and Portugal stemming from this international gathering, it is Newfoundland's view that elements of the Spanish and Portuguese fleets were removed from the regulatory area as a token gesture, only to return again. In response to the continued decline in fish stocks and the lack of action on the part of several countries, Canada has been forced to take more drastic measures to protect fish stocks on the Grand Banks. These have included arresting foreign vessels fishing on the Grand Banks just beyond Canada's 200-mile limit.

While initiatives are being undertaken on the international front, Canada, through its Fisheries Resource Conservation Council, has recognized that fishing mortality on fish stocks under Canadian jurisdiction have also been excessive. Difficult and drastic cuts to quotas have occurred. The repercussions throughout the industry and within communities along coastal Newfoundland and throughout Atlantic Canada have been devastating. The first of these measures, which preceded the formation of the FRCC, was the two-year moratorium on the northern cod fishery, announced on 2 July 1992. Following recent scientific advice, the moratorium has been extended until possibly the late 1990s. Groundfish fisheries in the Gulf and Scotia-Fundy areas have also been closed. Additional plant closures and a mass displacement of fishermen and plant workers can be expected, with serious economic and social consequences.

The plight of groundfish stocks in Atlantic Canada, and particularly the collapse of the northern cod fishery, has cast a dark cloud over the fishing industry and economy in the Province of Newfoundland. However, while the groundfish industry is reeling from severe resource shortages, there are several bright spots in the fishing sector. Shellfish species such as lobster, crab, and shrimp appear quite stable and landings have increased in recent years. These species are offering limited opportunities to some fishermen and plants that have suffered from the absence of cod. Pelagic species, highly migratory fish found in the upper water layers, such as herring and mackerel, appear healthy. With new markets and improved handling and processing technologies, these fisheries can provide greater economic opportunity.

Recent initiatives are focussing on such underutilized species as Icelandic scallop, Stimpson surf clam, grenadier, skate, spiny crab, and sea urchin. In addition, the Newfoundland aquaculture industry is growing at an encouraging pace, centred largely on Atlantic salmon, steelhead trout, blue mussels, Arctic char, and sea scallops. Cod enhancement is a novel concept that is receiving serious attention, as well. In response to the lack of raw material, the processing sector is also aggressively pursuing sources of groundfish from elsewhere in the world; fish plants now process fish from as far away as Alaska and the Barents Sea.

Nevertheless, despite these opportunities, the groundfish fishery will remain the engine of the Newfoundland fishery. As indicated, the groundfish fishery in Newfoundland is in grave condition and the present resource situation can only be reversed through effective stock rebuilding measures. In this context, the Government of Newfoundland and Labrador is seeking a more direct participation in fisheries management, which to date is dominated by the federal government.

The fishing industry and the economy of rural communities in Newfoundland and many parts of Atlantic Canada are in the midst of some extremely difficult times. The livelihood of thousands of fishermen and plant workers is hanging in the balance. Governments will be faced with the enormous task of providing the appropriate policies and response programs to facilitate social and economic adjustment within the region. One enduring characteristic of those who reap the "Northern Bounty" in the face of the hardships offered by the Northwest Atlantic is resiliency. Future bounties can only be secured, however, if the appropriate public policy measures are taken to rebuild and sustain seriously depleted fish stocks. For its part, the Government of Newfoundland and Labrador remains fully committed to the principles of effective resource management and sustainable fishing practices.

David Lewis worked for the Department of Fisheries, Food and Agriculture, Government of Newfoundland and Labrador from 1990 until

April, 1994. During this time he was responsible for administrative and supervisory activities related to the development, implementation and evaluation of comprehensive policies and programs for the fishing sector. **Mike Warren** has been employed for the past nine years with the Department of Fisheries, Food and Agriculture in the position of Fisheries Planning Supervisor.

HEATHER MACKENZIE

The Taste of Nova Scotia:

Marketing Regional Cuisine

THE TASTE OF NOVA SCOTIA is a province-wide restaurant marketing program that highlights Nova Scotia's many and varied food products, and, as well, markets our province as a "food destination." This unique foodservice marketing program is quality based, membership driven and works co-operatively with both the private sector and the government.

The experience of restaurateurs Jim and Donna Laceby, a husband and wife team, and members of the program, attests to the success of this venture. Donna Laceby operates the Amherst Shore Country Inn, overlooking the Northumberland Strait. It offers a daily dinner menu built around seasonal products and new local dishes such as Potato and Curry Soup with Red Oak Lettuce, Oven Steamed Salmon, and Raspberry Meringue Cheesecake. In Wolfville, Jim Laceby operates the Blomidon Inn, a restored nineteenth-century sea captain's mansion and has also built his menu around local products and dishes. Both properties have benefitted from the program as proved by an increase in the number of customers coming through their doors with the *Taste of Nova Scotia Dining Guide* in hand.

The Taste of Nova Scotia program was launched in 1989. The

program was designed to fulfil these main objectives: to raise the awareness and provide new uses for our quality local food products, and to promote the restaurants who utilized these foods on their menus. We also wanted to give both locals and visitors a truly Nova Scotian dining experience. The Nova Scotia departments of Tourism and Culture, Agriculture and Marketing, and Fisheries were all involved in the initial stages of development. Also instrumental in the formation of the program was the Nova Scotia Restaurant and Food-service Association, the Nova Scotia Chefs and Cooks Association and individual leaders in the foodservice industry. This group formed the Taste of Nova Scotia Steering Committee, which developed the criteria for the program.

Our culinary heritage combined with the harvests of our land and sea provides our chefs and cooks with an endless source of recipes and menu options. Nova Scotia has a wide variety of high-quality local products such as lamb, blueberries, pork, apples, asparagus, pumpkin, fresh herbs from the land and scallops, lobsters, mussels, oysters, sea urchins, and salmon from the sea. There are several micro-climates within the province which support, among other crops, three farm wineries. Two of these produce estate wines, while the third offers a variety of local fruit wines. Nova Scotia also has North America's only single malt distillery, in Cape Breton. The combination of traditional fishery catches with those of a growing aquaculture industry supplies a variety of fresh fish.

A wide range of products, from smoked salmon to cheese to European-style deli meats, have sprung from our natural resources. Often these products reflect our various cultural influences. The first English and French settlers in Nova Scotia discovered a sophisticated native Mi'kmaq culture which flourished on the fruits of the land and sea for 15,000 years before the settlers' arrival. Adding the influences brought by the Scots, Irish, Germans, Dutch, United Empire Loyalists and Blacks, Nova Scotia's rich culinary tapestry began to emerge. In the twentieth century, a new wave of immigrants from the Caribbean, Italy, Greece, the Middle East, Southeast Asia and India added to the ever-changing fabric.

Our favourite Nova Scotian recipes include traditional dishes such as blueberry grunt, seafood chowder, oatcakes, and rappie pie, as well as contemporary preparations of lobster, lamb, apples, and shark. Even in a province as small as Nova Scotia, there are distinctive pockets of regional cuisine. The South Shore is known for its German influence; the Annapolis valley area, known as the "breadbasket" of the province, has a strong French/Acadian cuisine, as does Cape Breton. Scottish influences are strong in both central Nova Scotia and Cape Breton. These influences all combine to fulfil the program's mandate of promoting Nova Scotia as a food destination with a long culinary heritage.

The Taste of Nova Scotia is a membership-based program founded on *quality* local foods, service, and hospitality. Each member restaurant must go through an assessment process to ensure that the quality criteria of the program are met. The criteria include use of local food products on their menus, quality of food preparation and presentation, professionalism in service, and the hospitality for which Nova Scotia is known. Current guidelines stipulate that at least six menu items or eighty percent of the menu must use food products found in Nova Scotia. Members are encouraged to purchase Nova Scotian food products when quality, freshness and availability are equal and price is competitive. Restaurants are also encouraged to reflect their area's cultural influences. After a restaurant has applied for membership, it is visited by two separate people incognito to ensure quality standards are met. The application must be approved by a membership committee made up of peers and final approval is given by the Board of Directors. But evaluation does not stop there: evaluators unknown to the establishment visit all members on a regular basis to ensure that quality standards are maintained.

The Taste of Nova Scotia program encourages member restaurants to provide their guests with comment cards, and our dining guide also includes these cards as a means of monitoring service. Our office receives thousands of comment cards every year from consumers who have dined at our member restaurants. These comment cards provide both the program and the individual restaurant measurable feedback, quickly pinpointing problem areas or areas of excellence.

The restaurant members in the Taste of Nova Scotia program offer a wide range of dining styles, from casual family dining to formal dining. They may include, for example, a take-out restaurant known to have served the best chicken burgers in the province for over 50 years, a small dining room found in a cosy inn, family-style restaurants, or formal dining establishments. They all have a common goal: each is committed to providing guests with a quality dining experience, using local food products.

The Taste of Nova Scotia program provides its members with information that will increase the awareness and use of local products. This may consist of sources of supply, storage and handling, or recipe suggestions. In providing this assistance, the program works directly with the actual producers, growers, processors, and distributors, facilitating the alliance between producers and end users. The program also encourages its membership to take advantage of staff training opportunities, in order to meet and exceed their guests' service expectations.

The program now has a steadily growing membership base which provides the foundation for the development of the marketing initiatives that promote the program's goals. The Taste of Nova Scotia markets locally, nationally, and internationally. Don Webster, who operates Thackaray's Restaurant & Bar and has been a member and supporter of the Taste of Nova Scotia from its inception, believes that the program provides members with a marketing edge. The quality standards that are enforced by the program ensure that visitors are not disappointed when they visit a member's operation. Moreover, visitors to the province can experience firsthand the essence of the province's cuisine. As a guest from Massachusetts wrote after visiting members, it was "the real thing and not an advertising gimmick."

Our key marketing tool is the *Taste of Nova Scotia Dining Guide*, which is distributed throughout the province. The guide gives general information about the trails (regions) of the province, the local foods, the cultural flavour, and recipes using local food products. Each member restaurant is listed by "trail" and the guide provides information on their location, house specialties, price range, hours of operation, and other points of interest.

The Taste of Nova Scotia program also works very closely with all types of media from print to television and has been featured in such publications as *Canadian Living* and *AAA*.

The Taste of Nova Scotia Society is now developing revenue-generating projects. One project was the *Taste of Nova Scotia Cookbook*, released in both Canada and the United States. This cookbook includes traditional and contemporary recipes featuring local cuisine, inns, chefs, and home kitchens. It gives readers insight into the people who produce and harvest our local foods and the cultural influences that have affected our culinary heritage.

The Nova Scotia Department of Agriculture and Marketing is currently developing a sister program, the Taste of Nova Scotia Quality Food Program, to showcase Nova Scotian food products for the retail and foodservice industries. This program will identify quality-branded Nova Scotian food products with the distinctive Taste of Nova Scotia logo at the grocery and/or specialty store level and other retail points such as Farmers' Markets. The two programs will work together to raise the awareness and use of local food products, both at home and abroad.

The Taste of Nova Scotia is a unique marketing program whose members are committed to providing their guests with a truly Nova Scotian dining experience. The program is young and growing and has endless opportunities in the future as it continues to market our province, its foods and people.

Heather MacKenzie is Executive Director of the Taste of Nova Scotia Society. She received her B.Sc. in Home Economics from Acadia University in 1973 and is a member of the International Culinary Professionals Association. She is also on the Board of Directors for the Nova Scotia Restaurant and Foodservice Association, and is a member of the Education and Training Committee for the Tourism Industry Association of Nova Scotia. Recent accomplishments include co-authoring the *Taste of Nova Scotia Cookbook.*

MENUS AND RECIPES FROM THE REGIONS

Canadian Menus and Recipes

NORTHERN BOUNTY, the conference in the fall of 1993, was a love feast. Canadians were ready for it! They descended upon Stratford, Ontario, from east and west, sharing recipes and ingredients, and *they ate together.*

The meals at the conference were spectacular events, created by some of Canada's greatest chefs, under the leadership of James Morris, co-director of the Stratford Chefs School. There was a public outcry for the menus and recipes from Northern Bounty the conference. That is why we have included this section in a book of papers about Canadian cuisine.

These recipes are unique! They reflect the regional character of Canada. We offer no substitutions for ingredients that can be found only in Vancouver or Halifax or places in between. The chefs who created these recipes used local, fresh ingredients and combined the traditional ways of preparing regional dishes for today's lifestyles. We have included a glossary of terms at the end of the recipe section should you wish to look up an unfamiliar ingredient.

We have not taken any shortcuts with the recipes. Chefs often say that they cook simple dishes. We know differently! The finished product may seem simple, but when it is examined, it is sometimes complicated enough to require the skill of a highly trained chef. One of our purposes in this section is to illustrate to readers how well-trained Canadian chefs are, and how greatly unappreciated. A chef's day begins early and ends late, because chefs are driven to please their customers and do their best. A great chef has a love of ingredients and how they work together. Chefs are the force driving our philosophy of *fresh* and *local* ingredients.

Appropriately, we begin with L'Ordre de bon temps, the first feasting society in the New World, founded by Samuel de Champlain, then move through the regions and menus that were part of the Northern Bounty conference.

Bon appétit!

The editors

L'Ordre de bon temps
The Order of Good Cheer

FOUNDED by Samuel de Champlain in 1606, the Order of Good Cheer became the first gastronomic society in the New World. Its purpose was to prevent the mysterious "land sickness" (scurvy), thought to be caused by ill-temper, idleness, and discontent. The French hoped that a winter of feasting and good times would be the best preventative medicine.

The setting for the Order of Good Cheer was the French Habitation in Port Royal, Nova Scotia. Surviving is this account of the feasting from Champlain's diary:

> We spent this winter very pleasantly, and had good fare by means of the Order of Good Cheer which I established, and which everybody found beneficial to his health, and more profitable than all sorts of medicine we might have used. This Order consisted of a chain which we used to place with certain little ceremonies about the neck of one of our people, commissioning him for that day to go hunting. The next day it was conferred upon another, and so on in order. All vied with each other to see who could do the best, and bring back the finest game. We did not come off badly, nor did the Indians who were with us.

During the feasts the French invited the Mi'kmaq chief Membertou and his followers to dine with them. The Mi'kmaq traditionally shared all of their food with whoever was in the vicinity, and from the Mi'kmaq the French learned the spirit of giving.

James Morris and Neil Baxter of the Stratford Chefs School created a dinner in the style of the Order of Good Cheer. A fairly good record exists of ingredients that would have been available in the fall of 1605, for most of the recipes they had to turn to French sources of that and other periods. Their goal was to recreate the general effect of an evening with the Order, rather than provide a meal that was historically correct. Morris and Baxter were guided by the knowledge that the members of the Order were quite sophisticated—Champlain was a visitor to the court of Henry IV, and one of the men's diaries mention roast meats from the cookshops of Paris. The diaries also provide much evidence of the French love for food and sauces, and we know that Champlain had ponds near the Habitation stocked with fish.

The Order of Good Cheer menu features products indigenous to Atlantic Canada: Jerusalem artichokes, shellfish, butternuts, and grapes. The recipes use popular regional cooking methods from that era in France—marinating and poaching, and pine-smoking. Prunes and Armagnac, regional products of France, and macaroons and cream puffs which were popular at the time, were also offered.

The Order did help to fend off illness during the winter, but more than anything else, its lasting benefit was the friendship between the Mi'kmaq and the French that continued for more than a hundred years. As others have found, the dining table is much better than a negotiating table for mediating conflicts between cultures. The spirit of the Order of Good Cheer is a culinary legacy to Canadians.

L'Ordre de bon temps
The Order of Good Cheer

*

Amuse gueule

Smoked Salmon Rolls with Fresh Salmon "Caviar"

*

Jerusalem Artichoke Soup

*

Maritime Seafood Salad

*

Roast Loin of Venison with Savory Wine sauce
Potatoes and Wild Mushrooms Boulanger
Roast Chestnuts, Butternuts, Fennel and Onions

*

Prune Tart with Armagnac Ice Cream

*

Petits Fours

Macaroons and Cream Puffs

SMOKED SALMON ROLLS WITH FRESH SALMON "CAVIAR"

1 lb.	cold smoked salmon	450 g
3½ sheets	leaf gelatin	3½ sheets
⅓ cup	fish stock	75 mL
2 Tbsps.	unsalted butter	25 mL
¼ tsp.	Tabasco sauce	1 mL
¼ tsp.	Worcestershire sauce	1 mL
1¼ cups	whipping cream (35%)	300 mL

Salt and freshly ground pepper, to taste
Salmon roe and fresh dill, for garnish

Chill all equipment, including bowl and blade of food processor.

Slice half the salmon into six 3 x 6 in. (7.5 x 15 cm) rectangles. Place each on piece of plastic wrap; refrigerate. Chop remaining salmon coarsely; set aside.

Soften leaf gelatin in a bowl of cold water until pliable, about 5 minutes. Warm fish stock in small saucepan. Drain and squeeze excess moisture from leaf gelatin; add to fish stock, stirring to dissolve completely. Refrigerate until cool, but not set.

Purée salmon chunks and butter in food processor until smooth. Do not overwork. Add fish stock, Tabasco and Worcestershire sauces. Process until blended. Transfer to large stainless-steel bowl. In separate chilled bowl, whip cream until it forms soft peaks. Fold half into salmon mixture. Fold in remainder. Season to taste with salt and pepper.

Spoon about 1 in. (2.5 cm) layer of salmon mousse into centre of each smoked-salmon rectangle. Roll slice salmon around the mousse with the help of the plastic wrap, until each edge meets. Twist ends of wrap tightly; chill rolls at least 1½ hours before serving.

To serve, unwrap rolls and place on chilled plate. Garnish with small spoonful of salmon roe and a sprig of dill.

Serves 6 as an appetizer.

JERUSALEM ARTICHOKE SOUP

This soup may be garnished with deep-fried parsnip chips made as you would potato chips.

2 Tbsps.	unsalted butter	25 mL
1	leek, white only washed and thinly sliced	1
1	celery stalk, thinly sliced	1
1	fennel bulb, thinly sliced	1
1 lb.	Jerusalem artichokes, peeled and thinly sliced	450 g
1	*bouquet garni* (bay leaf, thyme, and parsley)	1
6 cups	chicken stock	1.5 L
¼ cup	whipping cream (35%)	50 mL

Salt and freshly ground pepper, to taste
Parsnip chips, as needed, for garnish

Melt butter in a large, heavy-bottomed saucepan over medium heat. Add leek, celery, and fennel; cook, stirring, until soft but not brown. Add Jerusalem artichokes, *bouquet garni*, and chicken stock. Cover and bring to a boil; reduce heat and simmer until artichokes are tender. Let cool for 10 minutes. Remove *bouquet garni*. Add cream; purée in small batches until smooth. Return soup to pot; reheat gently. Season to taste with salt and pepper. Serve in warmed soup bowls, garnished with parsnip chips.

Serves 6-8.

ROAST LOIN OF VENISON WITH SAVORY WINE SAUCE

1 cup	olive oil	250 mL
½ cup	finely chopped carrot	125 mL
½ cup	finely chopped celery	125 mL
½ cup	finely chopped onion	125 mL
4	garlic cloves, minced	4
2	sprigs fresh thyme	2
2	bay leaves	2
3 lbs.	loin of venison, with bone	1.5 kg
2 Tbsps.	clarified butter	25 mL

Salt and freshly ground pepper, as needed
Savory Wine Sauce (recipe follows)

Make a marinade by combining olive oil, carrot, celery, onion, garlic, thyme, and bay leaves.

Remove venison loin from bone. Trim and discard fat and sinew. With cleaver, chop bone into 1 in. (2.5 cm) pieces. Reserve for sauce. Slice loin, against the grain, into 6 pieces about 2 in. (5 cm) in length. Arrange in single layer in deep, small casserole dish.

Pour marinade over venison. Cover; refrigerate 12-24 hours. Meanwhile, prepare the sauce (p.241).

To cook venison, remove pieces from marinade, pat dry, and sprinkle lightly with salt and pepper. Place sauté pan over high heat; add clarified butter. Sear venison quickly on all sides. Transfer entire pan to *preheated 400°F (200°C) oven* for 5-7 minutes or until cooked medium rare. Slice each portion thinly against the grain into 3-4 thin slices and serve with sauce.

Serves 6.

SAVORY WINE SAUCE

3 cups	beef stock	750 mL
2 Tbsps.	butter	25 mL
	Reserved venison bones	
¼ cup	minced shallots	50 mL
1	garlic clove, minced	1
1	sprig thyme	1
2	tomatoes, coarsely chopped	2
1 cup	dry red wine	250 mL
3 Tbsps.	sherry wine vinegar	45 mL
¼ cup	port	50 mL
2 Tbsps.	red currant jelly	25 mL

Salt and freshly ground pepper, to taste

Pour beef stock into saucepan. Bring to boil; reduce heat and cook, uncovered, until volume is reduced by half. Set aside.

Melt butter in large, heavy-bottomed saucepan over high heat. Add bones, brown quickly, stirring often. Add shallots, garlic, and thyme, cooking until soft and lightly coloured. Add tomato; cook several more minutes. Measure in red wine, sherry wine vinegar, and port. Bring to boil, cooking uncovered, until volume is reduced by half. Add concentrated stock and red currant jelly. Reduce heat to low, cover, and simmer for 1 hour, skimming as necessary. Remove from heat; strain and return to clean saucepan. Season to taste with salt and pepper. Refrigerate until needed. Reheat before serving.

Makes 1 1/2-2 cups (375-500 mL).

POTATOES AND WILD MUSHROOMS BOULANGER

⅓ cup	unsalted butter	75 mL
2 cups	sliced onions	500 mL
	Salt and freshly ground pepper, as needed	
2 Tbsps.	dried porcini mushrooms, soaked in water till soft and squeezed dry	25 mL
1 cup	sliced mushrooms	250 mL
3	large potatoes, peeled and thinly sliced	3
2 cups	well-flavoured chicken stock	500 mL

Melt 2 Tbsps. (25 mL) butter in sauté pan. Add sliced onion, sprinkling lightly with salt and pepper. Cook over medium heat until soft and lightly golden; set aside. In same pan, melt another 2 Tbsps. (25 mL) butter; add porcini and fresh mushrooms and sauté until golden. Add to reserved onions.

Arrange one-third potato slices in a buttered round 9 in. (22 cm) cake pan. Spread with half mushroom mixture. Sprinkle with salt and pepper. Top with another layer of potatoes; repeat layers, mushrooms, salt, and pepper. Add chicken stock to barely cover. Dot with remaining butter. Bake, uncovered, in *preheated 450°F (220°C) oven* for 60-75 minutes or until a golden crust forms. Every 5 minutes during baking, press top of potatoes with spatula to keep boulanger compact. Keep warm. Slice into wedges to serve.

Serves 8.

ROASTED CHESTNUTS, BUTTERNUTS, FENNEL, AND ONIONS

½ lb.	fresh chestnuts	225 g
⅓ cup	unsalted butter	75 mL
½ cup	chicken stock	125 mL
1 cup	sliced carrots	250 mL
½	celery root, peeled and sliced into ½ in. (1 cm) pieces	½
	Salt and freshly ground pepper	
3	sprigs fresh thyme	3
16	pearl onions	16
1 tsp.	granulated sugar	5 mL
½	fennel bulb, thinly sliced	½
¼ cup	butternut halves	50 mL

With a sharp knife, make a small X-shaped incision through the shell on the bottom of each chestnut. Cook in boiling water for 3 to 4 minutes. Drain and peel.

Over medium heat, melt 2 Tbsps. (25 mL) butter in large sauté pan. Add chestnuts, shaking pan to coat with butter. Add chicken stock; bring to a boil. Transfer pan to *preheated 400°F (200°C) oven* and bake, uncovered, basting frequently, until almost all liquid is absorbed and chestnuts are tender, about 20-25 minutes. Set aside.

Cut 2 large squares of aluminium foil. Place carrots in centre of one and celery root in centre of other. Sprinkle each lightly with salt and pepper. Add thyme and 1 Tbsp. (15 mL) butter to each. Seal tightly; place on baking sheet; bake for 40 minutes or until vegetables are tender and lightly caramelized. Remove vegetables from foil, discard thyme, and set aside to cool.

Make an X incision in the base of each onion. Bring a small saucepan of water to a boil; add onions. Cook for 1 minute, drain, and rinse in cold water. Peel onions, trimming any roots, but being careful not to trim off the root end. Transfer to large saucepan; sprinkle with sugar, salt, and pepper; cover and cook, over low heat, for 20 minutes, shaking pan occasionally. When tender add fennel; continue to cook until tender. Add butternuts, chestnuts, carrots, and celery root. Gently reheat, stirring carefully. Correct seasonings.

Serves 8.

PRUNE TART WITH ARMAGNAC ICE CREAM

The Filling

½ cup	pitted prunes	125 mL
2 Tbsps.	Armagnac	25 mL
1 cup	seedless Lexia raisins	250 mL
1 cup	water	250 mL
¼ cup	brown sugar	50 mL
1 tsp.	orange rind	5 mL
1 Tbsp.	lemon juice	15 mL
2 Tbsps.	orange juice	25 mL
3 Tbsps.	butter	45 mL

The Almond Cream

⅓ cup	unsalted butter	75 mL
½ cup	ground almonds	125 mL
½ cup	icing sugar	125 mL
2	eggs	2
1 Tbsp.	rum	15 mL
2 Tbsps.	pastry flour	25 mL
1	chilled unbaked 9 in. (22 cm) pastry shell in French tart pan	1

4	sliced pitted prunes, as garnish	4

Soak prunes in Armagnac overnight. Purée coarsely in food processor or blender. Set aside.

Combine raisins, water, brown sugar, and orange rind in stainless-steel saucepan. Cover, bring to boil; reduce heat and simmer for 10 minutes or until raisins are soft. With slotted spoon, remove raisins; set aside. Add lemon and orange juice to saucepan, cooking, uncovered, until the consistency of syrup (about 3 Tbsps./45 mL). Remove from heat; whisk in butter, prune purée, and soaked raisins.

Almond creme: in separate bowl, cream unsalted butter until fluffy. Beat in ground almonds and icing sugar. Whip in eggs, one at time, beating hard after each addition. Stir in rum and flour.

Spread prune filling on bottom of tart shell, smoothing the top. Cover evenly with almond cream and garnish with slices of pitted prunes.

Bake in *preheated 375°F (190°C) oven* for 30 minutes or until skewer inserted into the centre of the tart comes out clean. Let cool before serving with a scoop of Armagnac ice cream.

Serves 8.

ARMAGNAC ICE CREAM

4 cups	whipping cream (35%)	1 L
1½ cups	half-and-half cream (10%)	375 mL
12	egg yolks	12
1¼ cups	granulated sugar	300 mL
½ cup	Armagnac	125 mL

In a heavy saucepan, heat whipping cream and half-and-half until boiling. Vigorously whisk together eggs yolks and sugar in separate bowl. Slowly whisk in half of the hot cream. Return entire mixture to saucepan and cook, stirring constantly, over medium heat, until thick enough to coat a spoon. Strain, cover, and cool, stirring occasionally. Blend in Armagnac, transfer to ice-cream maker and freeze according to manufacturer's instructions.

Makes 2 quarts (2 L).

A Quebec Country Inn

IN A LIFETIME even the most intrepid traveller will stumble on only a handful of special, unspoiled places, those that smack of character; sites that eventually will deserve an historic marker. Hotel L'Eau à la Bouche is one, a superb little inn and restaurant sprawled across a hillside in Ste-Adèle. Here is tradition in the making, a new interpretation of Quebec's cuisine.

Pierre Audette and Anne Desjardins, a husband-and-wife team, opened L'Eau à la Bouche as a tiny restaurant thirteen years ago. Leaving their academic lives far behind, Pierre waited on tables, while Anne cooked and washed dishes (only on Saturdays did she hire a dishwasher). She created wonderful dishes with the customary ingredients of old Quebec. Quail, *foie gras*, sweet root vegetables, tender piglet (*cochonnet*), fresh Atlantic salmon, lamb, and goose all find their way through Anne's creative kitchen.

Here are a selection of recipes from L'Eau à la Bouche . . . a superb taste of the Laurentians and a great introduction to *la cuisine régionale au Québec.*

A Quebec Country Inn

*

Anne Desjardins, Chef
Hotel-Restaurant L'Eau à la Bouche
Ste-Adèle, Quebec

*

Escalopes of Fresh Atlantic Salmon
in a Phyllo Crust
with Fennel-infused Beurre Blanc
and Fennel Compote

*

Roasted Rack of Pork in a Sherry,
Thyme-perfumed Pear Sauce
Wild Rice

*

Hazelnut and Laurentian Maple Mousse Cake

*

Coffee and Sweets

ESCALOPES OF FRESH ATLANTIC SALMON IN A PHYLLO CRUST WITH FENNEL-INFUSED BEURRE BLANC AND FENNEL COMPOTE

1	large fennel bulb	1
1 cup	unsalted butter	250 mL
1¼ cups	dry white wine	300 mL
	Salt to taste	
1½ lbs.	Atlantic salmon fillet, skinless and boneless	750 g
4	sheets phyllo pastry	4
16	sprigs fresh fennel	16
2 Tbsps.	minced shallots	25 mL

Juice of ½ lemon
Additional fennel sprigs, for garnish

Wash fennel bulb. Cut stalks from bulb, reserving feathery leaves and bulb for compote. Chop stalks finely. In saucepan, melt ½ cup (125 mL) of the butter, allowing it to brown slowly. Add chopped fennel, cooking gently until soft and water has evaporated. With slotted spoon remove fennel and discard. Reserve butter.

Slice fennel bulb very thinly. In a heavy saucepan, simmer with 1/2 cup (125 mL) white wine until tender, about 3 minutes. Season with salt and 1 tsp. (5 mL) of the butter. Set resulting compote aside.

Slice salmon fillet diagonally into sixteen 1 in. (2.5 cm) thick portions. Cut each phyllo sheet into 4 rectangles. Brush each with fennel butter. Top with salmon escalope and fennel sprig. Wrap as you would a package. Brush with remaining fennel butter. Refrigerate until ready to bake.

Make Beurre Blanc Sauce by combining remaining wine and shallots in small saucepan. Bring to a boil and cook, uncovered, until liquid appears syrupy. Cut remaining butter into small cubes. Remove syrup from heat; whisk in butter a few pieces at a time. Season to taste with lemon juice and salt. Keep warm.

Bake salmon packets in *preheated 425°F (220°C) oven* for 6-10 minutes or until golden brown. Spoon sauce onto *warm* serving plates; top with salmon packets, garnishing with fresh fennel sprigs and Fennel Compote.

Serves 8.

ROASTED RACK OF PORK IN A SHERRY, THYME-PERFUMED PEAR SAUCE

8	small, sweet pears such as Seckel or *Poire de Cure*	8
	Juice of 1 lemon	
1 tsp.	unsalted butter, softened	5 mL
2 Tbsps.	minced fresh thyme	25 mL
3	garlic cloves, minced	3
¼ cup	minced shallots	50 mL
1 Tbsp.	Dijon mustard	15 mL
2	racks of *cochon du lait* —milk-fed suckling pig	2
1 tsp.	salt	5 mL
⅔ cup	dry sherry	150 mL
2 tsps.	sherry vinegar	10 mL
2 cups	veal stock	500 mL
½ cup	unsalted butter (second amount), chilled and cut into small cubes	125 mL

Fresh thyme, as needed, for garnish

Peel pears, leaving stems on. Carefully remove seeds by coring from bottom. Reserve peels and cores. Cover peeled pears with cold water and add lemon juice.

Mix together unsalted butter, 1 Tbsp. (15 mL) of fresh thyme, 2 of the minced garlic cloves, half the minced shallots, and Dijon mustard to make a "pommade." Rub onto the racks of pork and pears that have been patted dry. Place in roasting pan, sprinkle with salt, cover and bake in *preheated 425°F (220°C) oven* for 30-45 minutes or until internal temperature is 170°F (80°C). Remove meat and pears from pan; keep warm, loosely covered with foil.

On top of stove, heat roasting pan over medium, skimming any excess fat. Add reserved pear peels and cores, sherry, sherry vinegar, remaining shallots, and thyme. Cook, uncovered, for 5 minutes. Add veal stock and remaining garlic; bring to boil and cook 5 minutes longer. Strain into small pan. Whip in butter, a few pieces at a time, to create a smooth sauce. Season with salt to taste.

To serve, slice pork racks between each rib. Arrange 3 or 4 ribs on each plate and a baked pear. Garnish with fresh thyme.

Serves 8.

HAZELNUT AND LAURENTIAN MAPLE MOUSSE CAKE

Chef Desjardins serves slices of this cake in a pool of maple-sweetened apple compote and vanilla custard sauce. She garnishes the plates with apple chips she makes by thinly slicing an apple, dipping the slices into granulated sugar, and baking them at a high temperature in her convection oven until golden.

The Hazelnut Cake

¾ cup	finely ground raw hazelnuts	175 mL
2 Tbsps.	all-purpose flour	25 ml
2 tsps.	baking powder	10 mL

4	eggs, separated	4
¼ cup	granulated sugar	50 mL

The Mousse Filling

1 cup	dark maple syrup	250 mL
1 tsp.	gelatin	5 mL
6	egg yolks	6
1½ cups	whipping cream (35%)	375 mL
⅓ cup	warm apple jelly	75 mL

Stir together hazelnuts, flour, and baking powder. Whip egg whites until frothy. Whip in 2 Tbsps. (25 mL) sugar until stiff peaks form. In separate bowl, beat egg yolks with remaining sugar until thick and lemon coloured. Fold gently into egg whites. Sprinkle with hazelnut mixture, folding in until just blended and no dry spots remain. Spread evenly in an 8 in. (20 cm) parchment-lined, springform pan. Bake in *preheated 350°F (180°F) oven* for 30-35 minutes or until the top springs back when touched lightly. Cool.

In top of double boiler, combine maple syrup and gelatin. Let stand 5 minutes. Beat in egg yolks; place over rapidly boiling water. Cook, whisking constantly, until thickened. Cover; let cool. Whip cream until stiff; fold into cooled egg-yolk mixture.

Loosen cake from pan with sharp knife. Remove sides of pan, leaving cake on base. Split cake in half horizontally with sharp knife. Spread with warm apple jelly. Replace top. Transfer to larger parchment-lined 9 in. (22 cm) springform pan. Pour mousse over entire cake; cover, then freeze for at least 3 hours.

Serves 8.

An Ontario Feast of Fields

EVERY September the chefs of Knives and Forks, a coalition that links them with Ontario's organic producers, choose a meadow or a vineyard, dust off their portable stoves and grills, light an occasional bonfire, lug cartons and bins and boxes, tie on their aprons, and cook for the love of it. This Feast of Fields is a languorous two-mile-long Sunday stroll for roving gourmands, a celebration of Ontario's most unusual and finest ingredients, fine local wines, and brews.

The chefs of Knives and Forks are among Ontario's most accomplished culinarians, the organic producers among the most innovative. The Feast of Fields is their spirited statement in support of the organic movement and the celebration of organic food, and our collective dependence upon nature. All ingredients used for the occasion were either wild or organic.

In 1993, they chose to hold their gastronomic fair in the beautiful orchard of St. Ignatius College, just north of Guelph, a Canadian Jesuit-run 600-acre farm. This menu was drawn from that feast.

An Ontario Feast of Fields

*

Smoked Georgian Bay Splake
with Dilled Cucumber Sauce
Roman Trutiak

*

Multigrain Loaf
Uta Nagel

*

Sultan's Lamb Kebab
with Cape Gooseberry Chutney
Renée Foote

*

Yukon Gold Potato Fritters
Keith Froggett

*

Golden Beets and Grilled Onion Salad
Ellen Greaves

*

Apple, Grape, Elderberry,
and Black Raspberry Pie
Michael Stadtlander

SMOKED GEORGIAN BAY SPLAKE WITH DILLED CUCUMBER SAUCE

Roman Trutiak

2 Tbsps.	pickling salt	25 mL
¼ cup	granulated sugar	50 mL
2	8-10 oz./225-280 g fresh Georgian Bay splake fillets, skin on	2
1 Tbsp.	cracked black peppercorns	15 mL
⅔ cup	coarsely chopped fresh dill	175 mL

Sauce

¼ cup	chopped fresh dill	50 mL
½	English cucumber, grated	½
1 cup	plain yogurt	250 mL
2 Tbsps.	lemon juice	25 mL
1	clove garlic, minced	1

Mix salt and sugar. Place fillets, side by side, skin-side down. Sprinkle with salt mixture, coating evenly. Sprinkle with cracked peppercorns and dill. Layer one fillet on top of other, flesh sides together. Place in deep glass casserole. Cover tightly and refrigerate 4 hours.

Uncover fillets, gently removing dill and peppercorns. Rinse thoroughly under cold water; pat dry. Refrigerate fish, uncovered, for an hour to dry surface. Place fillets on top rack in smoker and gently smoke 6-8 hours over wood of your choice.

Stir together dill, cucumber, yogurt, lemon juice, and garlic. Refrigerate until needed. Spoon sauce onto smoked fillets.

Serves 8.

MULTIGRAIN LOAF
Uta Nagel

1 cup	cracked rye or wheat	250 mL
½ cup	linseeds (flax seed)	125 mL
½ cup	oatmeal	125 mL
½ cup	millet	125 mL
1¾ cups	boiling water	425 mL
4-5 cups	organic bread flour	1-1¼ L
2 cups	light rye flour	500 mL
2 tsps.	salt	10 mL
2 Tbsps.	instant yeast such as Fermipan	25 mL
1½ cups	lukewarm water	375 mL

Combine cracked rye, linseeds, oatmeal, and millet. Cover with boiling water; let stand 30 minutes.

In a large bowl, stir together, bread flour, rye flour, salt, and yeast. Beat in water and grain mixture, mixing to make a soft dough. Turn out onto floured board; knead 10 minutes, adding additional flour as required to make a soft, but not sticky, dough.

Cover and let rise on counter, at room temperature, until doubled in bulk. Knead a second time for 5-8 minutes or until dough is elastic. Divide in half and place in lightly oiled 5 x 9 in. (12 x 22 cm) bread pans or shape into rounds and place on greased baking sheets. Cover; let rise until doubled and bake in *preheated 375°F (190°C) oven* for 40 minutes or until richly golden.

Makes 2 loaves.

SULTAN'S LAMB KEBAB WITH CAPE GOOSEBERRY CHUTNEY

Renée Foote

1 lb	organic boneless leg of lamb	450 g
1 Tbsp.	chopped fresh thyme	15 mL
2 Tbsps.	chopped fresh rosemary	25 mL
¼ cup	chopped fresh basil	50 mL
2	garlic cloves, minced	2
½ cup	olive oil	125 mL

Wooden skewers, as needed
Salt and freshly ground pepper

Slice lamb into 2 in. (5 cm) strips, making diagonal incisions halfway through each strip, while taking care not to cut the meat into chunks. Lay meat flat in glass dish. Sprinkle with thyme, rosemary, basil, and garlic. Drizzle with olive oil. Cover and refrigerate overnight.

While meat is marinating, soak wooden skewers in water.

To barbecue, thread meat onto skewers, sprinkle lightly with salt and pepper, and grill over hot coals for 5-7 minutes or until medium doneness. Serve with Cape Gooseberry Chutney.

Serves 4.

CAPE GOOSEBERRY CHUTNEY

Renée Foote

2	plum tomatoes	2
2	beefsteak tomatoes	2
1	white onion	1
2 Tbsps.	safflower oil	15 mL
2	prune plums, pitted and chopped	2
1	Bartlett pear, peeled, cored, and chopped	1
1½ tsps.	salt	7 mL
2 tsps.	cinnamon	10 mL
1 tsp.	black cardamom seed, crushed	5 mL
½ tsp.	cayenne pepper	2 mL
2 Tbsps.	honey	25 mL
2 Tbsps.	vinegar	25 mL
2 cups	cape gooseberries, hulls removed	500 mL
½	bunch of dill, chopped	½

Preheat barbecue. Brush tomatoes and onion lightly with oil. Grill until skins are charred and onion is tender. Remove from grill; peel and chop coarsely. Transfer to large heavy saucepan. Stir in plums and pear. Bring to boil over medium heat; reduce heat and simmer, adding salt, cinnamon, cardamom, cayenne, honey, and vinegar. Stir in cape gooseberries; cook until soft and beginning to wilt. Add dill. Keep warm until ready to serve with lamb.

Makes 4 cups (1 L).

YUKON GOLD POTATO FRITTERS

Keith Froggett

4 cups	water	1 L
1 Tbsp.	lemon juice	15 mL
4 cups	grated Yukon Gold potatoes) (about 3 medium	1 L
1	egg	1
3 Tbsps.	flour	45 mL
1 tsp.	baking powder	5 mL
2 Tbsps.	grated onion	25 mL
1 tsp.	salt	5 mL
¼ tsp.	white pepper	1 mL
¼ cup	vegetable oil	50 mL

In large saucepan, bring water and lemon juice to boil. Add grated potato; blanch 30 seconds. Drain and cool under cold, running water. Drain and squeeze dry. Place potato in medium-sized mixing bowl. Stir in egg, flour, baking powder, onion, salt, and pepper. *Preheat skillet over medium heat.* Add oil when hot and drop on spoonfuls of potato mixture. Sauté until golden on both sides.

Makes 12 fritters.

GOLDEN BEET AND GRILLED RED ONION SALAD

Ellen Greaves

1	large red onion	1
⅓ cup	vegetable oil	75 mL
3 Tbsps.	balsamic vinegar	45 mL
	Salt and freshly ground pepper, to taste	
16	small golden beets, 2-3 in. (5-7 cm) in diameter	16
⅓ cup	popcorn seedlings	75 mL

Fresh herbs, for garnish

Cut onion into six wedges, leaving on a bit of root to hold pieces together. Place in small glass bowl. Whisk together oil and vinegar; season to taste with salt and pepper. Pour over onion, cover and refrigerate overnight. Remove onion from marinade and barbecue until wedges begin to soften. Return to vinaigrette, allowing to cool to room temperature.

Boil beets in their skins until soft. Peel and cut into bite-sized pieces; toss with half the vinaigrette from onion. Let stand at room temperature for 2 hours.

To serve, fan onion out, piling it high with beets. Garnish with popcorn seedlings and other fresh herbs.

Serves 6.

APPLE, GRAPE, ELDERBERRY, AND BLACK RASPBERRY PIE

Michael Stadtlander

3 cups	sliced apples, peeled and cored	750 mL
1 cup	Concord grapes, seeded	250 mL
1	2 in. (5 cm) vanilla bean, split and scraped	1
¼ cup	elderberries	50 mL
½ cup	maple syrup	125 mL
½ cup	black raspberries	125 mL
	Unbaked pastry for double-crust 10 in. (25 cm) pie	
1	egg	1
1 Tbsp.	milk	15 mL
2 Tbsps.	maple sugar	25 mL
1 cup	apple cider	250 mL
1 cup	crème fraîche	250 mL

Combine apples, grapes, and vanilla bean in saucepan. Cook gently over low heat until apples are soft. Add elderberries and maple syrup. Remove vanilla bean; stir in black raspberries. Pour filling into unbaked pie shell. Cover with latticework top.

Beat together egg and milk; brush over exposed pastry. Sprinkle with maple sugar. Bake in *preheated 375°F (190°C) oven* for 30 minutes or until crust is golden.

In small saucepan, bring apple cider to boil. Cook, uncovered, until syrupy. Brush over warm pie. Serve with crème fraîche.

Serves 8.

Cantonese City Style at Rundles

VISITORS to Canada are surprised to find Chinese restaurants in every city and town, and in nearly every tiny village across the country. These restaurants are the legacy of the Cantonese who first came here more than one hundred years ago to seek gold and find employment on the railways. When there was no more work in the mines and on the railways they took whatever jobs they could find. Though not trained to be cooks, many opened restaurants and their cuisine was home-style, country Cantonese. They adapted their recipes to the ingredients available to them and to suit the tastes of their Canadian clients. Descendants of these original immigrants still own most of the popular "chop suey" restaurants offering Chinese cuisine in Canada today.

With a second wave of Chinese immigration after the second world war, another kind of Cantonese restaurant cookery, "city-style" cuisine, became available in Canada. Practised by the Cantonese chefs who came in this second wave, it is generally for a sophisticated and mainly Chinese clientele. The Chinese luncheon menu, developed by James Morris and Neil Baxter of the Stratford Chefs School represents this cuisine. The menu is based on recipes using Chinese produce grown in Canada, and fish and shellfish from our west coast. Crabmeat is popular with Canadians in general, but geoduck and sea cucumber are enjoyed more by Chinese-Canadians than by others. To remove the mystery of these new and unusual foods, we have included precise directions for preparing them.

Cantonese City Style at Rundles

*

Chinese Cold Cut Platter
A Variety of Chinese Sausage, Ham and Jellyfish

*

Sweet Corn and Crabmeat Chowder

*

Stir Fried Geoduck and Sea Cucumber
with Shanghai Bok Choi

*

Braised Black Cod
with Pork and Garlic in a Sand Pot

*

Yong Chow Fried Rice

SWEET CORN AND CRABMEAT CHOWDER

16 cups	water	4 L
2 Tbsps.	salt	25 mL
1	3 lbs. (1½ kg) dungeness crab	1
¼ cup	unsalted butter	50 mL
1	small onion, diced	1
¼ cup	diced carrots	50 mL
1	celery stalk, diced	1
½	sweet red pepper, diced	½
1	sprig thyme	1
2	sprigs parsley	2
1	bay leaf	1
8 cups	water	2 L

Salt and freshly ground black pepper

To prepare crab: In large stockpot, combine water and salt; bring to a boil. Submerge crab in water; boil 10 minutes. With tongs, remove crab; let cool enough to handle. Twist off claws. Push centre section of crab out and remove soft gills. Using a knife, cut claws and centre section into pieces and pry white crab meat out. Reserve flesh and shell pieces separately.

To make crab stock: Melt butter in a 6 quart (6 L) pot; add onion, carrots, celery, and pepper. Stew vegetables over low heat for 15 minutes, stirring occasionally. Increase heat, add thyme, parsley, bay leaf, and crab shell pieces. Sauté, turning often. Add water; cover and bring to a boil; reduce heat and simmer for 30 minutes. Strain and reserve crab stock, discarding shells, vegetables, and herbs.

The Soup

3 Tbsps.	unsalted butter	45 mL
1	yellow onion, finely diced	1
½ cup	water	125 mL

8 ears	fresh corn	8 ears
1-2 tsps.	salt	5-10 mL
¼ tsp.	freshly ground pepper	1 mL
pinch	cayenne pepper	pinch
2	ripe red tomatoes, peeled, seeded, and diced	2
3 Tbsps.	chopped fresh chervil	45 mL

Melt butter in an 8 quart (8 L) soup pot. Add onion and water. Cover pot and sweat onion for 10 minutes over low heat. Shuck corn and with sharp knife cut kernels from cobs. Reserve 1 cup (250 mL) of kernels. Add rest to soup pot. Pour in crab stock, bring to a simmer, and cook for 5 minutes. Remove from heat; let cool 10 minutes. Purée soup in batches in a blender for a full 3 minutes. Season with salt, pepper, and cayenne.

Add reserved crab, tomatoes, and corn to soup; reheat gently. Serve in warm bowls; garnish with chervil leaves and additional freshly ground pepper.

Serves 8.

STIR-FRIED GEODUCK AND SEA CUCUMBER WITH SHANGHAI BOK CHOI

For ease of preparation, this recipe is divided into sections. The sea cucumber should already be soaked at the grocery store.

The Sea Cucumber

6 oz.	sea cucumber	200 g
6 qts.	cold water	6 L
8	garlic cloves	8
10	slices fresh ginger	10

6	green scallions, cut into ½ in. (1 cm) pieces	6

Prepare the sea cucumber: In a saucepan, combine soaked sea cucumber, half the cold water, 4 cloves garlic, 5 slices ginger, and half the chopped scallions. Bring to a boil, reduce heat and simmer for 45 minutes. Drain and repeat, cooking sea cucumber until soft. Drain well, cool and slice 1/8 in. (0.3 cm) thick. Reserve.

The Geoduck

3 oz.	geoduck, fresh or frozen, trunk (neck) section	100 g
1 Tbsp.	salt	15 mL
½ tsp.	soy sauce	2 mL
½ tsp.	sugar	2 mL
½ tsp.	potato starch	2 mL
⅛ tsp.	white pepper	0.5 mL
1 Tbsp.	rice wine	15 mL
1 Tbsp.	sesame oil	15 mL

Prepare the geoduck: Rinse geoduck under hot running water; peel off skin. Cut open; rub center of trunk with salt, reserving 1/4 tsp. (1 mL). Wash and clean thoroughly. Cut geoduck into 1/8 in. (0.3 cm) slices. Mix together the 1/4 tsp. (1 mL) salt, soy sauce, sugar, potato starch, white pepper, rice wine, and sesame oil. Pour this marinade over geoduck. Reserve.

The Stir-fry

2 lbs.	baby bok choi	1 kg
8	fresh shiitake mushrooms,	8
¼ cup	vegetable oil	50 mL
2	thin slices fresh ginger root	2
2 Tbsps.	pale dry sherry	25 mL
½ tsp.	chili oil	2 mL
½ cup	well-flavoured chicken stock	125 mL

1 Tbsp.	light soy sauce	15 mL
2 Tbsps.	cornstarch	25 mL
2 Tbsps.	cold water	25 mL

Prepare the stir-fry: Separate baby bok choi leaves; carefully remove sand and soil. Blanch in boiling water for 30 seconds. Drain and set aside.

Remove stems from shiitake mushrooms and slice caps thinly. Set a wok on high heat; add vegetable oil. Sauté ginger root slices briefly; remove and reserve. Add shiitake mushrooms; stir-fry until lightly coloured, adding more oil if necessary. Add bok choi; stir-fry quickly. Swirl in sherry, chili oil, chicken stock, and soy sauce. Combine cornstarch and cold water; add to wok. Add sea cucumber and drained geoduck; simmer for 1 minute or until everything has heated through. Do not overcook or sea cucumber and geoduck will toughen. Serve on a heated platter.

Serves 6-8.

BRAISED BLACK COD WITH ROAST PORK AND GARLIC COOKED IN A SAND POT

A sand pot is an inexpensive clay pot with a lid that can be found in an Asian market. We used one that holds about 2 1/2 quarts (2 1/2 L). Before the sand pot can be used, it must be seasoned. To do this, soak the pot in cold water for 24 hours. Then rub the outside of the pot with oil to the height of the handles. Fill it with water and bring to a boil. Drain and the pot is ready for use.

The Cod Steaks

4	black cod steaks, about 6 oz. (175 g) each	4

½ tsp.	salt	2 mL
½ tsp.	soy sauce	2 mL
½ tsp.	sugar	2 mL
¼ tsp.	white pepper	1 mL
1 Tbsp.	rice wine	15 mL
2 tsps.	sesame oil	10 mL
¼ cup	potato starch	50 mL
3 Tbsps.	vegetable oil	45 mL

Arrange black cod steaks in shallow pan. Combine salt, soy sauce, sugar, white pepper, rice wine, and sesame oil. Pour over cod steaks; cover and refrigerate for 2 hours.

Lightly pat black cod dry; coat with potato starch. Add vegetable oil to sauté pan; place over medium-high heat. Sear cod quickly on both sides. Reserve.

The Braising Base

2 Tbsps.	vegetable oil	25 mL
4	cloves garlic, peeled and crushed	4
4	dried Chinese black mushrooms, soaked until soft and sliced	4
1 lb.	white radish (daikon), peeled and sliced into 1 in. (2.5 cm) wedges	450 g
1 Tbsp.	Chu-hou paste	15 mL
2 Tbsps.	rice wine	25 mL
1½ cups	well-flavoured chicken stock	375 mL
½ cup	Chinese barbecued pork	125 mL
2 tsps.	oyster sauce	10 mL
2 tsps.	dark soy sauce	10 mL
¼ tsp.	sesame oil	1 mL

Prepare the braising base: Heat a 4 quart (4 L) sauce pan. When hot add oil, garlic cloves, and black mushrooms. Fry for 1 minute or until lightly coloured. Add white radish; continue cooking for another 2 minutes. Add Chu-hou paste and rice wine. Stir and cook for 30 seconds and then pour in chicken stock. Bring to a boil; reduce heat and simmer for 30 minutes or until radish has softened but still has some firmness to it. Add Chinese barbecued pork, oyster sauce, dark soy sauce, and sesame oil. Simmer for 5 minutes.

Place layer of braising mixture (about ⅓) in sand pot; place 2 cod steaks on top. Add another layer of braising mixture, then last 2 cod steaks. Top with remaining braising mixture. Cover and bring to a boil over medium heat. Reduce heat; simmer cod for 10-15 minutes or until meat pulls away easily from bone.

Serves 4.

YONG CHOW FRIED RICE

1/2 cup	vegetable oil	125 mL
1	egg yolk	1
3	eggs	3
2 Tbsps.	water	25 mL
1	egg white	1
1 Tbsp.	pale dry sherry	15 mL
1/2 tsp.	sugar	2 mL
1 Tbsp.	tapioca powder	15
1 tsp.	sesame oil	5 mL
1	garlic clove, crushed	1
6	black mushrooms, soaked and finely diced	6
1/2 cup	diced barbecued pork	125 mL
3 oz.	shrimp, cooked and diced	100 g
6 cups	cooked rice	1.5 L
1/2 cup	chicken stock	125 mL

4	scallions cut into 1/4 in. (0.5 cm) lengths	4
	Salt and white pepper, to taste	
1 Tbsp.	oyster sauce	15 mL

Heat 1 Tbsp. (15 mL) of oil in a skillet. Mix together egg yolk and whole eggs with a fork. Pour into hot pan. Cook until set, flipping before bottom layer begins to brown. Remove from pan, let cool, and roll up jellyroll fashion. Cut into thin slices about 1/4 in. thick. Reserve.

In small bowl, whisk together water, egg white, sherry, sugar, tapioca powder, 1 Tbsp. (15 mL) vegetable oil, and sesame oil. Set a wok over high heat. When very hot, add 2 Tbsps. (25 mL) oil and garlic. Discard garlic when browned. Add mushrooms and pork; cook for 1 minute. Add shrimp; stir-fry for 30 seconds. Remove and reserve.

Rinse wok; wipe dry. Set over high heat, and when hot add remaining oil. Add rice and sherry mixture. Turn rice repeatedly to ensure even heating, 5-7 minutes. When heated through, pour in half of chicken stock along edge of wok and stir. When absorbed, add remaining stock; stir again. Add meat; mix with rice. Add scallions; season with salt and pepper. Stir in oyster sauce, garnish with egg, and serve.

Serves 6-8.

A Chuckwagon Hoedown

STAMPEDE! *The* event is the chuckwagon race—wagons dash pell-mell around a circle and at the finish line the cowboy "cook" jumps out to be the first to get a fire going. Visitors to Calgary have seen cattle roping and fancy riding, but few outsiders have had a chance to witness a *real* pit barbecue done in authentic western style.

First you need a backhoe! With this machine you can dig a hole big enough to accommodate several cords of wood. You must carefully select hard wood or apple wood—fence posts are acceptable, but *don't* use any treated or creosoted wood. The cords of wood are set afire and burned down to coals several feet deep. In the meantime, the pit boss prepares the beef. It is cut into large chunks about 10 to 15 pounds each, wrapped in butcher paper, then in wet burlap, and tied securely. When the fire is perfect (allow 4 hours for this), the packages of beef are tossed onto the coals—yes, directly onto the coals. Quickly the pit boss manoeuvres a piece of tin over the pit and, as quickly, covers the tin with dirt. Not a wisp of steam emerges. The pit boss we met, Harry Smith, told us that the secret of the pit barbecue is to not allow any oxygen in. Oxygen will fuel the coals and burn the meat. The beef is left to cook, while onlookers pass the time with a little rye whisky (allow 12 hours here). At last, when it is time to open the pit, be cautious. Amazingly, the bundles are intact and hardly charred. The beef is unwrapped, sliced, and put onto enormous platters. These join a table laden with baked beans, fresh bread, salads, pickles and relishes, and there should be sixty pies and twenty cakes.

Chuckwagon Menu

*

Spicy Barbecued Beef Ribs

*

Ranch-style Baked Beans

*

Creamy Cabbage Coleslaw

*

Light-as-air Buns

*

Homemade Pickles and Relishes

*

An Assortment of Pies

*

Gallons of Coffee

SPICY BARBECUED RIBS

1½ cups	corn syrup	375 mL
1 cup	ketchup	250 mL
½ cup	Worcestershire sauce	125 mL
2 Tbsps.	dry mustard	25 mL
2 tsps.	ground ginger	10 mL
1 tsp.	chili powder	5 ml
1/2-1 tsp.	Tabasco sauce	2-5 mL
1 tsp.	minced fresh rosemary	5 mL
2	cloves garlic, crushed and minced	2
5 lb.	beef short ribs	2.5 kg

In a glass jar, shake together corn syrup, ketchup, Worcestershire sauce, and mustard. Add ginger, chili powder, Tabasco sauce, rosemary, and garlic. Cover and shake to mix well. Refrigerate for 1 hour to blend flavours.

Place ribs *on preheated barbecue.* Grill slowly until the desired degree of doneness. Brush with sauce during last 30 minutes of barbecuing.

Serves 5-6.

RANCH STYLE BAKED BEANS

4 cups	dried white navy beans	1 L
12 cups	cold water	3 L
1 lb.	salt pork, sliced	500 g
2	onions, minced	2
½ cup	tomato paste	125 mL
1½ cups	brown sugar	375 mL

1 Tbsp.	dry mustard	15 mL
⅓ cup	fancy molasses	75 mL

Wash beans thoroughly. Place in large saucepan. Cover with cold water and soak overnight. Bring to boil; reduce heat and simmer, covered, 1 hour.

Line large roasting pan or bean pot with pork slices. Set aside.

Add onions, tomato paste, brown sugar, mustard and molasses to beans and stir. Pour into prepared pan. Cover and bake in *preheated 325°F (160°C) oven* for 4-4½ hours, adding water if necessary and stirring occasionally.

Serves 10-12.

CREAMY CABBAGE COLESLAW

3 cups	shredded green cabbage	750 mL
3 cups	shredded red cabbage	750 mL
1 cup	carrots, peeled and grated	250 mL
1 cup	diced celery plus leaves	250 mL
2	green onions, chopped finely	2
¾ cup	mayonnaise	175 mL
⅔ cup	sour cream	150 mL
1 Tbsp.	granulated sugar	15 mL
1 Tbsp.	cider vinegar	15 mL
2 tsps.	dried dillweed	10 mL
1 tsp.	celery seeds	5 mL

Salt and freshly ground pepper, to taste

In a large bowl, toss together green and red cabbage, carrots, celery, and onions. In a separate bowl, whisk together the mayonnaise, sour cream, sugar, vinegar, dillweed, and celery seeds. Season to taste with salt and pepper. Pour dressing over cabbage mixture and toss lightly to mix. Cover and refrigerate for about 1 hour to let the flavours blend.

Serves 8-10.

LIGHT-AS-AIR BUNS

2½ cups	warm water	625 mL
1 cup	granulated sugar	250 mL
2 Tbsps.	active dry yeast	25 mL
3	eggs	3
2 tsps.	salt	10 mL
1 cup	vegetable oil	250 mL
8 cups	unbleached all-purpose flour	2 L

Additional flour for kneading

In large bowl, combine ½ cup (125 mL) of the warm water with 1 tsp. (5 mL) of the sugar. Sprinkle yeast over and let stand 10 minutes or until frothy. Whisk in remaining water, sugar, eggs, salt, and oil until thoroughly mixed.

Whisk in flour, a cupful at a time, beating in final amount with wooden spoon, to make soft sticky dough. Turn out onto well-floured surface. Knead for 4-5 minutes, dusting occasionally with flour, until dough is smooth and elastic. Place dough in well-oiled bowl, turning dough to grease all over. Cover dough with plastic wrap; let rise in warm place for 1½-2 hours or until doubled. Punch down dough and shape into rolls. Place 1/2 in. (1 cm) apart on well-greased baking sheet. Cover loosely and let rise until doubled and puffed, 1½-2 hours.

Preheat oven to 375°F (190°C). Bake rolls for 12-15 minutes or until hollow sounding when tapped on bottoms.

Makes 3 1/2 dozen.

DILLED CARROTS

Bunny Barss is one of Alberta's most popular food authorities. This recipe is adapted from her book *Come'n Get It: Favorite Ranch Recipes.* Bunny recommends that the carrots be about straight and about 3 in. (8 cm) long to make packing into jars easier.

2	garlic cloves	2
8	large sprigs of fresh dill	8
2 lbs.	baby carrots, washed and dried	1 kg
2 cups	white vinegar	500 mL
2 cups	water	500 mL
¼ cup	pickling salt	50 mL
½ tsp.	white pepper	2 mL
½ tsp.	mustard seed	2 mL

Put garlic clove and dill sprig in bottom of each of 2 hot, sterilized quart (1 L) jars. Pack small, whole carrots into each jar. Top with remaining dill.

In large saucepan, combine vinegar, water, salt, white pepper, and mustard seed. Bring to full boil, pouring over carrots to within 1/2 in. (1 cm) of top. Seal tightly and refrigerate for up to 1 month.

Makes 2 quarts.

SASKATOON PIE

Lucille Smith of Nanton, Alberta, is the wife of a professional "pit boss" and beef farmer, Harry Smith. Her special recipe for wild saskatoon berry pie follows.

4 cups	saskatoon berries	1 L
1 cup	gooseberries	250 mL
1 cup	granulated sugar	250 mL
3 Tbsps.	all-purpose flour	45 mL

Unbaked pastry for 10 in. (25 cm) double-crust pie

Put saskatoons and gooseberries into pie shell. Stir together sugar and flour; pour over berries. Cover with top crust; seal and crimp. Bake in *preheated 425°F (220°C) oven* for 15 minutes. Reduce heat to 350°F (180°C) and continue baking until berries are soft, about 30-40 minutes.

Serves 8-10.

SOUR CREAM PIE

Another Bunny Barss favourite, this unusual variation on old-fashioned raisin pie is one of the best!

1 cup	raisins	250 mL
3	eggs, separated	3
1 Tbsp.	all-purpose flour	15 mL
1 tsp.	cinnamon	5 mL
1 cup	sour cream	250 mL
½ cup	brown sugar	125 mL

1 tsp.	baking soda	5 mL
1	8 in. (20 cm) baked pie shell	1
¼ tsp.	salt	1 mL
⅓ cup	granulated sugar	75 mL

In a heavy saucepan, combine raisins, egg yolks, flour, cinnamon, sour cream, and brown sugar. Cook, stirring constantly, over medium heat until thickened. Immediately stir in baking soda. Pour puffed-up filling into pie shell.

Beat egg whites until frothy. Sprinkle in salt and continue to beat until soft peaks form. While beating, add sugar a spoonful at a time. Continue to beat until stiff and glossy. Pile onto hot filling, spreading meringue to edges. Bake in *preheated 350°F (180°C) oven* for 10-12 minutes or until delicately browned. Cool in draft-free place.

Serves 6-8.

A Wild and Wonderful Menu from British Columbia

SINCLAIR PHILIP has had an impact on West Coast British Columbia cuisine. Restaurateurs and chefs make pilgrimages to his inn, Sooke Harbour House, on Vancouver Island to learn from him and his wife, Frederica. His philosophy is simple, yet his cooking is sophisticated. He believes that *everything* on his menu should be grown or harvested around his inn. When he has time he likes to dive for the seafood his chefs cook—and there is a large saltwater tank outside the kitchen door; on one day you might see sea urchins and swimming shrimp, on another sea cucumbers and Red Rock crab. *Fresh* is another essential in his cookery. The inn is surrounded by raised beds of vegetables and herbs for the kitchen. Kiwi and passion fruit twine around the inn's pillars, and fragrant edible flowers grow in the window boxes. Just before your dinner, you may see the chefs in the garden choosing the herbs, greens, and flowers for your meal. Years ago Sinclair met Nancy Turner, an ethnobotanist who studies how the native people use plants in their diet. An edible-plant walk with Nancy in the bush or along the seashore is a favourite pastime for Sinclair. Some of the plants that he finds he transplants to his garden. This wild and wonderful collection of recipes is from Sinclair Philip and Sooke Harbour House.

Wild and Wonderful Menu from British Columbia

*

Red Rock Crab and Wild Mushroom Stuffed Pumpkin
with Stinging Nettle Sauce

*

Grand Fir Granite

*

Alder Cone Smoked Wild Grouse Breast
with Licorice Fern Root Glaze
and Juniper-Salal Berry Sauce

*

Steamed Blue Camas Lily Bulbs

*

Salad of Wild Greens

*

Salal Berry Cookies

*

Labrador Tea

RED ROCK CRAB AND WILD MUSHROOM STUFFED PUMPKIN WITH STINGING NETTLE SAUCE

The Pumpkins

4	baby pumpkins	4
1 Tbsp.	salt	15 mL
2 Tbsps.	honey	25 mL

Cut an opening in top of pumpkin large enough to insert stuffing, reserving top. Remove pulp and seeds. Fill medium-sized saucepan with water; add salt. Bring to a boil. Add pumpkins and lids and return to boil. Reduce heat; simmer for 3-4 minutes. With slotted spoon remove pumpkins from water; plunge into cold water. Drain and pat dry. Brush (inside and outside) with honey. Set aside.

The Crab Meat Stuffing

2 Tbsps.	unsalted butter	25 mL
3	organic shallots, peeled and finely chopped	3
1 clove	organic garlic, peeled and finely minced	1 clove
¾ cup	chopped wild mushrooms	175 mL
½ cup	fish stock	125 mL
½ cup	light, fruity white wine	125 mL
2 cups	Red Rock or other crab meat	500 mL
1 Tbsp.	chopped fresh lemon thyme, stems removed	15 mL
¼ cup	grated cheddar cheese	50 mL
4	crab legs and claws	4
2 Tbsps.	butter	25 mL

Stinging Nettle Sauce
(recipe follows)

Prepare the crab-meat stuffing: Heat butter in a saucepan. Add shallots and garlic and sauté until they are translucent. Add chopped mushrooms, fish stock, and wine. Bring to boil. Cook, uncovered, until volume is reduced by half. Gently stir in crab meat, chopped thyme, and grated cheese.

Spoon mixture into pumpkins. Place one crab leg and one claw into each pumpkin so that it protrudes. Set pumpkin lid on top.

Melt 2 Tbsps. (25 mL) of butter in a baking pan. Place pumpkins in pan. Leave in a *preheated 350°F (180°C) oven* just long enough to reheat—about 5 minutes.

Spoon Stinging Nettle Sauce around a plate and place pumpkin on the sauce.

Serves 4.

STINGING NETTLE SAUCE

Always wear gloves when handling raw nettles.

1 Tbsp.	salt	15 mL
6 cups	water	1.5 L
2 cups	stinging nettle leaves, tightly packed	500 mL
½ cup	light, fruity white wine	125 mL
½ cup	fish stock	125 mL
3 Tbsps.	butter	45 mL
½ tsp.	red or brown rice miso	2 mL

Freshly ground black pepper

Put the salt and water into medium-sized pot; bring to a boil. Add nettle leaves and return to boil for 1 minute. Drain and rinse under cold water. Drain again and squeeze out excess moisture. Purée leaves in an electric blender (or use a juicer) to make a paste.

Place wine and fish stock in a small saucepan; bring to boil. Boil, uncovered, over medium heat until liquid has a syruplike consistency. Add nettle paste, butter, miso, and pepper from a few turns of a pepper mill. Whisk until well mixed and frothy. Keep warm until ready to use.

Serves 4.

GRAND FIR GRANITE

2 quarts	grand fir needles, well washed	2 L
1 quart	water	1 L
1 cup	honey	250 mL

Fill 2 quart (2 L) container with grand fir needles. Bring water to boil and pour over needles. Weight down with several plates. Let steep for 12 hours. Strain through very fine sieve or cheesecloth. Stir in honey. Freeze in ice-cream freezer or in shallow pan in freezer, stirring often.

Makes 1 1/2 quarts (1 1/2 L).

ALDER CONE-SMOKED WILD GROUSE BREAST WITH LICORICE FERN FOOT GLAZE AND JUNIPER-SALAL BERRY SAUCE

At Sooke the chefs serve this with a salad of foraged wild greens and flowers such as amaranth, chicory, chickweed, lamb's quarters, orache, shepherd's purse, and sorrel.

2 Tbsps.	minced licorice fern root	25 mL
2 Tbsps.	Gewürztraminer icewine	25 mL
¾ cup	water	175 mL
3 cups	dried alder cones	750 mL
2	12 oz./350 g wild grouse breasts, bone in and skinless	2

Juniper-Salal Berry Sauce
(recipe follows)

In a small covered stainless-steel saucepan, gently simmer fern root in icewine and water for 20 minutes. Do not boil. Pour into glass jar; seal. Let stand at room temperature for 12 hours. Strain into small saucepan; boil, uncovered, on high heat until reduced to thick syrup. Set aside.

Heat alder cones in large saucepan over high heat until they smoulder. Reduce heat to low; place grouse breasts directly on top of smouldering cones. Lightly brush breasts with licorice fern root glaze; cover pan tightly. Smoke breasts for 3 hours or until cooked but not dry. Remove meat from bone. Serve with Juniper-Salal Berry Sauce.

Serves 4.

JUNIPER-SALAL BERRY SAUCE

1⅓ cups	water	325 mL
1½ cups	British Columbian Pinot Blanc wine	375 mL
3½ cups	salal berries	875 mL
1½ Tbsps.	maple syrup	20 mL
1½ Tbsps.	black peppercorns	20 mL
8	juniper berries	8
1½ Tbsps.	balsamic vinegar	20 mL

Pour 1 cup (250 mL) water and wine into bottom of perforated double boiler. Place salal berries in top section. Cover; simmer gently for 2 hours. Gently press berries with rubber spatula to extract remaining juice. Discard berries; reserving syrup in bottom of double boiler.

To salal syrup, add maple syrup, peppercorns, juniper berries remaining water, and balsamic vinegar. Bring to boil, then immediately remove from heat. Let stand before returning to heat. Cook, uncovered, until slightly thickened. If not using immediately, refrigerate until needed.

Serves 4.

SALAL BERRY COOKIES

1 cup	unsalted sweet butter, softened	250 mL
1 cup	wildflower honey	250 mL
2	large eggs	2
2 cups	whole-wheat flour	500 mL
2 cups	unbleached white flour	500 mL
1½ tsps.	baking soda	7 mL
1 cup	coarsely ground walnuts	250 mL

Cream butter with honey until fluffy. Add eggs, one at a time, beating well. Sift together whole-wheat flour, white flour, and baking soda; fold into honey mixture. Mix in walnuts. Form dough into a ball, wrap in plastic and refrigerate for 2 hours.

The Filling

2 cups	salal berries	500 mL
2 Tbsps.	honey	25 mL

Combine berries and honey in a small, heavy saucepan over low heat. Bring to a simmer. Cook for 5 minutes until thickened. Let cool.

Divide dough in half. Roll ⅛ in. (¼ cm) thick on a floured surface. Cut into rounds with a 3 in. (8 cm) cookie cutter. Place 1 teaspoon of filling in middle of each round and fold in half to form a semicircle; pinch edges closed. Transfer gently to a lightly buttered cookie sheet. Bake in *preheated 350°F (180°C) oven* for 10 minutes until lightly browned. Cool on wire rack.

Makes 4-5 dozen.

LABRADOR TEA

In a warmed medium-sized teapot, place a small handful (10-15 leaves) of dried Labrador Tea. Pour boiling water over (about 4 cups/1 L). Steep for about 10 minutes or until tea is lightly coloured and fragrant. Strain and serve. If desired, sweeten with honey.

GLOSSARY

Alder cones—the short, woody female "cones"—are actually the flowers of the red alder (*Alnus rubra Bong.*), which grows in moist woods and cleared areas throughout the Pacific Northwest and as far north as Alaska.[1]

Black cardamom is an aromatic spice native to India, with black seeds held inside a black pod. More pungent than either green or brown varieties, it is used in savory dishes only.

Blue camas lily bulbs are common to the southeastern portion of Vancouver Island and the Gulf Islands. The bulbs of the blue camas (*Camàssia quamash*) were a staple for the Coast Salish and some of the other local bands.[2]

Butternuts are the oily nuts from the butternut or white walnut tree native to North America. They are used primarily in pastries and desserts.

Cape gooseberries (*Physalis* spp.) are also called "ground cherries." These sweet, orange berries are covered with a papery husk and can be found in many farm markets across Canada.

Chili oil is simply vegetable oil in which hot red chili peppers have been steeped. A mainstay in Chinese cookery, this red oil can be purchased at most Asian markets.

Chinese black mushrooms are also known as "shiitake" and can be purchased in dried form at Asian markets.

Chu-hou paste is made from salt-fermented soybeans that have been ground to a paste and combined with flavouring ingredients. The paste adds depth and colour to stewed and braised dishes. Purchase it at Asian markets.

Cochon du lait or cochonnet is a small, milk-fed suckling pig the size of a lamb. It usually weighs about 75 pounds (34 kg) before butchering. Each rack of ribs yields 3-4 servings.

Geoduck (*Panope generosa*) is a giant clam that, because of its long siphon, buries itself deeply (30 in.-5 ft./75-150 cm) in the sandy ocean floor. It is sold live at many Chinese markets. The most prized edible portion is the long, meaty siphon, which is prepared by simply blanching and peeling.

Grand fir or balsam fir (*Abies grandis*) is collected by clipping the growing tips of the tree. The flat needles are lighter in colour on the underside.

Jerusalem artichokes (*Helianthus tuberosus* L.) have large, bumpy roots that, when peeled, are best eaten cooked. The plants can be found wild in many areas of North America and are easily cultivated. They are best grown in their own special area because they spread quickly.

Labrador tea (*Ledum groenlandicum Oeder*) is also known as swamp tea or Hudson's Bay tea. The short, leathery leafed plant grows around marshes and can be identified by its elongated, rolled-in leaves that have silvery fuzz on their undersides.[3]

Leaf gelatin is a clear, paper-thin sheet of gelatin used most often by professional pastry chefs. It may be found in gourmet or bakery-supply shops and sometimes in German specialty food stores. Three sheets will thicken 1 cup (250 mL) of liquid.

Lexia raisins are large, soft raisins usually purchased in bulk at health-food stores.

Licorice fern root is a small, licorice-tasting fern (*Polypodium glycyrrhiza*) that was used to whet children's appetites when they did not want to eat and as a flavouring for Labrador tea. The roots have a strong licorice flavour.[4]

Popcorn seedlings can be made by simply sprouting popcorn as you would mung beans or alfalfa seeds.

Potato starch is also called "potato flour" and is made from cooked, dried, ground potatoes. It is used as a thickener and in baked goods to give them a moist crumb.

Salal (*Gaultheria shallon* Pursh.) is a member of the heather family. Its dark blue to nearly black berries tend to be dry when fully ripe and were a major source of food for all of the coastal Indian groups. They were eaten fresh and dried.[5]

Saskatoon berries (*Amelanchier alnifolia* Nutt.) are the favourite berry of the Prairies and are also known as serviceberries.[6]

Sea cucumber (*Parastichopus californicus*) is a relative of both the sea urchin and the starfish. Easily harvested while scuba diving, the long, soft-bodied creature is used for the delicious strips of flesh that run the length of its interior. It is often seen dried in Chinese markets.

Splake, a brook and lake-trout cross, is found primarily in the freshwater lakes of Ontario, where it is being stocked. The light salmon-coloured flesh makes it one of Ontario's most prized fish.

Stinging nettles (*Urtica dioica* L.) are found across Canada and, if handled carefully when fresh, are a delicious green vegetable. Always wear heavy gloves when picking and preparing. Plunge into boiling water to blanch and immediately the stinging properties are removed.[7]

Tapioca powder is also called "tapioca starch" and is made from the root of the cassava (manioc). It is used as a thickening agent. Purchase it in Asian or African food stores.

CHAPTER NOTES

INTRODUCTION TO THE REGIONAL CUISINES OF CANADA

Our Northern Bounty
by Carol Ferguson

Endnote

1. Carol Ferguson and Margaret Fraser, *A Century of Canadian Home Cooking* (Toronto: Prentice-Hall Canada, 1992).

THE REGIONAL CUISINE OF BRITISH COLUMBIA

Traditional Native Plant Foods in Contemporary Cuisine
by Nancy J. Turner, Sinclair Philip, and Robert D. Turner

Selected Bibliography

1. Kuhnlein, Harriet V., and Nancy J. Turner. 1991. *Traditional Plant Foods of Canadian Indigenous Peoples: Nutrition, Botany and Use.* Volume 8, *Food and Nutrition in History and Anthropology,* edited by Solomon Katz. Philadelphia: Gordon and Breach Science Publishers.
2. Nuxalk Food and Nutrition Program. 1984. *Nuxalk Food and Nutrition Handbook.* Bella Coola, B.C.: Nuxalk Food and Nutrition Program and the Nutrition Nation Council.
3. Szczawinski, Adam F. and Nancy J. Turner. 1980. *Wild Green Vegetables of*

Canada. Edible Wild Plants of Canada No. 4. National Museum of Natural Sciences, National Museums of Canada, Ottawa.

4. Turner, Nancy J. 1975. *Food Plants of British Columbia Indians.* Part 1, *Coastal Peoples.* British Columbia Provincial Museum Handbook No. 34. Victoria, BC.

   ———. 1978. *Food Plants of British Columbia Indians.* Part 2, *Interior Peoples.* British Columbia Provincial Museum Handbook No. 36. Victoria, BC.

5. ———. 1979. *Plants in British Columbia Indian Technology.* British Columbia Provincial Museum Handbook No. 38. Victoria, BC.

6. ———. 1991. "Wild Berries." In *Berries,* edited by Jennifer Bennett. Toronto: Harrowsmith Books.

7. Turner, Nancy J., and Adam F. Szczawinski. 1979. *Edible Wild Fruits and Nuts of Canada. Edible Wild Plants of Canada* No. 3. National Museum of Natural Sciences, National Museums of Canada, Ottawa.

8. ———. 1978. *Wild Coffee and Tea Substitutes of Canada. Edible Wild Plants of Canada* No. 2. National Museum of Natural Sciences, National Museums of Canada, Ottawa.

THE REGIONAL CUISINE OF THE PRAIRIES

The Chuckwagon Tradition in Prairie Culture
by Beulah (Bunny) Barss

Bibliography

1. Barss, Beulah. 1983. *Come'n Get It.* Calgary: Western Producer Prairie Books.

2. Breen, D. H. 1972. "Ranching in the Northwest, 1875–1892". Ph.D. diss., University of Alberta, Edmonton.

3. Dary, David. 1981. *Cowboy Culture.* New York: Avon.

4. High River Pioneer and Old Timers Association. 1960. *Leaves from the Medicine Tree.* Lethbridge, AB: Lethbridge Herald.

5. Hughes, Stella. 1974. *Chuckwagon Cooking.* Tucson: University of Arizona Press.

6. McHugh, John O. 1976. "The Cattle Roundup," *Folklore of Canada,* by Edith Fowke. Toronto: McClelland and Stewart.

7. Nelson, Doug. 1993. *From Hotcakes to High Stakes: The Chuckwagon Story.* Calgary: Detselig Enterprises.

Canada's Breadbasket: Decades of Change
by Margaret Fraser

Bibliography

1. *Baking Made Easy.* 1938. Robin Hood Flour Mills Ltd.
2. Barer-Stein, Thelma. 1979. *You Eat What You Are.* Toronto: McClelland and Stewart.
3. Barss, Beulah. 1983. *Come'n Get It.* Saskatoon: Western Producer Prairie Books.
4. *Best Ever Breads.* 1993. San Francisco: Specialty Brands (Fleischmann's Yeast).
5. Ferguson, Carol, and Margaret Fraser. 1992. *A Century of Canadian Home Cooking.* Toronto: Prentice-Hall Canada.
6. Ferguson, Carol, and the Food Writers of Canadian Living Magazine. 1987. *The Canadian Living Cookbook.* Toronto: Random House Canada.
7. *From Saskatchewan Homemakers' Kitchens.* 1955. Compiled by Saskatchewan Homemakers' Clubs.
8. Gill, Janice Murray. 1993. *The Great Canadian Bread Book.* Toronto: McGraw-Hill Ryerson.
9. Henry, Sally. 1984. Taped talk on Flours. Presented at IACP Conference, Toronto.
10. *The Laura Secord Canadian Cookbook.* 1966. Compiled by The Canadian Home Economics Association. Toronto: McClelland and Stewart.
11. McCully, Helen. 1967. *Nobody Ever Tells You These Things.* Toronto: Holt, Rinehart and Winston Canada.
12. Nickerson, Betty. 1965. *How The World Grows Its Food.* Toronto: Ryerson Press.
13. Paré, Jean. 1981. *Company's Coming: 150 Delicious Squares.* Vermillion, AB: Company's Coming Publishing Ltd.
14. Scargall, Jeanne. 1974. *Pioneer Potpourri.* Agincourt, ON: Methuen Publications.
15. Scott, Anna Lee. 1928. *Cookery Arts and Kitchen Management.* Toronto: Maple Leaf Milling Co. Ltd.
16. Stechishin, Savella. 1957. *Traditional Ukrainian Cookery.* Winnipeg: Trident Press.

17. *When You Bake With Yeast.* Montreal: Standard Brands Ltd. (Fleischmann's Yeast).

To Travel Hopefully: Dining with the CPR in the West
by Robert D. Turner

Selected Bibliography

1. Canadian Pacific Railway. 1920. *Canadian Pacific Railway, Dining Car Service. Standards of Portions, Prices and Table Service.* Montreal: CPR.
2. Hart, E. J. 1983. *The Selling of Canada: The CPR and the Beginnings of Canadian Tourism.* Banff, AB: Altitude Publishing.
3. Hungry Wolf, Adolf. 1991. *Canadian Sunset: A Farewell Look at America's Last Great Train.* Glendale, CA: Trans-Anglo Books.
4. Kalman, Harold. 1968. *The Railway Hotels and the Development of the Chateau Style in Canada.* Maltwood Museum Studies in Architectural History, No. 1., University of Victoria, Victoria, BC.
5. Lamb, W. Kaye. 1977. *History of the Canadian Pacific Railway.* Toronto: Collier Macmillan Canada.
6. McKee, Bill, and Georgeen Klassen. 1983. *Trail of Iron: The CPR and the Birth of the West.* Vancouver: Glenbow-Alberta Institute and Douglas and McIntyre.
7. Robinson, Bart. 1973. *Banff Springs: The Story of a Hotel.* Banff, AB: Summerthought.
8. Turner, Robert D. 1977. *The Pacific Princesses: An Illustrated History of the Canadian Pacific's Princess Liners on the Northwest Coast.* Victoria, BC: Sono Nis Press.
9. ———. 1984. *Sternwheelers and Steam Tugs: An Illustrated History of the Canadian Pacific Railway's British Columbia Lake and River Service.* Victoria, BC: Sono Nis Press.
10. ———. 1986. *West of the Great Divide: The Canadian Pacific Railway in British Columbia, 1880–1986.* Victoria: Sono Nis Press.

THE REGIONAL CUISINE OF ONTARIO

Ontario Cooking: Cuisines in Transition
by Dorothy Duncan

Endnotes

1. P. B. Waite, *Canadian History* (Ottawa: Canadian Studies Directorate, 1988), 1.
2. William Lyon MacKenzie, *Sketches of Canada and the United States* (London: E. Wilson, 1833), 89.
3. M. A. Garland, "Some Frontier and American Influences in Upper Canada prior to 1837," *Transactions*, Part XIII (London: London and Middlesex Historical Society, 1929), 12-13.
4. Marilyn Barber, *Immigrant Domestic Servants in Canada* (Ottawa: Canadian Historical Association, 1991), 5.
5. J. M. Bumsted, *The Scots in Canada* (Ottawa: Canadian Historical Association, 1982), 16.
6. Anne Clarke, *The Dominion Cook Book* (Toronto: McLeod and Allen, 1899).
7. Margaret Taylor and Frances McNaught, *The New Galt Cook Book* (Toronto: George J. McLeod Ltd., 1898).
8. Reg Whitaker, *Canadian Immigration Policy* (Ottawa: Canadian Historical Association, 1991), 7.
9. Jean Burnet, *Multiculturalism in Canada* (Ottawa: Canadian Studies Directorate, 1988), 2.
10. John Macfie, *Parry Sound Logging Days* (Erin, ON: The Boston Mills Press, 1987), 148.
11. Ian Radforth, *Bush Workers and Bosses: Logging in Northern Ontario 1900–1980* (Toronto: University of Toronto Press, 1987), 98.
12. Franc Sturino, *Forging the Chain: Italian Migration to North America, 1880–1930* (Toronto: Multicultural History Society of Ontario, 1990), 105.
13. Peter Ward, *The Japanese in Canada* (Ottawa: Canadian Historical Association, 1982), 5.
14. Jean Burnet, "New Arrivals in the 20th Century and Their Food Traditions," *Consuming Passions* (Toronto: Ontario Historical Society, 1990), 256.
15. *Ibid.*, 256.
16. Edgar Wickberg, ed., *From China to Canada: A History of the Chinese*

Communities in Canada (Toronto: McClelland and Stewart, 1982), 152.

17. Bernard Vigod, *The Jews in Canada* (Ottawa: Canadian Historical Society, 1984), 7.
18. Jean Burnet, "New Arrivals," 258.
19. Franc Sturino, *Forging*, 186-7.
20. Dorothy Duncan, "Make it do—Make it over—Use it up," *Century Home* April–May, 1991, 21.
21. Dorothy Duncan, "The 20th Century Brought a Revolution to the Dinner Table," *Consuming Passions* 1982, 245.
22. Carol Ferguson and Margaret Fraser, *A Century of Canadian Home Cooking* (Scarborough: Prentice-Hall Canada, 1992), 127.
23. Jean Burnet, "New Arrivals," 260.
24. Okay Chigho, "Goudas Gold," *Business Journal* 82 (no. 9, 1990): 17.

Founding the Vintners Quality Alliance (VQA)
by Donald Ziraldo

Footnotes

1. Section 2:2, VQA Rules and Regulations. For these regulations, contact: Wine Council of Ontario, 35 Maywood Ave., St. Catherines, Ontario L2R 1C5. Telephone 905-684-8070, FAX 905-684-2993.
2. For information about VQA in British Columbia, contact: British Columbia Wine Institute, 1193 West 23rd. St., North Vancouver, British Columbia V7P 2H2. Telephone 604-986-0440, FAX 604-986-2625.

THE REGIONAL CUISINE OF QUEBEC

Quebec Goes Country
by Johanna Burkhard

Source List

1. A copy of *Along the Vintners' Trail* is available from Vignoble de l'Orpailleur, 1086 Route 202, P.O. Box 339, Dunham, Quebec J0E 1M0, or call 514-341-1982.

2. Québec cidreries: contact Robert Demoy, Verger Du Minot, 376, chemin Hovey Hill, Hemingford, Quebec J0L 1H0. Telephone 514-247-3111.
3. Game meat and bird suppliers: contact Gibier Canabec, 2115, Range Ste-Ange, Ste-Foy, Quebec G2E 3L9. Telephone 418-872-4386 or 1-800-663-2373.
4. Quebec goat-cheese makers: contact Ginette Menard, Syndicate of Goat Breeders of Quebec, U.P.A.., 555, boul. Rolland Therrien, Longueuil, Quebec J4H 3Y9, or call 514-679-0530, ext. 288.
5. Information on regional cuisine and farm-gate producers: contact Rose-Hélène Coulombe, MAPAQ, 201, boul. Crémazie Est (4e), Montreal, Quebec H2M 1L4. Telephone 514-873-2364.
6. Quebec Food Certification Program: contact Pierre Daigle, MAPAQ, 201, boul. Crémazie Est (4e), Montreal, Quebec H2M 1L4. Telephone 514-873-4410.
7. Tables Champêtres: Fédération des Agricotours, C.P. 1000, Succ., Montreal, Quebec H1V 3R2. Telephone 514-252-3138.

Quebec's Culinary Traditions: An Overview
by Yvon Desloges

1. See E. Leroy Ladurie, "La verdeur du bocage," in *Le territoire de l'historien*, 190-192, 208-214, on the place of game at special occasions and in its symbolic relations.
2. Robert Sauzet, "Discours cléricaux sur la nourriture," in J. C. Margolin et R. Sauzet, *Pratiques et discours alimentaires à la Renaissance* (Paris: Maisonneuve et Larose, 1982), 248.
3. Yvon Desloges and Marc Lafrance, "Game as Food in New France," in Peter Benes, ed., *The Dublin Seminar on New England Folklife*. Annual Proceedings 1993, Boston University, forthcoming.
4. Paul-Louis Martin, *Histoire de la chasse au Québec* (Montréal: Boréal, 1990), 21. This information is corroborated by probate inventories of both Quebec City residents and those of the Richelieu Valley.
5. J. Lalemant, "Relation de 1662–1663," in *Relations des Jésuites*, vol. 5: 30. Lahontan, *Nouveaux voyages dans l'Amérique septentrionale*, La Haye, 1703, vol. 1 (28 May 1687) 94. Boucault, "Etat présent du Canada, 1754," in *RAPQ, 1923–24*, 23.
6. ANQQ (Archives nationales du Québec à Québec), NF25, liasse 10, #440 3/4, 30 april 1710.
7. J. Lambert, *Travels through Lower Canada and the United States of North America into the years 1806, 1807 and 1808*, London, 1810, vol. 1, 78.

8. A. Vallée, "Cinq lettres inédites de J. Frs. Gauthier. . ." in *Mémoires et comptes rendus de la Société royale du Canada*, IIIe série, vol. 24, 1930, section 1, p. 25, 30 oct. 1750.
9. On this debate, see C. Fischler, *L'omnivore*, 39-59; see also M. Harris, *Good to Eat: Riddles of Food and Culture* (New York: Simon and Schuster, 1985), 13-18.
10. Y. Desloges, *A Tenant's Town: Québec in the 18th Century* (Ottawa: Environment Canada, 1991), 147-149.
11. This situation parallels that of Fort Frederica in Georgia in the middle of the eighteenth century. On this subject, see E. Reitz and N. Honerkamp, "British Colonial Subsistence Strategy on the Southeastern Coastal Plain," in *Historical Archaeology*, vol. 17 (no. 2, 1983): 4-26.
12. ANQQ, M5/2:269-270, Ordonnance de Bégon, 28 Jan. 1717.
13. NAC, (National Archives of Canada), MG23, A1, vol. 2: 1824–1903, Lieut. Marr's Remarks upon Québec . . . from 1768 to 1772.
14. Quoted in J. Hamelin and F. Ouellet, "Outillage et rendements agricoles," in C. Galarneau et E. Lavoie, eds., *France et Canada français du XVIe au XXe siècle* (Québec: Presses de l'université Laval, Cahiers de l'Institut d'histoire, no. 7, 1966), 97 and 102.
15. NAC, MG23, GVI, Songe 69: 163-164, Boisseau, Nicolas-Gaspard, Mémoires. For a further and more complete survey of husbandry practices in France and England, see A. Bourde. 1967. *Agronomie et agronomes en France au 18e siècle*, 2 vol. Paris: SEVPEN.
16. See J. Hamelin and Y. Roby, *Histoire économique et sociale du Québec, 1851–1896* (Montréal: Fides, 1971), 6-38.
17. M. Lafrance and Y. Desloges, *A Taste of History: The Origins of Québec's Gastronomy* (Montréal: La Chenelière, 1989), 103-104.
18. Henry, John Joseph, "Campaign against Québec 1776," in Kenneth Roberts, *March to Québec 1776.* Journals of the members of Arnold's Expedition, Portland: Down East Books, 1980.

The Art and Science of Good Bread
by James MacGuire

Bibliography

1. Boily, Lise, and Blanchette, Jean-François. 1979. *The Bread Ovens of Québec.* Ottawa: National Museums of Canada.
2. Calvel, Raymond. 1990. *Le goût un pain.* Paris: Éditions Jérôme Villette.

3. Calvel, Raymond. 1964. *Le pain.* Paris: Presses Universitaires de France.
4. Caron, La Mère. 1903. *Directions diverses données en 1878 par la révérende Mère Caron, alors Supérieure Générale des soeurs de la chasité de la Providence pour aider ses soeurs à former de bonnes cuisinières.* 6th ed. No publisher listed.
5. David, Elizabeth. 1977. *English Bread and Yeast Cookery.* Harmondsworth, Middlesex, England: Penquin Press.
6. Dupont, Jean-Claude. 1974. *Le pain d'habitant.* Montréal: Éditions Le Méac.
7. ———. 1865. *La nouvelle cuisinière Canadienne.* Montréal: C. O. Beauchemin et Valois.
8. Malouin, Paul-Jacques. [1767] 1984. *Description et détails des arts du meunier, du vermicelles, et du boulanger.* Reprint of the Paris edition of 1764–1767. Geneva: Slatkine Reprints.
9. Parmentier. [1778] 1981. *Le parfait boulanger ou traité complet sur la fabrication et le commerce du pain.* Reprint of 1778 Paris Edition. Marseille: Jeanne Laffitte.
10. Poilâne, Lionel. 1981. *Guide de l'amateur de pain.* Paris: Robert Laffont.

MENUS AND RECIPES FROM THE REGIONS

An Ontario Feast of Fields

For more information read:

Smoking Salmon and Trout by Jack Whelan. Aerie Publishing, Deep Bay, Vancouver Island, R.R.#1, Bowser, B.C. VOR 1GO
First printed in 1982.

Glossary

Reference for notes 1–7

Turner, Nancy J. 1975. *Food Plants of British Columbia Indians,* Part 1, *Coastal Peoples.* British Columbia Provincial Museum Handbook, No. 34, Victoria, BC.

INDEX

Index

Index

RECIPE INDEX